T0305417

Aspen and the American Dream

The publisher and the University of California Press Foundation gratefully acknowledge the generous support of the Barbara S. Isgur Endowment Fund in Public Affairs.

Aspen and the American Dream

HOW ONE TOWN DEALS
WITH INEQUALITY IN THE ERA
OF SUPERGENTRIFICATION

Jenny Stuber

UNIVERSITY OF CALIFORNIA PRESS

University of California Press
Oakland, California

© 2021 by Jenny Stuber

Library of Congress Cataloging-in-Publication Data

Names: Stuber, Jenny M., 1971– author.
Title: Aspen and the American dream : how one town deals with
    inequality in the era of supergentrification / Jenny Stuber.
Description: Oakland, California : University of California Press, [2021]
    | Includes bibliographical references and index.
Identifiers: LCCN 2020043882 (print) | LCCN 2020043883 (ebook)
    | ISBN 9780520306592 (cloth) | ISBN 9780520306608 (paperback)
    | ISBN 9780520973701 (epub)
Subjects: LCSH: Equality—Colorado—Aspen. | Middle class—
    Colorado—Aspen. | Housing—Colorado—Aspen.
Classification: LCC HM821 .S765 2021 (print) | LCC HM821 (ebook)
    | DDC 305.8009788/43—dc23
LC record available at https://lccn.loc.gov/2020043882
LC ebook record available at https://lccn.loc.gov/2020043883

Manufactured in the United States of America

29 28 27 26 25 24 23 22 21 20
10 9 8 7 6 5 4 3 2 1

For my Papa,
Don Stuber,
Known to many as "Cool D"

Contents

Figures and Tables

TABLES

Introduction

THE IMPOSSIBLE MATH OF ASPEN, COLORADO

Paradox and contradiction are at the heart of social life and, consequently, of keen interest to sociologists like me. The tensions and contradictions that run through the upscale resort town of Aspen, Colorado, can be illustrated with a simple question: How is it possible for a town to exist where the median household income is about $73,000, but the median home price is about $4 million? Conventional wisdom among financial advisors is that a household earning $73,000 per year can reasonably afford a home in the $225,000–$325,000 price range—not the $4 million price tag found in Aspen. The paradoxical relationship between local incomes and the price of real estate is what I call "The Impossible Math of Aspen, Colorado." Aspen is a place where many residents own homes with values in excess of $10 million, but the majority of the town's nearly 7,400 residents cannot afford a home even far below the median price. Yet they live there, nonetheless. The navigation and resolution of this paradox is the subject of this book. I show that what solves the impossible math equation between incomes and home values in Aspen—the "X-factor" that makes middle-class life possible—is a process of place-making that involves the careful orchestration of diverse class interests within local politics and the community, with the overarching goal of maintaining Aspen's value and preserving its authentic small-town character. This is achieved through a highly regulatory and extractive land use code that provides symbolic and material value to highly affluent investors and part-year residents, as well as less-affluent locals, many of whom benefit from an array of subsidies—including the extensive affordable housing program that houses middle- and upper-middle-class locals—that redistribute economic resources and make it possible for them to live in one of the most unequal communities in the nation.

These analyses take as their point of departure the 2016 moratorium on development, in which the Aspen City Council pushed the pause button on development so that officials could rewrite the land use code. The land use code, produced by local politicians and their urban planning staff, plays a significant role in place-making and is also a tool that mediates the seemingly disparate interests of Aspen's middle-class workers and its ultra-wealthy residents and visitors. In a technical sense, the land use code governs where buildings with different uses (retail, residential, industrial) can be placed, how big they can be, and what they must look like. As a centerpiece of urban political economy, these codes spell out whether developers are entitled to tax abatements or incentives or whether, as in Aspen, they must pay mitigations or exactions. In a symbolic sense, the land use code constitutes, according to anthropologist Constance Perin, a "moral system that both reflects and assures social order" by allocating membership and belonging within a community.[1] It does so by establishing a hierarchy of uses and regulating access to meaningful social roles, including homeowner and entrepreneur. Finally, the land use code structures class relations: by creating opportunities for business ownership and residency, it shapes material interests, dictating both the profitability and the costs associated with these roles, and shapes where and how different groups come in contact with one another.

The 2016 revision of Aspen's land use code provides insight into the process of place-making and how class relations structure and are structured by place-making. During this instance of place-making, Aspen's politicians, urban planners, developers, the local business association, and citizens came together to negotiate the look and feel of this quaint, yet exclusive mountain town. The city council's decision to rewrite the land use codes was a reaction to locals' anxieties that they were no longer in control of their community and that outside forces were increasingly dictating not just the look and feel of their community, but also the criteria for belonging. These outside forces can be glossed by a single word: *supergentrification*. In response, stakeholders' efforts focused on how to craft building sizes and shapes that would both preserve precious mountain views *and* make space for locally serving businesses, and how to "rightsize" building mitigations so that owners and developers are not disincentivized from economic activity but are still obligated to make meaningful contributions to affordable housing. This book tells the story of how the Aspen City Council sought to rewrite their land use code, which dictates both the material and symbolic form of the town, and how they attempted to balance the divergent class interests of the local stakeholders in an effort to answer the question, "Aspen for whom?"

This book tells a story that is of interest to sociologists, urban planners, and policy makers who study land use codes, as well as anyone interested in how communities function amid rising social inequality. In many ways, Aspen challenges the conventional wisdom of what we know about politics, place, and economic inequality. The conventional wisdom, drawn from scholarly research on social class, place-making, and urban development, is that a place like Aspen should not exist. That is, a place should not exist where the median income is $73,000 per year, but the median home price is nearly $4 million. The dynamics posed by neoliberal economic policies and supergentrification should impact Aspen as they have impacted New York, London, and other global cities: elevating the interests of business, decreasing taxation and the provision of government services, and paving the way for displacement and exclusion. These dynamics should make it impossible for a community to exist where the incomes earned by local residents are fundamentally at odds with housing prices, and where working locals still exert considerable influence on how the town operates.

And yet this version of Aspen does exist—at least for now. Aspen, as it currently exists, is a place where global elites own second (or third, or fourth) homes that they visit during the winter and summer "high seasons." They ski majestic mountains in the winter and in the summer hobnob with celebrities, intellectuals, and other global elites during the Aspen Ideas Fest, the Food and Wine Classic, and the Music Festival. It is also a place inhabited by 7,400 year-round residents, some quite affluent themselves, but most of whom hold the ordinary jobs that make any small town function. They are doctors and nurses who staff the hospital; teachers and librarians who attend to children and others wanting to learn; law enforcement and first-responders who keep Aspen safe and orderly. There are, of course, plenty of people who work the jobs that make Aspen a world-class resort, especially in hospitality, real estate, architecture, and the building trades. These are the year-round residents whose $73,000 household incomes place them above the national average, but who are priced out of local, free-market housing. While other scholars have studied Aspen and the very similar community of Jackson Hole in Teton County, Wyoming, those scholars have examined the tensions between the uber-wealthy and lower-income Latinos. While such work is important, it has largely ignored the middle- and upper-middle-class residents who form the core of such communities. Indeed, 75 percent of Pitkin County's residents earn between $25,000 and $200,000 annually. This book centers their experiences, and examines the curious relationship between the affluent global elites and Aspen's working locals, focusing on how local stakeholders strive to craft a town that operates *both* as an exclusive enclave and as an authentic community with a middle-class core.

While Aspen is currently home to a substantial middle- and upper-middle-class population, for many locals there is a sense that they are losing control of their beloved town, ceding ground to global elites. Locals see their town becoming a place where tenants of $20 million condominiums can lodge noise complaints against the brewpub or the exercise studio next to whom they purchased a unit, and threaten to drive out local business owners and their patrons. The existential threat posed to Aspen's middle-class locals is supergentrification—a global economic force impacting elite resort towns and major metropolitan areas alike. Supergentrification refers to the process whereby an already gentrified neighborhood is further upscaled, so that homes, restaurants, and retail establishments that once catered to middle-class residents are replaced by those that cater to an increasingly affluent clientele. Within the resort economies of the west, geographers have referred to this as "Aspenization."[2] Locally, evidence of supergentrification is captured in the oft-repeated description of a place where "the billionaires are pushing out the millionaires." This facet of

Aspen and the tensions it poses are abundantly clear in the town's two newspapers, *The Aspen Times* and *The Aspen Daily News*, which circulate widely throughout town. On the one hand, these free daily papers are made possible by revenues generated from the glossy real estate advertising inserts that depict majestic mountain estates and sleek downtown condos with price tags in excess of $10 million, as well as with advertisements on interior pages for boutiques selling jewelry, vintage watches, and furs; high-end restaurants; and blue-chip art galleries. On the other hand, these newspapers' front-page reporting captures ongoing political struggles, like the battle against a new hotel, the effort to ban luxury chain stores, and demands for more affordable housing. Every day, newspaper readers confront the ways in which class tensions and understandings play out in Aspen: the city that sells luxury and aspiration as its core brand is also a place where locals push back against supergentrification. This book documents a year in the life of place-making in Aspen, Colorado. Drawing from a rich set of qualitative data collected during a year of ethnographic field work, I show how local politicians and other stakeholders attempt to balance the seemingly divergent interests of these two groups while striving to preserve the unique small-town character—one part exclusiveness, one part accessibility—that has become Aspen's international brand. It examines urban planning as a tool for place-making and, in this context, for managing supergentrification; it is through this same tool that class interest and class relations become institutionalized in place.

THE STUDY OF PLACES AND PLACE-MAKING

The fact that Aspen's middle- and upper-middle-class locals coexist is not an accident: it is the result of a carefully calibrated process of place-making. The notion of place-making asserts that places do not exist in themselves; instead, they are made. But what is a place? A place is more than a physical location or point on a map. Places are more than the statistical or geographic units designated by the US Census Bureau or other such entities. According to Thomas Gieryn, places have three co-occurring elements.[3] First, a place has a geographic location; it is a unique spot in the universe, with both finitude and elastic boundaries. Aspen, for example, is located in Pitkin County and has decipherable municipal boundaries, but its imagined boundaries extend to adjacent communities like Snowmass, Woody Creek, and Basalt. Second, a place has material form, grounded in physical features, both natural and built by humans. The physical place of Aspen is bounded by the mountains that rise up around the built environment and the Roaring Fork River that parallels Highway 82 into and out of town. Equally, it is made up of structures that house its commercial, residential, and government functions. Finally, places are invested with meaning and value. As such, places are not merely stages or backdrops for human activity; rather, they emerge as they are "interpreted, narrated, perceived, felt, understood, and imagined."[4] And yet these interpretations are labile and contested. In Aspen, millennials and other recent arrivals sometimes accuse those who arrived in the hippy heyday of the 1970s of wanting to encase the town in amber; the latter, conversely, worry that newcomers don't adequately understand the progressive, low-growth politics that made Aspen the special place that it is. Likewise, Aspen means something different to the local law enforcement officer living in subsidized housing than it does to the billionaire who visits the family compound a few weeks each year. Each individual or group participates in place-making, and may have different ideas about what Aspen is, what its virtues and problems are, and how its essence—and their interests—should be preserved.

The idea that places are not fixed entities hints at the notion of place-making. As used here, *place-making* refers to an ongoing accomplishment wherein community stakeholders, possessing varying material and symbolic interests and resources, come together and negotiate the meaning and materiality of that place. It occurs through the recursive interaction of structural and cultural elements; the intertwining of the material and ideational. Drawing on Anthony Giddens's theory of structuration, Harvey Molotch, William Freudenburg, and Krista Paulsen propose a model of place-making where *place-character* emerges from a "lashing-up," in which existing structures (e.g., laws, policies, norms, etc.) and human action (meaning-making, contestation, interaction) continuously intersect and interpenetrate.[5] On an informal level, this lashing-up plays out in an affluent tourist's decision to return to Aspen for their annual ski vacation; on a formal level, it occurs in local government's decisions about whether to approve the building of a new hotel or impose new mitigations on developers. Place-making is an "unending series of adjacent and recursive choice-point moves," where the resulting configuration is "not predetermined, but is formed in a path-dependent way as each actor, with more or fewer resources at his or her command, shapes a new social structure by drawing upon the simultaneously enabling and constraining hand of the old."[6] Through these processes—which can take place over decades or during a single city council meeting—geographic locales take on distinct place characters.

Although place-making is an ongoing process, there are moments when this process is thrown into stark relief. The building moratorium and rewriting of the land use code that played out in Aspen during 2016 is one such moment—albeit, a yearlong one. The attendant proposal to regulate chain stores, which emerged midway through the moratorium from citizens frustrated by the council's efforts to address the needs of local shoppers and business owners, is another. In place-making processes like these, stakeholders with different material and symbolic interests come together to negotiate the meaning and materiality of a place, and do so within a context where some groups have more power than others. Power, in this case refers to political influence, economic influence, cultural legitimacy, social capital, and more. A long-time citizen-activist or architect in Aspen may have less economic power and influence than a developer, but their claims to cultural legitimacy—what geographer Eugene McCann calls *discursive power*—may have substantial resonance in conversations about Aspen's land use code.[7] With these different forms of power at play, social-class groups and interests can influence the place-making process in nuanced ways.

PLACE AND THE POLITICS OF SOCIAL CLASS

There is no doubt that Aspen is an affluent place, as well as an unequal place. With a median home price around $4 million and the most expensive luxury real estate market in the United States, there are significant barriers for anyone who wants to become a part of the community in a long-term way.[8] The downtown shopping district also caters to affluent tastes. The pedestrian mall is dotted with Gucci, Dior, Prada, Ralph

Lauren, and Dolce and Gabbana. There is not a J. Crew, Zara, or Gap, anywhere in sight. Aspen is also highly unequal. Ranked among the top ten most unequal communities in the United States, the median household in the top 1 percent earns seventy-two times more than the median household among the bottom 99 percent; within the United States as a whole, this ratio is 26:1.[9] And yet from another vantage point, Aspen is a community composed largely of middle- and upper-middle-class residents, where only 10 percent of the population earns more than $200,000 annually. These analyses focus on Aspen's attempts to be a place where middle- and upper-middle-class locals coexist alongside global elites, where urban planning plays a starring role in the place-making process and the institutionalization of class interests.

Affluent People and the Politics of Exclusion

Aspen and the American Dream provides a novel understanding of how affluent places "do" social class. By "do" social class, I mean the routine ways of understanding social class, as well as the ways that class interests and interactions are institutionalized through cultural norms and concrete policies. Much of the existing literature portrays affluent communities in a homogeneous light, with elites operating in predictable ways. Existing scholarship depicts elites using place-making tools to protect their cultural and economic interests. One way they do this is through exclusion. As with gating, a form of exclusion that erects a boundary and restricts access to individual properties or entire communities, exclusion can operate both physically and symbolically.[10] In *Fortress America: Gated Communities in the United States*, Edward J. Blakely and Mary Gail Snyder write that setting boundaries through gating "is always a political act" because, by virtue of their construction, "someone must be inside and someone must be outside."[11] With restrictive covenants that govern what owners can and cannot do with their properties, gated communities are also a regulatory scheme that protects property values and supports claims to exclusivity.

Along with materially protecting property values, the gates that surround affluent communities "symbolize distinction and prestige and create and protect a place on the social ladder" allowing residents to proclaim, "I am the kind of person who can afford to live in this distinctive community."[12] Choon-Piew Pow shows that gated communities in Shanghai became increasingly popular in the early 2000s as developers began to market them as a means to live the good life and fulfill the aspirations of conspicuous consumption made possible by liberalization of the Chinese economy. Once inside—whether in Shanghai or London—residents can, through social closure, build social and cultural capital. The nonmaterial benefits of gating are highlighted in Kathryn Wilkins's historical account, where during the nineteenth century, residents of London's affluent West End neighborhoods shut themselves in—rather than shutting others out—so that they could drink, dance, and revel with anyone who was anyone in British society.[13] Gates, then, can help residents to distance themselves from the hoi polloi and facilitate the building of homophilous social networks.

When physical barriers are elusive or nonexistent, members of affluent communities can use other strategies to exclude unwanted elements and mark membership within a community. One approach is to draw upon what geographers James S. and Nancy G. Duncan call "the invisible walls of zoning."[14] Through their influence on zoning policies and the land use code, community members can shape the look and feel of a place, and regulate which types of activities take place where. A number of studies have profiled the efforts of affluent community members to control growth, often through exclusionary zoning.[15] By implementing exclusionary zoning practices that increase minimum lot sizes and setbacks (distance between the primary structure and the right of way) and preserve open space and wetlands, affluent residents seek to preserve the look, feel, and charm of their communities. As Justin Farrell shows in his work on ultra-wealthy residents of Teton County, Wyoming, efforts to preserve the beauty of the natural landscape also create scarcity: scarcity of land available to develop, which further increases property values and perceptions of exclusivity.[16]

In their ethnography of Bedford, New York, an old money New York City bedroom community, Duncan and Duncan provide a cultural critique of exclusionary zoning.[17] Rather than overt acts of class domination, Duncan and Duncan argue that affluent residents articulate landscape preferences —for mature trees, open space, and wetlands—in ways that depoliticize them, imprinting on them the veneer of mere aesthetic preferences, rather than snobbery or racism. "Bedford is a site of aesthetic consumption practices," they write, "in which the residents achieve social status by preserving and enhancing the beauty of their town. They accomplish this by highly restrictive zoning and environmental protection legislation and by preserving as much undeveloped land as possible through the creation of nature preserves."[18] Instead of considering residents' donations of forests and wetlands as an act of charity or a reflection of deeply held environmental values, Duncan and Duncan, argue that affluent landowners benefit themselves: through their donations they receive both tax breaks and the opportunity to have a meadow or forest within walking distance, if not within view of their kitchen window or patio. Justin Farrell argues these same points in his portrayal of wealthy environmental activists and their contributions to local land trusts in the Grand Teton mountains.

These ethnographies of privilege and place portray class dynamics as antagonistic, where the politics of exclusion typify elites' efforts to influence policies that would erase or marginalize less-affluent community members. Ironically, the presence of affluent residents increases demand for lower-skilled and lower-paid laborers, yet these same affluent residents may also oppose efforts to increase the affordable housing or social services upon which these laborers rely.[19] Although affluent residents welcome the labor power that less-skilled workers bring—many of whom are Latino— they do not welcome their visibility or their long-term relocation. An extensive body of literature details the politics of NIMBY-ism—"not in my backyard"—in the form of middle- and upper-middle-class residents' opposition to affordable housing in their communities. In Duncan and Duncan's work on Westchester County and Corey Dolgon's work on the Hamptons, we find affluent residents mounting campaigns against day laborers' ability to assemble in highly visible locations. Residents of Westchester County encouraged local businesses to post anti-loitering signs and, in the case of Mount Kisco, New York, successfully urged the city to relocate the meetup spot for day laborers to a less conspicuous place beyond the town square. Residents also succeeded in passing an "anti-panhandling" ordinance, which required workers to obtain permits to solicit work in public places. This law passed, in part, based on the rhetoric that Latino day laborers waiting to be hired are tantamount to beggars, threatening pedestrians who would otherwise do business in the town square.

When it comes to social class exclusion, dynamics are especially complicated in Aspen. As in other affluent communities, many people experience exclusion in Aspen due to its expensive housing market. Yet during my time in Aspen, I discovered that class integration exists alongside class exclusion. In fact, the idea that Aspen offers members of different social classes the opportunity to intermingle is a beloved part of local lore. On seemingly countless occasions during my research, people boasted of the ability of the rich and famous to sidle up to the bar in the legendary Hotel Jerome and not be hounded for their fame, but to be able to fly under the radar and converse with the bartender and other (ostensibly not-so-rich-and-famous) locals. I regularly observed both elites and non-elites actively participating in Aspen's vast array of arts and cultural events. Nowhere is this more evident than at the Eero Saarinen–designed music tent, a destination for classical music enthusiasts throughout the summer's famed Music Festival. Inside the tent sit subscribers with season tickets, while both affluent and non-affluent concert goers, who pay nothing to hear the same music, populate the outdoor grounds. What is interesting about Aspen is that concert goers who enjoy glasses of rosé while sitting on blankets for free outside the music tent may claim that their experience is not only more fun than sitting inside the staid tent, but perhaps even more legitimately "Aspen," given the mixing of classes and sense of unpretentious luxury. Conversations with locals also reveal complicated class relations in Aspen. Whereas some locals characterize relations as "class warfare," with the rich waging war on the not-so-rich, others described these relationships as symbiotic, with the affluent and less-affluent gaining something of value from each other. A number of locals even described class relations in Aspen as exploitative—yet saw middle-class locals as benefitting from, if not exploiting, wealthy residents and part-year visitors, due to their reliance on tax revenues that fund local programs, especially the housing program that allows working locals a place to live outside of the exclusionary free market.

Affluent Place-Makers and the Pursuit of Profit

At a structural level, the existing research similarly portrays monied interests as having a relatively narrow set of goals. Seminal theories of urban political economy, for example, situate economic elites and their economic interests as the preeminent shapers of cities. For Marxist geographer David Harvey, the city was as central as the factory for capitalists' control over society, with cities being built to advance profit motive and the needs of production.[20] The centrality and normativity of elites' interests are illustrated in John Logan and Harvey Molotch's *growth machine* theory, which argues that "the political and economic essence of virtually any given locality, in the present American context, is growth."[21] A pro-growth agenda is pushed, Logan and Molotch argue, by economic elites and the government officials they co-opt, who seek to maximize the *exchange value* of a place—its economic value in terms of how much it can be rented or sold for. To do so, cities provide tax abatements and other incentives to lure companies to locate there and expand jobs, the quality of the workforce, and ostensibly the tax base. At times, local residents may oppose the efforts of monied elites in an effort to preserve or maximize its *use value*: that is, its value as a place for habitation. Yet local residents are typically no match for the growth machine, which benefits from the deep pockets and continuous, institutionalized support of local political regimes.

This view of monied and politically entrenched interests seeking to maximize monetary returns is evident in studies of economic development and urban branding. Miriam Greenberg's *Branding New York*, Kevin Fox Gotham's *Authentic New Orleans*, and Alessandro Busà's *The Creative Destruction of New York City* all show growth machine coalitions, led by *place entrepreneurs*, whose primary interest is selling a place and maximizing its economic value.[22] This group includes the rentier class, made up of real estate owners and developers, who stand to cash in when a place expands or rebrands. Politicians often join with economic elites as place entrepreneurs. As shown by Miriam Greenberg and Alessandro Busà in their case studies of New York City, local politicians cultivate seamless networks with economic elites, fostering public-private partnerships that allow them to implement neoliberal economic development strategies that use tourism and intensification of FIRE (finance, insurance, and real estate) industries as substitutes for traditional neighborhood-based development. Urban growth and place-making are augmented by *city producers*—media, marketing, civic groups, and nonprofit organizations—who use their social,

political, and economic leverage to influence place-making, often by lobbying developers and legislative bodies.[23] They are the tourist bureaus and
chambers of commerce who coin slogans and craft marketing campaigns
to sell New York as cosmopolitan and safe, New Orleans as authentic, and
Colorado as offering a mix of relaxation and adventure.

Despite its applicability to large global cities competing for a slice of
the economic pie, growth machine theory fails to describe place-making
dynamics in Aspen, Colorado. With respect to branding and the role of
city producers and place professionals, it is true that much effort has been
spent crafting an image of Aspen as a funky mountain town, home to
nature-lovers like John Denver and gonzo outlaws like journalist Hunter S.
Thompson. Moreover, many dollars are spent by the Aspen Chamber and
Resort Association (ACRA) to sell Aspen as simultaneously luxurious and
unpretentious; a place to renew your mind, body, and spirit—an ethos
known as the Aspen Idea.[24] Further, consistent with David Harvey's for-
mulation of the city, place-makers in Aspen have found ways to appropriate and extract surpluses from its distinctiveness, trading on the symbolic
capital embedded in its charming historic streetscape and awe-inspiring
mountain views.[25] Yet Aspen is not a place where the local government
deploys tax breaks or other incentives to lure development and jobs.
Indeed, it sometimes seems as if Aspen is bent on extracting as much as
possible from developers. So entrenched is this ethos that council member Adam Frisch describes Aspen city government as a "mitigation industrial complex," with tight regulations and steep fees, designed to ensure
that developers offset the impact of their projects, such as the increased
wear and tear on highways and the need for new housing that comes with
job creation. If Aspen had a flag, Frisch has said, its motto would read:
"Development Pays Its Own Way."

Aspen, perhaps, more closely reflects the principles of *regime theory*,
which argues that places are made through the cooperation of economic
and political elites, rather than the cooptation of political elites by economic elites. In his profile of Atlanta, Clarence Stone shows economic
elites forming coalitions with other stakeholders, namely politicians and
civic groups, to exercise power.[26] Regime theory is especially applicable
in communities with diverse and, perhaps, segmented constituencies.
In Atlanta, for example, economic power has been held historically by

Whites, while political power has been held by the majority Black population. Without cooperation between these two stakeholders, little would
get done. Together, these groups focus on more than economic growth. In
Atlanta, stakeholders mediate divergent—and sometimes contradictory—
interests as they jointly strive to accomplish the city's material priorities,
in the form of economic growth, and its symbolic priorities, in the form
of civic pride and racial harmony. In contrast to growth machine theory,
regime theory shows that local actors have disparate interests, some economic and rooted in exchange value and others focused on quality of life
and use value, yet they must work together to achieve their goals.

Regime theory is equally applicable to Aspen, where the major cleavage
is not racial in nature but breaks down in terms of social class. In Aspen,
middle- and upper-middle-class year-round residents hold political power,
while wealthy developers and part-time residents hold economic power.
Their interests, however, are interlocking; both focused on maintaining
Aspen's value. By preserving Aspen's "golden goose"—its built environment
and place character—place-makers are able to craft a municipality that
simultaneously provides a return on investment to its affluent constituencies and funds the affordable housing program and other amenities that
make the lives of middle- and upper-middle class residents possible.

The way that social class dynamics play out in Aspen is partially reflective of the fact that residents of the United States can only register to vote
in one locality at a time. In Aspen, many part-year residents use their primary residence—whether in Houston, New York, Chicago, or Seattle—for
voting purposes and remain relatively uninvolved in local politics. This
concentrates political power in the hands of less-affluent, year-round residents, many of whom seek to preserve a progressive approach to politics
that dates back to the 1970s. As in other cities with a progressive approach
to politics, formal political goals in Aspen tilt toward use value and an
emphasis on quality of life and away from exchange value and an emphasis on growth. Progressive cities operate, according to Pierre Clavel, at the
intersection of two dynamics: a broad, participatory base of activism and
the implementation of redistributive polices (progressive taxation and
regulations on the free market, such as rent control).[27] While progressive
politics have emerged in old industrial cities like Hartford, Connecticut,
and Cleveland, Ohio, as well as scenic, lefty communities like Berkeley,

California, and Burlington, Vermont, what they have in common is a pro-
fessionalized approach to urban planning, built on the premise that "the
public had created property values and other forms of social wealth, and
therefore that the public should control" and ostensibly benefit from their
use.[28] Progressive cities implement growth controls on the assumption
that developers "generate externalities, neighborhood effects, or spillovers"
from their economic activities, and that "these offenses must be publicly
controlled, either by preventing them in the first place or by otherwise providing relief for the victims."[29] Because economic development increases
traffic, the need for waste management, and demand for housing, developers must offset the impacts of their activities. This includes building housing for the workers *their* developments create, distributing transit passes
for workers on the move, and, in some cases, mitigating environmental
impacts. Progressive cities re-center the needs of citizens, providing a
counterbalance to the pro-growth inclinations of business elites.

Alas, not every municipality can effectively employ progressive politics
or growth controls. In their case study of Santa Cruz, California, Richard
Gendron and G. William Domhoff show that managed growth can be successful in "in demand" places characterized by a perfect combination of
demographic traits and non-substitutable geographic advantages.[30] Progressive politics can take root in small and exclusive meccas, home to very
wealthy populations with the means to survive low densities and limited
growth (e.g., Palm Beach, Beverly Hills, Martha's Vineyard), and in areas
inhabited by populations with high levels of education and social and cultural capital—like Berkeley, California, or Boulder, Colorado—who use
their cultural legitimacy and sophistication to lobby developers and politicians to meet residents' needs. According to Harvey Molotch, "antigrowth
movements are probably more likely to succeed in those places where volunteer reform movements have a realistic constituency—a leisured and
sophisticated middle class with a tradition of broad-based activism, free
from an entrenched machine."[31] Such conditions are present in Aspen,
where the percentage of locals with college degrees is double the national
average, thereby facilitating a high level of political engagement. Moreover, developers and other wealthy interests have not, as of yet, formed
a coherent political lobby; to the extent that they oppose the progressive
impulses of local government and planning officials, they do so in ad hoc

ways, using law suits reactively, rather than proactively seeking to influence policy.

Since the 1970s, progressive politics in Aspen have centered on downzoning and the protection of rural open space, accompanied by redistributive policies that fund programs for locals. My argument sheds light on
why Aspen has been a fertile setting for growth management and how
local place-making efforts have resulted in land use policies that strive
to meet the needs of middle- and upper-middle-class locals *and* return
value to economic elites. I provide a spin on theories of progressive politics
and growth management, and show that, as Warner and Molotch found
in Santa Barbara and Santa Monica, "regulation fosters certain kinds of
development that otherwise would not take place, and thus even if some
projects are lost to the locality completely, other projects—better ones—are
gained as substitutes."[32] In Aspen, ever-more exclusive boutiques, restaurants, and hotels are prioritized over attracting a wider base of visitors to
stay in chain hotels and purchase T-shirts with witticisms like "How's Your
Aspen?" and "Pot-agonia"—a play on the cannabis culture and a popular
brand of outdoor clothing. In this context, local officials and stakeholders have sought to limit growth, but not revenue generation. Indeed, the
degree and kind of taxes and fees levied in Aspen are almost unparalleled
by other US communities—a strategy that is all the more effective due to
the fact that those who pay the bulk of these revenues are visitors and part-
year residents who are not registered to vote in Aspen. Rather than a purely
progressive politics or growth management strategy, Aspen seems to pursue a hybrid growth agenda, with efforts yielding quality over quantity.

Class Relations in the Age of Supergentrification

Despite the lore of interconnected class relations and a history of progressive politics, middle- and upper-middle-class locals are finding it
increasingly difficult to make Aspen their home. That is because a wave of
supergentrification threatens to overtake the town. Gentrification refers
to the process whereby middle-class individuals—the gentry—move into
an urban area and displace working-class locals. Supergentrification
takes this process to a higher level. The ever-escalating rents in the posh
neighborhoods of New York, San Francisco, and London are evidence of

Figure 1. Signs of supergentrification at the Old Aspen Drug. Photo by Jenny Stuber.

supergentrification, as less-affluent residents are displaced from neighborhoods they once called home. When a $20 million third-floor condo is
purchased, to be occupied for just a few weeks of the year, it is clear that
supergentrification has come to Aspen. It is also evident in the Banana
Republic being replaced by Louis Vuitton, Dolce and Gabbana moving
into the space once occupied by the Gap, and Aspen Drug—a beloved
pharmacy that also sold tchotchkes and souvenirs—getting shuttered and
gutted to make room for Moncler, a high-end Italian sportswear company
selling down jackets whose prices start around $1,500 (figure 1).

Supergentrification impacts not only the economic realities of a place,
but also its feel and sense of character. Although they may be drawn to
a community based on its charm and character, newcomers typically do
not have deep social or emotional ties to that place, and long-term residents worry that they may not respect its historic value. Charm, character, or cachet may attract them to a place, but once there, global elites
demand a level of familiarity and exclusivity that tends toward upscaled

homogenization. People who are members of the exclusive dining club Casa Tua in Miami embrace the same establishment when they find it in Aspen. It's a pleasant surprise when visitors discover Matsuhisa in Aspen, where they can order sushi that is every bit as delicious as the sushi they have enjoyed at the founder's restaurant, Nobu, in Beverly Hills. The fact that Matsuhisa and many international luxury boutiques are located in Aspen's red stone Victorian buildings gives them a sense of local flavor and authenticity, yet their very presence also provides a sense of comfort to those with upscale global tastes.

Although the concept of gentrification has been in the vernacular since British sociologist Ruth Glass coined the term in 1964, supergentrification reflects a newer set of economic processes.[33] It is the product of global economic forces, especially those fueled by neoliberalism and the deregulation of financial markets that gained speed in the early 1990s. According to British geographer Loretta Lees, supergentrification emerged from "intense investment and conspicuous consumption by a new generation of super-rich 'financifiers' fed by fortunes from the global finance and corporate service industries."[34] It was fueled, Sharon Zukin notes, by "speculation in a neoliberal market system: an increasing volume of investment capital seeking profitable returns, an increasing array of financial instruments to channel investment into risky deals and an increasing anxiety on the part of city governments to maximize resources so they can compete for the money and prestige that are conferred by deal making."[35] The flood of private money into cities and into resort towns like Aspen, impacts how they operate and for whom. Today, considerable debate exists over the various types of gentrification—classic gentrification, retail gentrification, tourist gentrification, and the like—yet Loretta Lees, Tom Slater, and Elvin Wyly assert that the point of continuity running through all of these iterations is the displacement of one social class for another, and a fundamental remaking of class dynamics on the landscape.[36]

Supergentrification, for some scholars, is a logical consequence of the neoliberal city. As described by Jason Hackworth, within the neoliberal city, redevelopment of the urban core and public-private partnerships have become the go-to means of bolstering city finances that have lagged due to declining federal investments.[37] In the neoliberal city, tax subsidies are used to lure development, especially development in tourism, high-end real estate, and retail endeavors, in the hopes that these will become primary sources of revenues. A roll-back of city services, privatization of social services, and entrepreneurialism in city management also characterize this approach.[38] In cities like London, New York, and San Francisco, the increased flow of capital encourages private investment in older properties; after evicting current residents, global investors renovate these properties and rent or sell them to a higher-paying clientele.[39] These residents demand a higher level of consumption, resulting in further upscaling. Simultaneously, less-advantaged residents are displaced and dwindling social services means that their needs go largely unmet.

Urban scholar Rowland Atkinson and his coauthors refer to this landscape of minimal regulation and minimal provision of social services as the "minimum city."[40] It takes root in locales where disinvestment and neglect have left properties unoccupied, a gap existing between current residents' ability to pay and what could be commanded if refurbished. With governments and property owners seeking reinvestment, the flood of global capital settles where it finds preferential fiscal arrangements—often a reduction in property transaction fees. In extreme cases, this gives rise to the plutocratic city, where funding for social services has been bargained away and the very objectives of the city, Atkinson and coauthors argue, "come to be identified and aligned with the presence of wealthy elites while wider goals, of access to essential resources for citizens, have withered."[41] There, the state is co-opted by economic elites, and a "butler class" of professionals—lawyers, accountants, politicians, and more—emerges to help them achieve their goals.

While it would appear easy to apply the notions of supergentrification and neoliberalism to any locale experiencing significant upscaling, it is not entirely clear how these terms apply to Aspen. With respect to supergentrification, it is clear that global elites have brought their money to Aspen and use it to express their consumer desires. It is also clear, as in the neoliberal city, that the majority of tax revenues have been "outsourced" and off-loaded onto high-end home buyers and part-year residents or tourists. It is less clear, however, that in coming to Aspen, these global elites have brought their neoliberal business models or their efforts to influence local governance. Aspen, moreover, is characterized by an abundance of well-funded social programs, in contrast to existing models of the neoliberal city. For these reasons, a new model is needed to capture how the politics of social class influence place-making in Aspen.

Despite Aspen's atypical patterns, newer threads in the literatures on social class and gentrification help make sense of what's going on in Aspen. First, with respect to gentrification, Loretta Lees has led the push for studies that identify points of similarity and difference as gentrification has gone "planetary"—evolving from a localized phenomenon spearheaded by urban pioneers to a global phenomenon led by state actors.[42] She and her collaborators advocate for approaches to gentrification that maintain the focus on understanding how new infusions of capital transform class relations, while permitting mutations and elasticity in exactly how this concept plays out.[43] Aspen, for example, was never a desolate urban frontier, ripe for reinvestment. Yet it has been a safe landing spot for global capital, a place where the production of space has catered to progressively more affluent users.[44] Consistent with Lee, Shin, and Lopez-Morales's call for studies of how municipal governments respond to gentrification, I focus on how local officials have used the tools of the land use code to create a "sense of place" amid upscaling and emerging class tensions.[45]

Empirically, Japonica Brown-Saracino has pushed this research forward, demonstrating that gentrifiers cannot be painted with a broad brush.[46] Her ethnographic work profiling gentrification in four distinct communities complicates understandings of how social class works in place, especially in terms of how gentrifiers' material interests map onto their ideological interests. She shows that despite their relative affluence, the type of gentrifier she called *social preservationists* sought to align their understandings of place with the less-affluent, long-time residents whose culture and lifestyles attracted them to the neighborhood.[47] This appreciation leads social preservationists to want to preserve the character of their neighborhoods and the businesses operated by old timers, even if doing so limits the appreciation of their property values. Her work challenges the notion that affluent newcomers operate in ways that would strictly enhance their economic capital.

Work by British cultural geographers and scholars of social class suggest that the notion of class itself needs to be reimagined. Modifications to the concept are needed as scholars continue to examine how class functions across domains, and not just in employment and workplace relations, where the concept originates. British scholar Beverley Skeggs, for example, distills the concept down to its essence, arguing that "class" simply and generically names a struggle.[48] Moving beyond a priori categorizations of class, Benson and Jackson theorize that class is relational, situational, and context dependent.[49] As Imogen Tyler writes, drawing on the work of Jodi Dean, the point of continuity is that: "Class, in whatever historical context or popular, technical or political idiom it is communicated . . . is a recognition of the unequal distribution of resources (economic and symbolic) and the accompanying processes 'of exploitation, dispossession, and immiseration that produces the very rich as the privileged class that lives off the rest of us.'"[50]

Gentrification and supergentrification constitute such a struggle, Michaela Benson and Emma Jackson write, namely "a struggle over space through which practices over valuation and ownership are writ large."[51] Class, in this regard, is a social process, not a social position; this perspective frees up analysts to attend to class struggles and dynamics without being wedded to orthodox definitions where, for example, gentrification involves the displacement of working-class persons by middle-class persons. These insights pave the way for this study of Aspen, and the complicated ways in which local stakeholders grapple with extreme inequality within the context of supergentrification. These analyses produce a model that helps us understand not just how class relations play out in this resort community, but how they may play out elsewhere.

THE ARGUMENT: PLACE-BASED CLASS CULTURES

This book explores the making of an idyllic mountain town, one that both reflects and defies the conventional wisdom about how social class works in affluent communities. As a relatively affluent community with a rich quality of life, Aspen achieves what many American communities can only dream of: a place where residents enjoy low levels of unemployment, higher-than-average incomes, and extensive opportunities for health and recreation. It is also a place that garners considerable interest from investors, vacationers, and second-home owners. But beneath the surface of this idyllic town are significant tensions and contradictions. This book explores these tensions and contradictions, investigating the ways in which community stakeholders and groups with divergent class interests intersect and attempt to resolve these tensions. Using extensive field notes taken at more than one hundred hours of official city meetings, along with more than 75 in-depth interviews, I highlight how local residents and elected officials use political institutions and the tools of urban planning to create a town that has a distinct identity and considerable value as a brand—one that strives to satisfy the aspirations of middle-class locals and global elites, alike.

Yet balancing these class-interests is challenging, especially in a context where market forces make it difficult for the majority of year-round residents to gain a foot hold in the local housing market. One key component that makes middle-class life in Aspen possible—thereby resolving this impossible math equation—while also attending to the desires of investors, vacationers, and second homeowners, is the land use code that guides local development. I show that through Aspen's carefully negotiated land use code, global elites gain something of considerable worth: the ability to invest in and enjoy living, working, or vacationing in a community that makes a concerted effort to preserve its charm and character—as well as what is perhaps most important, its economic value. The negotiation of Aspen's land use code—which is one setting in which class relations get institutionalized—ensures that buildings remain small in scale, pedestrian friendly, and historically appropriate. I show that by creating scarcity and attending to the aesthetics of the built environment, Aspen's city council, in tandem with its city planners, and with attention to the needs and prerogatives of local developers, strives to preserve the unique character that many associate with this historic mountain town, while simultaneously ensuring a limited supply of the "Aspen brand" that many find so desirable.

What year-round middle- and upper-middle-class residents gain through these negotiations is the ability to fulfill an American Dream: the opportunity to live in a place that offers an extraordinary quality of life and the chance to become a long-term resident or homeowner— even when free-market forces are stacked against them. Their place in Aspen is achieved through a highly regulatory land use code that effectively redistributes economic resources from the uber-wealthy to the less affluent—albeit largely middle- and upper-middle-class—locals.

These redistributive processes impact shoppers at boutiques like Gucci and Prada, who pay a supplementary sales tax; buyers who pay a 1.5 percent Real Estate Transfer Tax (RETT) on home purchases; and property developers, who pay considerable mitigation rates on their projects. These taxes and fees, in turn, fund a city budget of nearly $120 million and other pots of money for local programming, where a disproportionate amount is paid by affluent people for whom Aspen may be only a part-year home.

These revenues sustain the extensive affordable housing program that allows middle- and upper-middle-class locals to make Aspen their home. These tax revenues also fund an extensive public transportation system and supplement the public schools, whose quality is seen by many residents as comparable to private prep schools. Benefits are extensive enough that some have referred to locals as a "subsidy class." These monies also allow the city to buy up parcels of land through its "Open Space and Trails" program, which both provides recreational space for visitors and locals and restricts the supply of land for local development, further driving up the value of the land that can be developed.

Ultimately, I argue, Aspen constitutes a unique case where the downward distribution of economic resources seems to work—albeit within limits. The supply of affordable housing, alas, does not meet demand; thus, many locals live farther "down valley" and endure long commutes to work. But rather than give tax cuts to the wealthy with the hope that doing so will stimulate economic growth, Aspen imposes various "tax hikes" on the wealthy to achieve its community goals. High mitigation fees are required of property developers, motivated by the belief that development must "pay its own way"—offsetting their impact on demand for housing, transportation, and infrastructure, and delivering value back to the community. In municipalities driven by the growth machine, developers may be courted with subsidies and other incentives. Yet, in Aspen, neither affluent developers nor luxury home buyers have overtly pushed back against these extraordinarily intentional efforts at social engineering and their associated costs. Instead, they appear largely content to pay the high costs associated with being part of this upscale mountain town.

To make sense of these processes—many of which stand in contrast to existing understandings of how class is done in place—I develop the concept of *place-based class cultures*. This concept brings together the material, symbolic, and institutionalized dimensions of place. It asserts that places and their local cultures are the result of four distinct elements: cultural beliefs about what a particular place is like; discourses that frame understandings of class and class interactions in that place; ways in which class interests are socially and politically institutionalized; and finally, framing these processes, demographic traits and material conditions that establish how class operates and can be understood. Although the model of place-based class cultures can be applied to class struggles and the politics of place across an array of settings, the analyses provided herein speak most directly to exclusive resort communities, like Teton County, Wyoming; Nantucket, Massachusetts; and Carmel, California. These analyses can help us understand how, for example, struggles over affordable housing or chain retailers may play out differently, based on how social class is embedded and expressed in local cultures and politics.

Throughout, I show that the ability to extract resources from wealthy constituents is the result of a carefully calibrated process of "place making" —one designed to preserve Aspen's identity as an authentic mountain town. It hinges on Aspen's storied history as a silver mining town in the 1880s, as the birthplace of the modern ski industry in the 1950s, and as a haven for outlaws, bohemians, and celebrities in the 1970s. This history now comingles with its present, which is part playground for international elites and part work-a-day town with a year-round population of doctors, journalists, teachers, emergency responders, architects, hospitality professionals, and even a few remaining outlaws and bohemians. By offering an agent-oriented approach to place-making, I demonstrate that Aspen's ability to weave together the interests of its diverse class constituents is not a foregone conclusion; rather, it is the result of ongoing work by local stakeholders—citizens, government officials, developers, and vacationers—and the balancing of class interests to preserve the town's unique feel and value; that is, to "Keep Aspen, Aspen," as a local political campaign advocated.

These analyses are about Aspen, Colorado—a concrete municipality and place on the map, as well as an imagined community with flexible boundaries. Empirically, these analyses focus on the people who live and work in Aspen and the immediately surrounding communities, and especially about the people and process involved in crafting the place called

Aspen. This book is also specifically about those who have chosen Aspen and the immediately surrounding communities as their home, and who have done so not because of the bountiful work opportunities, but for the lifestyle it affords. For these reasons, this is largely a story about White people, crafting what Rich Benjamin might consider a "whitopia."[52] Eighty-eight percent of Aspen and Pitkin County residents are White, and although the county does not collect information on racial or ethnic demographics, it is likely that a similar percentage of those availing themselves of the local affordable housing program, managed by the Aspen Pitkin County Housing Authority (APCHA), are White as well.[53] The housing authority requires documentation of legal residency in the United States, which many locally employed Latinos cannot produce; it also places occupancy limitations in units, which do not accommodate the complex kin structures and multigenerational families among Latinos. Despite their residential absence, Latinos' presence is very much felt in Aspen and the Roaring Fork Valley: their labor fuels the service and construction industries. Moreover, as I elaborate upon in chapter 1, it is their residential absence that creates the conditions that allow the working locals to participate in a coherent class-based politics. The racial homogeneity of the community, its unmarked Whiteness, likely operates as a key resource for providing subsidized housing and access to the Aspen Dream. Next, I outline how the book's argument unfolds, chapter by chapter.

CHAPTER OUTLINE

Chapter 1 accomplishes two goals. First, I situate the research setting, describing the history of Aspen as well as its geographic and demographic characteristics. Second, I establish the theoretical framework for these analyses and spell out the notion of place-based class cultures. I describe each component in the model of place-based class cultures and show how it operates as a tool for understanding how places are made, how conflicts over place emerge, and how these conflicts may be resolved. Additionally, I apply the model to Aspen and the Roaring Fork Valley, and show how it establishes the framework within which the city council sought to rewrite the land use code.

Chapter 2 provides a detailed look at why so many people are drawn to Aspen and how they manage to make sense of living in such an extraordinarily unequal place. Rather than focusing on either lower-income service workers, as Lisa Sun-Hee Park and David Pellow did in *The Slums of Aspen*, or the uber-elites, as Justin Farrell did in *Billionaire's Wilderness*, I focus on the substantial portion of the population that can be called middle- or upper-middle class. Although progressive local leaders have tried to provide housing and economic opportunity to working locals, many of them struggle to climb job ladders and find stable, affordable housing. I show that some residents respond to these challenges by substituting the "Aspen Dream" for the "American Dream": a set of moves through which they assert that the symbolic and lifestyle benefits associated with living in Aspen outweigh the economic costs. These residents' voices provide insight into how and why working locals weigh the economic and symbolic benefits of living in a place, and how a locale's place-based class culture—both in terms of cultural narratives and the institutionalization of class interests and interactions—shapes their experiences.

Chapter 3 returns more directly to the question of place-making and establishes the context in which Aspen's city council declared a land use moratorium during the spring of 2016. In halting development, the city council spearheaded a process by which the community renegotiated its identity through the land use code. I show that the land use moratorium was an effort to reset the pendulum of local development, which many locals felt had swung too far in favor of wealthy developers and the forces of supergentrification. Council members expressed anxieties of their own, concerned that downtown was becoming "sterilized," as affluent outsiders bought up $15 million penthouses, allowing the commercial spaces below to remain empty. With condos that were occupied for only a few months out of the year, and vacant store fronts, the council embraced 2016 as a year of place-making and the chance to reset the pendulum with the goal of preserving community values and advocating for working locals.

Chapter 4 focuses on how Aspen residents and city officials used the land use moratorium as a chance to reassert Aspen's identity as an authentic mountain town. They did so by revising the Commercial Design Standards, which establish the look and feel of local development and architecture. With respect to place-based class cultures, these efforts play a role in both reflecting and creating place narratives, claims about what Aspen is like. I show that these negotiations accomplished two interrelated goals. First, they reinforced building rules that seek to balance elegance and exclusivity with authenticity and "messy vitality." Second, they sought to preserve the Aspen brand by limiting building sizes and creating open spaces for citizens and visitors to enjoy the mountain scenery. Collectively, these efforts protect developers, investors, and vacation homeowners who may be looking for a safe place to land their millions; these regulations simultaneously generate considerable revenues, that fund affordable housing and allow locals to enjoy the community year-round. In this way, these efforts institutionalize the class interests of wealthy investors, residents, and visitors.

In chapter 5, I examine how the Aspen City Council, in conjunction with developers and business interests, reconciled the tensions and contradictions that emerged from the proposed changes to the land use code. The council sought to implement policies that would encourage new development and upgrades of existing commercial spaces, while also generating mitigation fees that fund the affordable housing program and provide economic opportunity for locals. These analyses show how the council responded when they discovered the unintended consequences of their proposals, and how they attempted to adjudicate the fact that their proposed policies would have disparate impacts on middle-class locals and the more affluent investors and visitors. These efforts continue to highlight the linkages that exist between cultural discourses on Aspen and utilization of the land use code to institutionalize class interests.

Although Aspen city council was addressing issues of community character and economic opportunities for locals through the moratorium process, some citizens felt that they weren't doing enough. Chapter 6 explores the efforts of a local citizens' group to enact even more restrictive measures aimed at providing more opportunities for locals to start their own business or shop at locally serving stores. Aspen's citizen-activists targeted high-end retailers like Gucci and Prada, accusing them of altering Aspen's sense of authenticity and driving up commercial rents. I show how this effort—which resulted in the passage of new regulations on chain stores—highlights the issue of place-making in Aspen and how the Aspen City Council and other stakeholders engage the question, "Aspen for whom?"

If chapter 6 considers the question of "Aspen for whom?" one needs to answer that question not just in terms of social class, but also in terms of race and ethnicity. Chapter 7 does just that, exploring how migrants and longer-term Latino residents experience life in the Roaring Fork Valley. I examine their experiences, asking how they navigate life within this extremely White, extremely expensive community. In contrast to the narratives presented by Lisa Sun-Hee Park and David Pellow in *The Slums of Aspen* and Justin Farrell in *Billionaire's Wilderness*, these Latinos describe feeling safe in the local area, and find it a suitable place to pursue the American Dream. Although they have fears of law enforcement—especially federal law enforcement—and have felt the cold shoulder of some Anglos, they generally provided positive accounts of their lives in the Roaring Fork Valley. I situate their experiences within the context of the local place-based class culture, and suggest that the ways in which class is "done" in Aspen provides a level of comfort for these newcomers to the United States.

The conclusion considers the limits and possibilities of crafting a community that attempts to meet the needs of residents and visitors representing diverse class interests. While the Aspen City Council and local voters exert considerable force in place-making, influencing the shape, feel, and function of the town, the free-market continues to operate with a logic of its own, pushing real estate values and the cost of doing business ever higher. The free-market both permits and constrains what can be accomplished in Aspen, and sets in motion—sometimes with great force —the pendulum swing that locals perpetually seek to rebalance. Finally, I suggest that what happens in Aspen might, necessarily, stay in Aspen. Because few communities are blessed with Aspen's natural beauty, and because few communities have an active and powerful middle-class base that is largely unchecked by more affluent interest, it is unclear whether there are lessons here for other communities typified by great wealth and significant gaps between the super-rich and everyone else, cities like San Francisco, Boston, and London, or posh resorts and retirement communities like Carmel, California, and Martha's Vineyard, Massachusetts.

1 Place-Based Class Cultures

At a pivotal moment in the process of rewriting the land use code, long-time Aspen resident and community activist Toni Kronberg made an incisive observation during a city council meeting. Reacting to the efforts of community members to regulate high-end chain stores—a topic I return to in chapter 6—she said: "The thing that complicates this [discussion over restricting chain stores] is our communities. We really have three communities here. There is the resort community of people who come visit here; the local community, who are year-round; and the second-home owners, who have the multimillion-dollar homes. We have three communities here, and we're all trying to work together." Her statement captures what may be the central challenge of place-making in Aspen: as a community comprised of three distinct constituencies, with seemingly disparate interests, it is difficult to fashion a place that serves each group's interests. Whereas some are drawn to Aspen to shop at luxury chains, others are in desperate need of more accessible retail options; the latter, however, benefit from the significant taxes paid by the former. Given their different material realities, these constituencies differ in how they are impacted by the decisions that shape the look and feel of buildings, determine what goes inside of them, and assess how much developers should mitigate for the right to build in Aspen. Despite the challenge of trying to mediate the seemingly disparate interests of these groups, Aspen and its stakeholders have one asset that assists their place-making endeavors: relative consensus over how class should be "done."

In this chapter I introduce the conceptual framing that guides my understanding of place-making in Aspen and the role that urban planning and the land use code play in institutionalizing class interests. This framing helps explain the initial decision to revise the land use code, how this process unfolded, and how it was resolved. The notion of *place-based class cultures* captures how places "do" social class. It provides a model for understanding how social class is implicated in notions of place and processes of place-making. While some research has explored community conflicts over class interests, and has even examined how the material and symbolic dimensions of class animate these tensions, this work goes further in offering a model that explicitly centers social class in understandings of how places work. The notion of place-based class cultures brings together the material and symbolic aspects of social class and considers how social class interests become institutionalized. This chapter describes this model and articulates how it works in Aspen. The remainder of this book draws on this model to understand the impetus, process, and outcome of Aspen's most recent land use code revisions.

Before presenting the model of place-based class cultures, some definitions are in order. Central to the model is the concept of social class. Although foundational to the field of sociology, there is perhaps no concept that is more widely contested. While I bracket many of the debates surrounding social class—how many there are, for example, and whether it should be conceptualized as categorical or gradational—my use of the term attends to its material *and* symbolic dimensions. The material dimensions of social class are captured by measures of wealth and income. These financial assets are valuable because they can be used to acquire goods or services, accumulate additional financial assets, and enable social action. In terms of its symbolic component, my conceptualization of social class owes a debt to Max Weber and Pierre Bourdieu.[1] Writing in the first decades of the twentieth century, German theorist Max Weber conceptualized one's position in the social structure as deriving from one's material resources, but also reflecting nonmaterial elements, namely status and power. From this standpoint, the ability to engage in class action has as much to do with having esteem and deploying influence as it does with possessing financial resources (market position). Writing in the 1970s, approximately sixty years after Weber, French theorist Pierre Bourdieu added to understandings of the symbolic aspects of social class.[2] Social and cultural capital, he theorized, derive from one's position in the class structure and can also be used to affect one's position. A person's cultural capital includes material objects denoting class position, as well as the cultural meaning given to those objects. It also includes institutionalized and embodied forms, so that educational credentials and how one acts and interacts—a concept captured more fully in Bourdieu's notion of *habitus*—both represent and reinforce one's class position.[3] Calling these resources "capital" underlines the manner in which they operate as a form of currency—one that can be activated in a system of exchange, resulting in the further accumulation of social, cultural, or financial capital. Notions of cultural capital are crucial for understanding how class is done in Aspen—and anywhere else, for that matter—since it shapes notions of who belongs in the community, whose interests count, and how discourses can be used to get things done. In Aspen, symbolic resources like cultural capital do not perfectly align with financial capital, giving them an autonomous and powerful role in place-making.

Because the notion of place-based class cultures frames social class as something that is done—an accomplishment—I view class relations and the role of social class in place-making as contingent. Although the dominant classes have more financial resources than the subordinate classes, and can use these resources to influence how class interests and relations are understood, I do not view these processes or outcomes as automatic. Like Bourdieu, I see the material and symbolic aspects of class as analytically, interactionally, and structurally distinct. Given the autonomous role of social and cultural capital, class relations and class interests can play out in surprising ways, and may even give subordinate classes the power to shape place-making processes. This happens in Aspen, I show, where less-affluent locals make claims of authenticity, which impact the decision-making of local governmental bodies. Moreover, like British theorists of class Beverley Skeggs and Imogen Tyler, I see "class" not as an identity or a discrete social location, per se, but as an emergent phenomenon that arises from localized struggles.[4] This localized and contingent character means that understandings of class and class action can arise in surprising ways, as they do in Aspen.

The notion of "culture," as used in the model of place-based class cultures, derives from William H. Sewell Jr.'s emphasis on culture as a dialectic that unites *meaning* and *practice*.[5] In his classic essay "The Concept of Culture(s)," Sewell states: "System and practice are complementary concepts: each presupposes the other. To engage in cultural practice means to utilize existing cultural symbols to accomplish some end. The employment of a symbol can be expected to accomplish a particular goal only because the symbols have more or less determinate meanings—meanings specified by their systematically structured relations to other symbols. Hence practice implies system. But it is equally true that the system has no existence apart from the succession of practices that instantiate, reproduce, or—most interestingly—transform it. Hence system implies practice."[6] Culture, in this sense, functions as a set of tools that can be applied to different kinds of problems. In fields of contestation, where multiple players are involved—like Aspen's year-long moratorium—goals and values shift through the recursive deployment of "strategies of action," where culture is both one reason for this morphing and a tool used to respond to it.[7] Culture, then, is not an autonomous social structure that exists alongside other social institutions, like the family, politics, and economics; rather, it is a system of meanings and practices that suffuses all aspects of human actions and all social institutions. This structure is both durable and flexible: while it establishes a frame within which understanding and action take place, differing degrees of consensus, cohesion, and power mean that the structure is also subject to change.

Within community and urban sociology, notions of culture and its structuring capacity are captured in the model of *place character* developed by Harvey Molotch, William Freudenberg, and Krista Paulsen.[8] Drawing on Anthony Gidden's theory of structuration, which sees human action (agency) and social structure as fundamentally linked, Molotch and coauthors describe the processes by which places take on a durable character:

In their structure-making actions, humans draw, per force, from existing conditions—that is, from structures resulting from their prior actions. Thus, as people take action they make structures, and every action is both enabled and constrained by the prior structures. All this occurs in an unending series of adjacent and recursive choice-point moves. . . . The resulting configuration, at any moment or place, is thus not predetermined, but is formed in a path-dependent way as each actor, with more or fewer resources at his or her command, shapes a new social structure by drawing upon the simultaneously enabling and constraining hand of the old.[9]

While these authors do not explicitly name culture and practice as the forces that structure these choice-point moves, they state that the "symbolic and ideational" realms inform the "stored up human activities" that give rise to place distinctiveness, suggesting a close alignment with Sewell's conceptualization.[10] Both of these perspectives inform my notion of place-based class cultures. Within this model, social class functions as a symbolic resource, as well as a material resource, so that institutional spheres—like local government and the land use code—are structured simultaneously by meaning and the allocation of economic resources.[11] In sum, to say that a *place* has a *class culture* means that social class deeply informs both individual and collective ways of doing and understanding, and that these elements "lash up" and become institutionalized, which then shapes class interests and the distribution of life chances.

PLACE-BASED CLASS CULTURES: THE MODEL

The centerpiece of these analyses is the notion of place-based class cultures. I developed this concept, which is comprised of four core components (see figure2), after conducting more than eighty interviews and one hundred hours of structured observations within Aspen, Colorado, and the surrounding Roaring Fork Valley. The four components of this model reflect scholarly understandings of culture, as outlined above, and models of place-making, like those developed by Harvey Molotch and his coauthors, and Japonica Brown-Saracino.[12] Although Molotch and his coauthors argue that cultural frames guide action, and that these frames result in the durable accomplishment of place, they say little about what kinds of

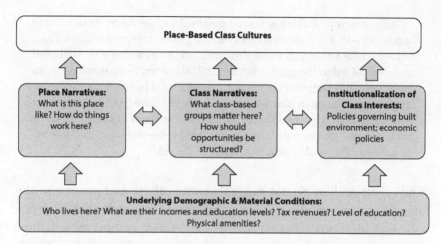

Figure 2. Place-based class cultures.

frames guide this process; I suggest that social class is one of these frames. Japonica Brown-Saracino's model of *sexual identity cultures* also informs my work, in that it foregrounds identity and demographics as integral to place character, what she calls the *socioscape*. Her work is critical for asserting that there is no one queer "idioculture," so that sexuality is done differently, depending on a community's demographic and cultural milieu. My work builds on this concept, showing that social class and affluence also operate in place-specific ways. My contention is similar to Butler and Robson's finding that social class does not manifest the same within all neighborhood contexts, and that middle-classness has different expressions and utilities; there are, in essence, multiple middle-class habituses.[13] Compared to these scholars, however, I pay greater attention to the formalized ways in which identity cultures become institutionalized and how they are embedded in norms and policies, like the land use code. Like Molotch and his coauthors, my model foregrounds how culture operates as a resource that people can draw upon or seek to modify to accomplish individual or collective goals, and how it eventually becomes institutionalized. My model also captures something subtly stated by David Harvey in his essay, "The Right to the City": "The question of what kind of city we want cannot be divorced from the question of what kind of people we want to be, what kinds of social relations we seek, what relations to nature we cherish, what style of life we desire, or what aesthetic values we hold."[14] For this reason, my work insists on examining the interpenetration of narratives about who lives in a place and how that place is institutionalized.

The first element that makes up the model of *place-based class cultures* is cultural beliefs about what a particular place is like; these *place narratives* are the origin stories or cultural touchstones that narrativize a place and are used to highlight its distinctiveness. Second are discourses that frame understandings of how social class operates in that place. Third, the model attends to the ways that class interests are socially and politically institutionalized, shaping informal norms and formal policies. Framing this are the demographic and material traits that establish the conditions of possibility for how class operates, how it can be understood, and what can be accomplished in that place, given these demographic and material conditions. In what follows, I describe and illustrate each component and show how they inform place-making in Aspen. I start with the locale's material conditions and demographic traits by way of introducing the setting for these analyses.

Underlying Demography and Geography: Setting the Stage

Material conditions and demographic traits, along with the physical features of a particular locale, establish the conditions of possibility that shape place-making efforts and how social class operates. Together these traits structure the parameters of what can or cannot be accomplished. Demographically, is the population relatively poor and the tax base low? Geographically, does the locale have valuable features that can be monetized to advance local interests? When it comes to Aspen, one must acknowledge the obvious: it is spectacularly beautiful. Tucked high in a mountain valley, Aspen has snowy peaks, vibrant fall foliage, and a flowing river that provide year-round leisure opportunities. These features attract outdoor enthusiasts—some who hike, bike, and ski those trails, and others who appreciate the same features from the vantage point of a sidewalk café. Aspen, like other beautiful locales—think of Santa Barbara or St. Bart's—could not be just anywhere. Whereas other locales have ports or mineral reserves or other natural features that stimulate the economy, Aspen's landscape is its biggest resource, constituting both use value and exchange value, giving it opportunities that other communities cannot easily replicate. This is important to understand when asking whether Aspen's strategy for addressing class interests can be exported elsewhere.

A town of 7,400 year-round residents, Aspen is demographically unlike most rural towns of its size. It is a place that skews toward the highest levels of affluence, with minimal persistent poverty and limited presence of the working poor. As shown in table 1, the town's residents are twice as likely to have a bachelor's degree and earn household incomes that are 30 percent higher, compared to national averages. The percentage of households earning more than $200,000 annually is twice the national average. Poverty rates are about a third lower than the national average and fewer households meet federal definitions of "low income." Unemployment rates are lower, as well. When describing Aspen's economic landscape, two additional figures are worth mentioning. First, it ranks among the most unequal communities in the United States. In Aspen, a member of the top 1 percent earns, on average, $72 for every dollar earned by a member of the bottom 99 percent; the average for the United States is $26 to 1. Second, at $1,366,000, the threshold for making it into the top 1 percent is three times higher than the national average. And while 90 percent of Aspen residents earn incomes below $200,000, its quaint Victorian neighborhoods and the mountains that rise up from town are inhabited by some of the wealthiest people in the world. Paradoxically, then, Aspen is both a solidly middle or upper-middle-class community and one of extreme affluence.

How Aspen's economic base and its political base intersect also make it unique. Although members of the uber-wealthy own homes in Aspen and consider it a part-time residence, they can file taxes and register to vote in only one place. Therefore, the exorbitant incomes of many part-year Aspenites are not included in the figures presented in table 1, nor do they vote in local elections. Aspen's primary political constituency, then, are year-round residents—75 percent of whom earn incomes between $25,000 and $200,000. These locals are, moreover, extremely politically engaged and left-leaning. About 75 percent of the electorate turned out in the 2016 presidential election, and 70 percent of them voted for Hillary Clinton, the Democratic candidate.[15] Even municipal elections have voter

Table 1 Select Demographic and Economic Traits

	Aspen, CO	Pitkin County, CO	United States
Median household income	$72,793	$71,244	$60,293
Households earning more than $200,000	10.4%	10.1%	5.7%
Households earning less than $24,999	15.8%	13.5%	22.3%
Ratio of incomes, top 1% to bottom 99%	—	72.2 (times)	26.3 (times)
Income threshold for top 1%	—	$1,366,427	$421,926
Average income of top 1%	—	$6,620,969	$1,316,985
Average income of bottom 99%	—	$97,714	$50,107
Percent with bachelor's degree or higher	63.7%	63.1%	31.5%
Percent in poverty	7.5%	6.8%	11.8%
Unemployment rate	3.9%	3.6%	5.2%
Percent White (non-Latino)	60.4%	85.7%	84.4%
Municipal budget per capita	$18,084	$8,273	$2,368 (Jax, FL)
			$1,812 (Duval County, FL)
Retail sales per capita	$13,443	$19,950	$42,735

U.S. Census, 2020a, 2020b; Apartment List, 2020; Sommeiller and Price, 2019.

turnout upwards of 60 percent. Local politicians rarely run with party affiliations, yet it is fair to describe the majority as liberal or progressive. These demographic characteristics make for a complicated dynamic: While the political and economic interests of year-round residents may differ from Aspen's uber-wealthy part-year residents and visitors, local officials must consider both groups in their place-making efforts.

Although 88 percent of Pitkin County residents are White, Hispanic residents make up an important segment of the broader community, especially those who commute into Aspen to work. Aspen itself is less than 10 percent Hispanic, but just thirty minutes down valley, in Carbondale,

48 percent of the town's 6,900 residents are Hispanic.[16] Many of these people travel to Aspen to work, have a stake in its social, economic, and political fortunes, and are instrumental to the town's day-to-day functioning. While some Hispanic residents are local voters and participate in not-for-profit groups to advocate for their well-being in housing, education, and health care, they exert limited formal political pressure.

Demographically, Aspen's racial homogeneity plays an important role in how it does social class. The fact that income is the central axis of differentiation undergirds the relatively uniform discourses about what Aspen *is* and how social class works there. Moreover, stark differences in economic capital are interwoven with similarities in cultural capital, so struggles over social class are characterized by points of similarity and difference. The relatively homogeneous discourses that emerge, in turn, conceal the racial and ethnic diversity that does exist, potentially leading to blind spots in local governance and place-making efforts. In addition, the lack of racial difference surely impacts how the politics of redistribution work in Aspen. As suggested by Louise Seamster, it is not a coincidence that liberal, low-growth policies emerge from cities that are often overwhelmingly White.[17] The political scientist, Martin Gilens, similarly notes that Americans' limited support for redistributive welfare policies in large measure results from racial animus, with voters associating these programs with primarily Black recipients.[18] In Aspen, it is likely that racial cohesion allows class solidarities to congeal. These class solidarities, then, provide support for redistributive policies—support that might be more muted if the community were more racially and ethnically diverse. As long as subsidized housing is for "people like us," Aspen's Whiteness can serve as resource in how class politics play out.

Finally, what makes Aspen especially unique compared to other towns of its size is the scope of its municipal budget. With a budget of $120 million in 2019, this equates to more than $16,000 per capita. This compares to $2,300 for Jacksonville, Florida, and even $13,000 for the peer resort community of Vail. The Pitkin County budget adds another $8,200 to that figure. These monies come from property taxes and sales tax revenues, which include supplemental levies for community projects. Although some of these monies are sequestered by the state for broader infrastructure projects, this extraordinarily large budget provides relatively unparalleled opportunities for place-making and promoting the well-being of residents and visitors.

Aspen Exceptionalism: Narratives about Place

If geographic and demographic traits structure the conditions of possibility for shaping a place-based class culture, those possibilities begin to take shape through local narratives about place. Japonica Brown-Saracino defines place narratives as "the stories residents tell about their city to themselves and others."[19] These narratives contain stories about how this place came to be, what it is like, and how it is distinctive. These narratives can be as simple as a motto on a bumper sticker—"Ithaca is Gorges," for example—or expressed in more complex histories and origin stories. Because, as Brown-Saracino states, these narratives include accounts of "who and how to be in a place," they also provide a script that ostensibly guides action and behavior.[20] This connection to praxis—a patterned way of doing or being—is evident in Molotch and coauthors' nod to Raymond Williams when they write: "People's sense of character and tradition make up the local 'structure of feeling,'" which is a part of the "lash-up" of structuration.[21] Narratives about place, then, are both cause and effect of how place-based class cultures become institutionalized, and how places maintain their distinctiveness. My insight into these narratives derives largely from interviews with twenty-four elected officials and people whose jobs explicitly involve place-making (land use lawyers, architects, etc.), along with forty interviews of middle- and upper-middle class locals, and sixteen Latino service workers.[22] In our conversations, I found that notions of authenticity and exceptionalism run through their discourses.

I first visited Aspen at age five, when my dad moved there after my parents' divorce. Aspen is like "Disneyland for adults," my grandmother told me, prior to departure. Although I didn't understand it at the time, her sentiment captured Aspen's association—especially during the 1970s—with adult forms of fun and excitement, namely drugs and a more libertine approach to sex. Even then, I knew that Aspen was home to many celebrities, as documented in *People* magazine's profiles of its then-famous residents. Today, Aspen's reputation for glitz and glamour continues. Many of the locals I spoke to, however, took pains to distinguish the Aspen seen by others and the one experienced by locals. Payton Dillon, a twenty-something who grew up in Aspen, articulated this distinction by comparing visitors to locals: "They are all wearing fur coats and driving in Range Rovers and stuff," she said, and "the locals, we have a Subaru and a 1974 Jeep, and everybody is just, you know, normal." Locals routinely eschewed the glamourized image of Aspen. Instead, they took pride in it being a "real place," one with a sense of character and authenticity.

Aspen's character and authenticity date back to the town's "humble beginnings"—a phrase used on the Aspen Chamber and Resort Association's (ACRA) website—in the 1870s, with the discovery of bountiful silver mines in the surrounding mountainsides. Prospectors, encouraged by then governor Frederick Pitkin, flooded the area, displacing the migratory Ute Indians and building a full-service town. By the early 1890s, Aspen's population peaked at about twelve thousand and was sustained by local newspapers, opera houses, and other big-city amenities. In 1893, due to rampant speculation and the passage of the Sherman Silver Purchase Act, the silver bubble burst. What ensued was a four-decade period known as the "Quiet Years," remembered today as a time of grit and resilience, where the population dipped to around seven hundred and locals burned once-grand furniture to warm their homes. Although Aspen's historic silver boom lasted only fourteen years, it left behind the city's urban grid and an enduring aesthetic orientation, evident in the quaint miners' cabins, Victorian mansions, and stately municipal buildings protected by a vigorous, yet innovative, historic preservation commission.

Today, that sense of authenticity is frequently invoked in discourses that draw boundaries against other seemingly similar places, especially the nearby ski resort, Vail, Which was established as a purpose-built resort abutting Interstate 70 in the early 1960s. Many Aspenites denigrate Vail, characterizing it as fake and corporate. Payton Dillon, who grew up in Aspen and attended college in Switzerland, took pride in her town's unique heritage. When Aspen emerged as a ski destination after the destitution of the Quiet Years, she said, "It was like all these skiers from Europe came here . . . [and] they put their heart and soul into it. And it was very organic. Where Vail was kind of, 'Let's build a kind of Swiss mountain town.'" Greg Clendenning, a beverage distributor who arrived in Aspen in the mid-1970s, echoed this point, saying that

Figure 3. Alpine authenticity at Aspen's Mountain Chalet Hotel. Photo by Jenny Stuber.

developers "put [Vail] up over the weekend and tried to make it look like a Tyrolian village." Historian William Philpott affirms these distinctions in his recounting of Colorado's emergence as a premier vacationland. Vail, he said, "was no suburb, but it sprang from the same historical context," with its "carefully orchestrated, corporate-controlled, thematic plan."[23] Travel writers in the late-1960s described Vail as plastic Bavaria, Hansel and Gretel meet Howard Johnson, and a Hollywood set of a tiny Austrian village.[24] Whereas Aspen embraced messy vitality, Vail was square; so square that the resort's management company banned beards among its workers.[25] Capturing the fundamental distinction between the two communities, Clint Jones, a Denver native who has lived in Aspen since the early-1990s, said, "Vail is ski area with a town built around it, and Aspen is a town that happened to have a ski area." Figure 3 represents Aspen's version of Alpine Authenticity, with the *Mountain Chalet* hotel dating back to 1954.

In addition to viewing Vail as contrived and hokey, Aspenites maligned its scale, with tall buildings blocking views of the mountain. The sacredness of small-town character and mountain views is institutionalized in Aspen's building codes, which form a recursive loop that informs discourses about place. This is evident in Aspen's continual battle to adjust building heights—which at their highest allowed four stories, in contrast to Vail's eight- to ten-story buildings—and in formal discourses like those offered by the Aspen Area Community Plan. This community-planning vision document states: "The image of Aspen as an organized façade needs to be injected with the 'messy vitality' that originally created Aspen's renowned cultural and social diversity. Aspen as a community should avoid an environment that is too structured, too perfect, and that eliminates the funkiness that once characterized the town."[26] In the not-so-humble opinion of real estate professional Dennis Diamond, Aspen embodies a sense of exceptionalism: "Even though a lot of these other resorts would never say it, they're Aspen wannabes. . . . They're very envious of what we have, and they all want to try to be all of that, or pieces of it."

If notions of authenticity form the backbone of locals' place narratives, discourses surrounding "The Aspen Idea" play a significant supporting role. Born from the mind of Elizabeth Paepcke—wife of Walter Paepcke, Chicago industrialist founder of modern-day Aspen—the Aspen Idea is the ethos that "body, mind, and spirit" should guide the town's existence. Together with Austrian skier Friedl Pfeifer, Walter Paepcke harnessed the local beauty, founding the Aspen Ski Company in 1946. Just as significant was the Paepckes' cultural impact, through their contributions to the Aspen Institute, the Aspen Music Festival and School, and the Aspen Center for Physics. According to historian William Philpott, Paepcke believed that teaching the arts and humanities "could cure humankind of its addiction to technology, science, and power." Accordingly, Paepcke sought to "turn Aspen into a cultural retreat, where visitors would mingle with artists, philosophers, and musicians" and solve the problems of the Cold War.[27] Today, these cultural institutions are housed at the Aspen Meadows, a Mid-Century Modern–style campus, designed by European artists and immigrants, some who fled Europe during the Second World War. The ethos of "body, mind, and spirit" is evident each summer as global elites and intellectuals travel to Aspen for an array of world-class cultural programming. The centerpiece of the summer high season is the Aspen Ideas Fest, where for nearly $4,000, ticket holders can experience a week of lectures from diplomats, policy makers, artists, and opinion leaders. During the remainder of the summer, music enthusiasts enjoy classical and jazz performances at a music tent designed by Finnish modernist, Eero Saarinen.

Discourses on Aspen's cultural and intellectual amenities emerged in my conversations with local residents and place-makers, when asked what makes Aspen unique and what keeps them living there in spite of the brutal housing market. Like many others, Dennis Diamond, who has lived in Aspen since the early 1980s claimed, "I get to live in one of the best places on the planet, bar none." He, too, saw Aspen's identity rooted in its cultural amenities: "There is no small town in the world, certainly in the United States, that has everything that we have. . . . Every town now has their little music festival, or they have their film festival, and, you know, they have other sorts of cultural things, but nobody has what we have"— meaning all of it, together. Although virtually everyone embraced Aspen's authenticity and the city itself inscribed the value of "small-town character" in its planning documents, city employee Maggie Carson reflected on the evolution of this term: "Aspen's small-town character isn't as a small mining town anymore; it's this kind of international visionary-type town that has Victorian roots, but also very important modern roots—in skiing, in the arts, in culture." It is this mix of cultural amenities, situated in a small town of 7,400 residents, that prompted retired journalist Glenn Sweeney to describe Aspen as "the only small town in America . . . [where] you could live in the splendor of nature, with an intellectual and a cultural life that you could only get in a city." Yet, the flip-side of attracting big city amenities and world-class citizens is that housing local residents and maintaining an authentic feel becomes increasingly difficult.

Finally, a central theme in Aspen's place narrative emerges from a third historical moment. Drawing on the town's emergence as a hippy-hotbed in the early 1970s, these discourses frame Aspen as politically progressive and full of unique characters; a place where celebrities, artists, and renegades can sidle up to the bar at the Hotel Jerome and enjoy a drink, unmolested, with a band of quirky locals. A hands-off approach to drug enforcement began in that era and continues to this day. Harkening back to his early years in Aspen, former mayor John Bennett (1991–1999), told me: "[In the early 1970s] we were in the midst of a counterculture war here that echoed the same counterculture war that was going on across the world. Here, the issues were sharply defined and it came down to questions like, Do we want to pave this city over and turn it over to what Hunter [S. Thompson, gonzo journalist] referred to as 'the greed heads' of the world, or do we want to preserve it, and keep it a really special, cool place . . . not just sell out to the developers and the commercial interests." Former mayor Bill Stirling (1983–1991) similarly aligned Aspen with an anti-capitalist spirit, claiming that "no one came [in the early 1970s] to make anything off of Aspen; we didn't come to capitalize on Aspen." In the early 1960s, locals organized a "Mothers March" through downtown, protesting the increased price in youth ski tickets, from 75 cents to $2; the demonstration culminated in burning effigies of the ski company's presidents.[28] *Aspen Times* journalist Peggy Clifford admonished the Aspen Ski Co., "Life is not a business and the town is not a corporation."[29] The sentiment was that the "quest for profits should not be allowed to rob locals of the recreational lifestyle that was rightfully theirs."[30] It is a sentiment that continues to animate Aspen politics, even if global market forces serve as a powerful check on this aspiration.

Under the banner of "Freak Power," gonzo journalist Hunter Thompson and biker-lawyer Joe Edwards worked to institutionalize this ethos into Aspen's politics, mounting two political campaigns in 1970, for Pitkin County Sheriff and Mayor of Aspen, respectively. Joe Edwards was especially agitated by the town's anti-vagrancy laws, which cracked down on idle hippies. These laws were passed by Aspen's old guard who remembered the bleak Quiet Years and pushed a pro-growth agenda. Although they lost their elections, the battle tilted in their favor when Michael Kinsley and Dwight Shellman arrived a few years later. As I detail later in this chapter, their leadership ushered in a progressive political framework that continues to guide place-making efforts, especially foregrounding the rights of locals. Today, many political leaders praise this generation of leaders for encoding "social engineering" into Aspen's political DNA.

Outside the political realm, memories of these political figures and the milieu they inspired are alive and well. Also arriving in the early 1970s, local journalist Jesse Hanks described his initial impressions of the town:

"There were a lot of people leading unconventional lives with unconventional goals, living in unconventional places, so that was the spirit of the town: unconventional. It was not your average American town, and even for the people who were seen within the context of Aspen as having the most settled, conventional lives, [they] were not really your average American. Even the ones with families and everything else, they'd come to this kind of offbeat outpost where normal expectations were not the normal American expectations." While most Aspenites I spoke with told me that the true gonzo spirit was dead and lives on via a nostalgic but thin aesthetic appreciation, they described Aspen as a place that continues to attract unique characters. Employed as a history educator and "Aspen's biggest cheerleader," Rosie Sorrentino reflected that "the people who are attracted to this valley are kind of outside-the-box thinkers, to begin with; people who don't like to just follow the path that is expected. People that don't want to work nine to five . . . who are risk takers" and come to a place "where everything is done at a heightened level." What that means is that alongside the progressives, bohemians, and creative types are people with mental health issues and substance abuse problems—much like Hunter S. Thompson, himself.

The narratives that local residents draw upon span a hundred and fifty years, and characterize Aspen as a real, authentic place that draws amazing artists and progressive figures, gathering them into an exceptionally beautiful place. The word *community* emerged time and again in conversations with locals, explaining why they chose to make Aspen their home. "I came for the skiing," millennial political activist Skippy Mesirow (elected to city council in 2018) told me, "but I stayed for the sense of community." Elsewhere, residents commented upon and marveled at the scope of philanthropy and generosity. For the deeply intellectual yet witty architect Clark Demming, "Aspen's a very narcissistic place. It loves itself and everything about Aspen is just honey to the bees." Speaking out of earnestness rather than cynicism, local political figure and holder of odd jobs, André Lewandowski said: "It's the best place ever; I love Aspen. It's changed a lot over the years, and it's changed a lot since I've been here, . . . but Aspen's interesting because you go on vacation and when you're headed home, you're psyched. You can't wait to open your door and be home." While many locals lamented the lack of affordable housing and other challenges associated with living in a rarefied resort economy, they asserted that the social, cultural, political, and natural features of Aspen mean that at the end of the day, "My life is better than your vacation." In the next chapter, I return to the challenges confronted by working locals. With respect to place-making processes, discourses of Aspen exceptionalism reflect notions of what Aspen is and should continue to be; when the validity of these discourses is threatened, these cultural understandings inspire efforts to reaffirm and reinscribe these treasured and taken-for granted assumptions.

Aspen Egalitarianism: Narratives about Class

The model of *place-based class cultures* centers on understandings of social class, seeing them as both an input and output in how class interests are institutionalized. Class, in this sense, is shaped by both material resources and cultural resources. As a cultural resource, narratives about social class address questions like: What is the social class of the people who live here? How many classes are there? How do class or status groups intersect and interact? What are their interests and their stake in the community? Demographic, political, and material conditions enable and constrain the power of these narratives to become institutionalized. The work of Japonica Brown-Saracino and British scholars complicates understandings of how social class works in place, especially in terms of how residents' material interests map onto their ideological interests. Moreover, who comprises a social class and how they seek to identify and activate their interests is a contingency.[31] Once again drawing on this set of interviews, I find that when it comes to understandings of social class in Aspen, two things are evident: one, there is high degree of consensus around these understandings; and two, there is anxiety over the sense that once-egalitarian class relations have given way to dislocation and foreign ways of doing class.

Aspen locals are well aware of the connotation beyond its borders as a place of affluence, glitz, and celebrity. Several millennials who had grown up in Aspen, for example, said that they hesitate to tell people outside of Aspen precisely where they were raised. Instead, they told new college friends that they "grew up in Colorado" because, as medical student Eugenia Rappaport said, "people have assumptions about it and I don't feel like getting into it." For these young adults, maintaining silence or ambiguity around their hometown origins was an effort to counteract the eye-rolls or the need to explain that Aspen is a normal place to live, even if it is, as Eugenia acknowledged, "incredibly wealthy . . . [and] an entitled and privileged place." Locally, however, many residents emphasized its lack of pretension.

"The origin myth of Aspen," architect Clark Demming told me, is that it is a place where "miners can rub shoulders with millionaires— billionaires, now, but millionaires, back when the phrase was coined." The central location for this storied rubbing of shoulders is the Hotel Jerome, which opened in 1889 and is listed on the National Register of Historic Places. Today, its rooms rent for nearly $1,000 in winter, requiring a minimum stay of five nights. Yet, when former mayor John Bennett arrived in Aspen in 1970, with a band of "merry pranksters" who set out to "discover America" when Yale shut down during student protests: "You could walk in the Jerome Bar, which was the watering hole of choice for all of my friends, and lined up at the bar would be, you know, carpenters, ski instructors, and bus boys and waiters and waitresses, and billionaires, and Hunter Thompson. Hunter would be holding court at the end of the bar, and Jack Nicholson might be with a beer and a hat pulled down over his head so, no one even knew who he was. . . . It was this incredibly egalitarian place, I just loved it! Looking back on these times, Bennett characterized Aspen as 'the most class-free place [he'd] ever been.'"

Long-term locals described the workplace as another site for class mixing. Bennett eventually bought a bookstore, about whose customers he said, "We had Jack Nicholson and we had the local dishwasher from the restaurant next door, and they all hung out together." Jesse Hanks, a New Yorker who arrived after graduating college in the early 1970s, described his experiences: "I was pumping gas on Main Street and, you know, I was a grease-covered kid, . . . but some of the same people who would drive in, I'd pump gas for them and then I'd wind up seeing them at parties in the evening and they were, you know, some of the more well-established, well-to-do people in town. But there was tremendous mixing across all the different—I'd say across different social divisions, but there really weren't so many social divisions." Instead, he said, "it felt like the kind of a town where everybody was sort of, you know, equal is a hard thing to say, but there was a level of equality." Clint Jones, an artist and private chef, took this sentiment several steps further. Reflecting on recent experiences rather than nostalgic reflections he said, "Every client I have has become— they're family." He has flown on clients' private jets, stayed in their New York apartments, and attended family celebrations. These friendships have emerged, Clint said, "not because I'm a professional peer or financial peer," but because "[I'm] trustworthy and safe" and not trying to get anything from them. Whereas scholar Justin Farrell characterizes such claims among Teton County's uber-wealthy as an effort to assuage their class guilt, here such claims emerge from the mouths of working locals.

Claims to Aspen's egalitarianism are sometimes attributed to the intellectual joie de vivre of the town's spiritual cofounder, Elizabeth Paepcke. When former mayor John Bennett met her in the early 1970s, he recalled her saying: "My worst fear would be the day when Aspen becomes nothing but rich people. . . . She was a wealthy person," Bennett continued, "but she didn't hang out in country clubs; . . . she had a ton of working friends, and what she really liked were artists and intellectuals. She didn't give a damn what your income was; she wanted to know what your coefficient of creativity was." The idea of a creativity coefficient reflects Paepcke's Aspen Idea of mind, body, and spirit, an idea reinforced by journalist Jesse Hanks's characterization of those who gave Aspen its energy in the 1970s. Money "wasn't the defining factor in [the Paepckes'] lives," he told me. They tended "to have a lot more interests than just accumulating the money—because this was not a place exclusively for wealthy people at that point, it was a place where people mixed and there was an emphasis on arts and thought and intellect."

While Aspen locals widely acknowledged that many tremendously wealthy people live and vacation there, their class discourses asserted that Aspen wealth is—or should be—uniquely unpretentious. This preference for "unpretentiousness" seemed to escape the attention of the national advertising company that was hired by the Aspen Ski Company in 2016 to promote their four local ski mountains. The agency proposed a marketing campaign with copy reading "The Rich Life," in a diamond-encrusted font. This motto was quickly rejected by Ski Co., who saw it as entirely out of step with the Aspen brand. Despite the presence of many luxury retailers and homes selling for $30 million, locals routinely described the unassuming nature of wealth in Aspen. "No matter how much money you have," architect Woody Bateman asserted, "when you come here, you shed all that stuff." In Aspen, class is done in a low-key way. "If you owned a Lamborghini," Woody continued, "you would not take that thing here. You would be with your jeans and your Jeep or whatever, because there is a desire to blend in with the local people." Plenty of opportunities allow for free or low-cost class mixing. Like many other locals, John Bennett looks forward to summer's annual music festival. While subscribers and ticket holders sit in reserved seats inside the tent, other enthusiasts enjoy bottles of rosé sitting on blankets outside. Seated "outside for free," Bennett and his wife see "multimillionaires and, you know, and waiters and waitresses from our favorite restaurants. Everybody's sitting out there, and that's great. It's really cool." Justin Farrell critiqued similar discourses of authenticity and class mixing among Teton County's billionaires, seeing them as a moral front that justified the accumulation of wealth and exploitation of the natural environment.[32] The difference in Aspen is that these claims are being made by working locals—not billionaire elites. This suggests a more widely shared understanding of the discourse, which suggests that either such claims are indeed part of the local fabric or that working locals somehow misinterpret the nature of their relationships with the wealthy people around them. I prefer the former interpretation.

Extending the notion that Aspen embodies an unpretentious expression of wealth, others claimed that social class distinctions in Aspen can also be ambiguous. This, too, is partially attributable to Aspen's "laid back" culture, as land use lawyer Brian Cottrell put it, where even lawyers, politicians, and developers go to work in "biking shorts or hiking clothes or jeans and a polo." Not once did I observe anyone in city council chambers wearing a jacket and tie. While they may wear Brooks Brothers or Brioni suits for business in their hometowns or larger cities, many professionals in Aspen wear a uniform of outdoor brands like Marmot and North Face. A journalist in his late-twenties, Mason Ward described how the casual outdoor culture can obscure class differences. Local residents, he said, are: "[P]eople with super-high levels of education, maybe who grew up with money, who are taking this route, 'I want to work for a nonprofit and I want to spend a lot of time outside.' But they choose not to live ostentatiously. There's some ostentation here in Aspen, but then there's this whole segment where you're not totally sure where people fall because maybe what they're displaying is just kind of normal, White, educated—this uniformity where you ski and do yoga—and your class could be anything!"

While many Aspen locals have high levels of education and, therefore, some degree of privilege, the outdoor aesthetic—which is not cheap, but certainly more affordable than the garments sold in the town's designer boutiques—levels out distinctions among those whose cultural capital allows them to blend into an undifferentiated privileged class. Claims of egalitarianism, then, rest on a Bourdieusian approach to class: while working locals and affluent visitors and part-year residents may differ in their economic capital, they have shared cultural capital. In addition to the fact that many working Aspenites graduated from selective liberal arts colleges and Ivy League universities, they almost universally share a love of outdoor recreation and an appreciation for the environment, and in many cases also share an interest in contemporary art and classical music. These shared interests allow them to blend.

Despite these claims of class egalitarianism, members of the Aspen community have very different material circumstances. Aspen is among the most unequal communities in the United States, after all. Yet when asked directly about how classes relate to one another, most described a positive, symbiotic relationship. Rosie Sorrentino, who came to Aspen in 1999 as a manager in the hospitality industry, described class differences this way:

> Well, I jokingly say there are two kinds of people in Aspen: There are those with three jobs and those with three homes. But we need each other. . . . You know, without *them* [wealthy, part-year residents and visitors], *we* [less affluent locals] don't have the opportunity to be here—and I am one of "we," not "them." It's about supporting each other, you know? The gardener takes care of the lawn and keeps it looking nice for you. The ski instructor gets to have a job because you're going to pay X amount of dollars to ski with him for a week. So, it really works both ways.

Ce Ce Catalano, a thirty-something who does in fact work three jobs, echoed this point. "My jobs wouldn't exist without real-estate. Real estate is what funds all of the media and most of the marketing in this town. I wouldn't be able to live here without it." Clint Jones, another holder of three jobs, rebuffed any suggestion of class exploitation: "I like the 1 percent; the 1 percent allows me the life I like to live. I'm not rich or wealthy or anything like that, but I look at what I do for a living and it's like, I couldn't do that anywhere else." As a private chef, he estimates that he earns 40–50 percent more locally than he would elsewhere.

Class tensions were not entirely absent from residents' discourses, yet, rather than a distaste for wealthy people, these discourses typically focus on conflicts surrounding development. Conflicts sometimes emerged between year-round residents seeking to limit growth and those who fuel growth, namely developers, visitors, and part-year residents. Woody Bateman, an architect, tapped into these tensions, but asserted that potentially conflictual class relations should be reframed as interdependent: "I don't want to sound negative, but one thing that does bother me is the hypocrisy. We are the poster child for trickle-down economics. We completely exist because very wealthy people come here and employ us, all of us. But we're against wealthy people; we're against development—and yet that's where it all comes from. I think that the conversation could be more honest if we admit what's happening and not vilify people for being a real estate agent or whatever."

As I discuss below and in chapters 3 and 6, tensions over locals' interests and how class is done in Aspen have intensified in recent years. A few, like thirty-something beverage distributor Scott Bailey, questioned the assumption that the wealthy benefit the local economy, whether through taxes or philanthropic contributions. "There's a lot of rich people here who don't contribute anything," he told me. "They're up [in their homes] on Red Mountain; they have a chef; they don't come into town." Most of the residents I spoke to, however, spoke of the role that affluent outsiders play in making their lives possible. According to Doug Donaldson and Tanya Reyes, leaders in the local faith community, wealthy churchgoers disproportionally fund their parish's activities—enabling wonderful music programs, for example—despite the fact that they are not year-round residents. Council member Adam Frisch frequently invoked the town's extraordinarily large $120 million municipal budget—85 percent of which, he speculated, derived from spending by visitors and other non-year-round residents—as trickling down in the form of subsidies to affordable housing, education, and recreational opportunities that benefit the middle classes.

As global capital markets have expanded and wealth has flooded into Aspen, new discourses have emerged, forcing locals to make sense of what happens now that "the billionaires are pushing out the millionaires." The sentiment that things have changed since the idyllic, egalitarian 1970s was nearly universally held—especially by those who arrived during that period. Journalist Glenn Sweeney characterized present-day Aspen as "the most class-ridden structure I've ever seen." "It was so ideal," he lamented, but due to "rampant capitalism, people started getting more money than they ever needed or dreamed of." Perhaps most offensive to longtime locals is the tendency of Aspen's newer wealthy arrivals to self-segregate. Rather than heading into town to "rub shoulders" with locals, affluent visitors now hire private chefs to cook for them in their $25 million mountain estates. Jesse Hanks worried about this impact on class relations and the local economy, fearing that some part-year residents "fly in a lot of their food supplies, so they're not even shopping [in the local grocery stores]." Ironically, the success of the town's affordable housing program also seems to have exacerbated class segregation. With the expansion of this program, rather than build units in the historic core or above local businesses, larger complexes with more units have been built on the edge of town, which seems to inhibit class mixing in bars, restaurants, and the pedestrian malls.

The fear that ostentation and glitz have replaced unpretentiousness and funkiness worried some Aspenites. Instead of flying under the radar, Jesse Hanks characterized Aspen's newer wealth as wanting their names on the buildings they have endowed with charitable contributions. "This town feels like every nook and cranny has been scrubbed clean with a toothbrush," he lamented. Now that "money dominates everything . . . that funky character has been pushed way out of town, further and further down valley to Carbondale and beyond." Much of what Aspen holds sacred, namely its storied funkiness and history of class mixing, feels increasingly elusive. The fact, however, that local interests have been encoded into the town's progressive politics, provides the possibility that these older class relations might be reaffirmed and re-institutionalized through revisions to the land use code.

The Institutionalization of Class Interests

Place-making is not merely about discourses—it is also about the durable ways in which place is institutionalized. Institutionalization, here, refers to the process by which place gets encoded formally, through laws and policies, as well as informally, through routines, norms, and recognized ways of doing things (e.g., making claims, lobbying for change). As illustrated in figure 1.1, discourses about place and social class intertwine with their institutionalization, so discourse can make laws and policies possible, while laws and policies, in turn, permit—or constrain—available discourses. There are, of course, additional influences on the institutionalization of class—changes in underlying economic conditions, for example—but these discourses, I argue, are central elements of place-making. The dialectic between discourses and policy is clearly illustrated in a statement drawn from the Aspen Area Community Plan of 2000— the vision document that both captures sentiments of what Aspen *is* and establishes a legal framework for implementing that vision through urban planning: "Aspen has flourished because it has accepted people for who they are and not for whom we think they should be. A stratified class system is foreign to Aspen and is in opposition to our concept of a healthy valley. Valuable 'accidental' cross-cultural interaction is now being blocked. Encouragement of a more classless and interactive Aspen is necessary if we are to have a spirited community."[33] In this final section, I illustrate how class interests have been institutionalized in Aspen. Focusing on zoning, taxation and fees, political involvement, and policy development, I show that the rights of locals—especially middle- and upper-middle-class locals—have been enshrined in local politics. Global market forces have been a formidable opponent in recent decades, however, threatening taken-for-granted ways of doing and understanding class in Aspen.

Progressive is a word often used to describe Aspen's political landscape, especially the landscape from which the current social and political terrain has grown. Rooted in the arrival of countercultural "seekers" during the late 1960s and early 1970s, the progressive ethos was institutionalized through hard-fought political campaigns that unseated the old-timers who controlled Aspen. One figure in "the battle for Aspen"—as Hunter S.

Thompson called it—was Joe Edwards (1972–1980), whose successful campaign for county commissioner worked from the premise that, in the words of former mayor John Bennett, "We who live here, we who live in the Valley, have the right to say what kind of place it will be." The political efforts of Edwards and his contemporaries—the trio of Dwight Shellman, Stacey Stanley, and Michael Kinsley—have resulted in four policy pillars that many local politicians and residents seek to defend. First among these is the effort to control growth. Far from Logan and Molotch's urban "growth machine," the effort to limit growth has been evident since the Pitkin County commissioners "downzoned" the county in the 1970s, restricting density and population growth. At the time, the county's zoning regulations permitted fifty-five residential units per acre; if built to capacity, these regulations would have allowed the county's population to swell to nearly four hundred thousand residents. Edwards and Shellman worked to limit residential growth, allowing one unit per ten acres in rural portions of the county. This downzoning worked hand in hand with a "growth management quota system" (GMQS), which limited growth by scoring applications for residential and commercial developments based on aesthetics, sustainability, and alignment with community goals. Other efforts to manage growth included restricting the square footage of homes, prohibiting commercial development outside the urban growth boundary, protecting mountain views, and setting aside rural lands for open space and public recreation rather than private use. Geographer William R. Travis claims that over the years, Aspen and Pitkin County have "led the West in terms of [innovative] planning solutions."[34]

Today, the low-growth legacy remains and is defended as a fundamental premise in "keeping Aspen, Aspen." Indeed, the desire to limit growth and preserve town character—by restricting building sizes, preserving views of the mountain, and protecting rural spaces—are fundamental priorities in Aspen's urban planning. Yet as I show in chapter 5, efforts to control growth can butt up against other goals. For example, the desire to limit building sizes and concentrate commercial development in the urban core make it difficult to fulfill simultaneously the goal of providing affordable housing within the same scarce area. Additionally, by limiting the size of buildings and land available for development, real estate prices increase. Within a low-growth context, conflicts may emerge over how to adequately serve the needs of locals while also attracting the people who pay the taxes that make local life possible.

A second policy pillar that shapes class relations and class interests in Aspen is the ambitious affordable housing program, another achievement of '70s-era progressive politicians. The median home price in 2018 hovered around $4 million, well out of reach of 90 percent of locals, who earn less than $200,000 annually. Even in the early 1970s, affordable housing was failing to keep up with the expanding resort economy. In 1974, Pitkin County commissioners voted to develop a housing authority—now the Aspen Pitkin County Housing Authority, (APCHA)—believed to be the first government-led workforce housing program in the nation.[35] Colloquially called "employee housing," the program maintains nearly three thousand units in a town with 7,400 year-round residents; some are rental units, other can be purchased. Figure 4 shows an example of an affordable housing complex. Employees become eligible by working at least fifteen hundred hours each year, within the county. This, along with income and family size, qualifies them to bid on units ranging from studio apartments to five-bedroom homes. A typical two-bedroom townhome might sell for $270,000, while a typical two-bedroom apartment might rent for $1,300 monthly. Excluded from participation are those who earn more than $300,000 annually and those who have more than $900,000 in assets. You may need a moment to digest this fact: yes, an individual earning $300,000 a year—a member of the top 1 percent in many US communities—qualifies for subsidized housing in Aspen. One important source of funding from this program comes from mitigations paid by developers. Ever since 1993, developers have "offset" the demand for housing that is created when their projects—whether an office building, a hotel, a mixed-use development—produce jobs that need to be filled. Over the years, the amount that developers are responsible for has increased. At the onset of the 2016 moratorium, the code mandated a rate of 60 percent, meaning that developers had to either create new housing onsite for 60 percent of the new workers their projects generate, or pay an equivalent fee to build housing offsite. A second source of funding is the real estate transfer tax (RETT), which imposes a 1.5 percent tax on real estate transactions in Aspen, two-thirds of which funnels into a fund used to build affordable housing.[36] Initially passed by the county commissioners

Figure 4. Affordable housing units at Fairway 3 in Snowmass (approximate purchase price: $275,000). Photo by Don Stuber.

in 1990, voters have renewed the RETT numerous times. Local voters' support for additional taxation is fairly unsurprising, given that they are relatively unlikely to be the ones who purchase homes and contribute to the fund.

Premised on maintaining its identity as a "lights-on" community, the affordable housing program is a bedrock institution, allowing "local characters" to live in town and contribute to the town's much touted authenticity. The Aspen Area Community Plan institutionalizes this sentiment, specifying that housing projects need "to further [a socioeconomic] mix and to avoid segregation of economic and social classes."[37] Today, locals and even the founders of the program are split on whether the program has grown too large or should continue to expand. It is undeniable, however, that demand outpaces supply, given that less than 15 percent of local workers are able to find housing within Aspen's free-market sector.[38] How to address the unmet demand is more of a political question than an economic one, since $7 million from the RETT and perhaps $3 million from sales taxes pour into the housing fund each year. Whereas NIMBY-ism ("Not In My Backyard") in other communities reflects efforts at class exclusion, to the extent that opposition to new affordable housing exists in Aspen, it typically reflects the desire to preserve mountain views. More-over, some residents and local politicians fear that creating more affordable housing will simply drive more demand, thereby stimulating population growth and re-creating the problem it attempted to solve. The third rail of local politics, the affordable housing program and its supporters continue to evolve the program so that it fulfills the mandate, spelled out in the AACP, of facilitating locals' ability to live in close proximity to work. For accountant and Aspen native Donald Ranstead, who raised his children in one of the program's single-family homes, the program amounts to a "*huge* subsidy to keep town character alive"—one that serves the interests of working locals, but in less obvious ways also serves the interests of uber-wealthy developers, visitors, and part-year residents, contributing to the sense of authenticity and character that fuels the Aspen brand.

A third policy pillar in Aspen, and one that structures class relations is the "pay to play" approach to development. During his tenure, Aspen city council member Adam Frisch was famous for saying, "If Aspen had a flag, its motto would read 'Development Pays Its Own Way.'" Stated more simply by Mayor Steve Skadron (2013–2019), "This is a town that hates development." The local attitude insists that instead of economic incen-tives and tax abatements, those wishing to develop in Aspen must offset the impacts of their activities. As explained in the Aspen Area Commu-nity Plan of 2012, "private sector development should not place a finan-cial burden on the tax-paying public."[39] Many communities have such fees, designed to offset environmental impacts, as well as the increased demand for housing, schools, social services, and infrastructure created by development. Because mitigations increase a developer's cost to develop, they can be used as a tool to control growth and thereby influence local character, as shown in Kee Warner and Harvey Molotch's case study of three California communities.[40]

While many communities impose mitigation fees, they differ in how extensive and intensive they are in terms of types of mitigations levied and the percentage levied. Maggie Carson, an employee in Aspen's urban plan-ning department, believes that Aspen has "the highest mitigation of any community in Colorado and other peer communities outside of Colorado." In addition to affordable housing mitigations, fees are also extracted for environmental and transportation impacts. Large commercial projects in Aspen may be assessed anywhere from $2 to $5 million in mitigation fees. A typical residential project may incur $250,000–300,000 in building fees alone, according to real estate professional Dennis Diamond. Mitigations have become so extensive and such a widely used tool to shape growth patterns that council member Frisch has dubbed Aspen's land use code, "the mitigation industrial complex."

The use of mitigations is not merely a technical aspect of urban planning. Indeed, they are a tool that structures class relations. For year-round locals—most of whom are middle or upper-middle class—these mitigations make life in Aspen both possible and enjoyable. These funds, along with other local taxes, help build affordable housing, facilitate free or low-cost public transit, and foster access to nature. Mitigations in Aspen are a tool for economic redistribution, giving rise to what architect Mitch Nelson called the "subsidized class"—working locals who benefit from the housing, education, and recreational subsidies that flow from tax levies and development fees. If Aspen were like many communities in the United States, wealthy stakeholders might push back against these extractions. But as Maggie Carson explained, "Maybe we're able to do that [impose extensive mitigations] because we're Aspen and people always want to come here." Despite the institutionalization of a "mitigation industrial complex," some locals had become concerned that too many developers were negotiating their way out of mitigation fees and being absolved of their responsibility to the community. This concern was especially apparent with regard to affordable housing mitigation. As I show in the next chapter, this sentiment played an important role in the city council's decision in 2016 to rewrite the land use codes and align them more directly with community values.

Finally, not every instance of the institutionalization of class interests derives from local politics or local norms; federal policies also affect how class is emplaced. The fourth policy that structures class relations and class interests in Aspen, and contributes to its unique place-based class culture, derives from the fact that people can vote in only one locale. People who own multiple homes must decide where they will pay income taxes, homestead their houses, and register to vote. Colorado is considered moderately tax-friendly; some high-net-worth individuals might domicile there, as opposed to the state of their primary residence, for tax purposes.[41] And while it is impossible to know the percentage of part-year residents who are registered to vote in Aspen, the fact that municipal elections historically have taken place in May and national elections in November—quiet months in the off-season—suggests that the numbers are low. Consequently, those who vote on ballot initiatives (often tax levies and referenda on development projects) and elect the officials who structure the political side of place-making, are disproportionately the year-round residents who differ materially from the area's part-year residents. Aspen, then, is a place where those who shape the town's economic fortunes and those who shape the town's political fortunes are somewhat different groups. Yet, rather than thinking of these groups as having fundamentally different interests, given their different material and class locations, Aspen operates more like Atlanta, as profiled by Clarence Stone: a place where seemingly opposed stakeholder groups must cooperate with one another to build a successful community, even if their interests seem to differ.

With electoral power in the hands of middle- and upper-middle-class residents, Aspen and Pitkin County generally support "progressive candidates." While many residents feel that the progressivism of recent leaders pales in comparison to the political godfathers of the 1970s, elected officials still favor slow-growth policies and routinely pledge to protect, if not expand, affordable housing. Voters themselves show an almost limitless appetite for passing new tax levies, whether for transportation, education, or fire services. The strong support for higher taxes makes sense, given locals' support for quality-of-life issues and the fact that tax revenues are paid disproportionately by wealthy visitors and part-year residents. Those uber-wealthy constituents, however, lack a formal political voice, and have not mounted a coordinated opposition to the fees, taxes, and mitigations that seem to escalate ever higher. For Jim DeFrancia, a longtime developer and descendent of an Aspen silver miner, the lack of opposition makes perfect sense: "This little town's got like a $100 million a year budget. I mean it's astonishing, right? And it's all paid for overwhelmingly by people who don't vote here and who take little or no interest in the local politics— 'cause to them, it's just the cost of living and they really don't care. So that leaves us as locals to benefit, right?" For many of the uber-wealthy who make Aspen their home or playground, taxes and extractions amount to a rounding error, and they, too, benefit from intensive social engineering. The fees that subsidize Aspen's affordable housing program, schools, recreation, and social services, are made possible by an intensely protected Aspen brand, one that derives from growth controls, historical preservation, and aesthetic regulations. All of this, together, supports the assertion that Aspen has one of the "thickest land use codes" per capita. "[T] he question," for council member Frisch, "is whether Aspen has thrived *in spite of* or *because of* us doing more tinkering than most communities anywhere in the world." He concludes, though, that "it's a little bit of both, but mostly we are great because of it."

CONCLUSION

Collectively, the place-narratives and policy pillars described in this chapter comprise Aspen's *place-based class culture*. They form a set of interconnected elements, framed by local demographic and material conditions, that shape how social class is understood and therefore "done" in a particular place. How a place does social class, in turn, shapes its place character and how local stakeholders attempt to adjudicate class interests. While this model can be translated to almost any community, the dynamics seen here are most applicable to places that are relatively affluent, unequal, and homogeneous—like many resort communities—and have an active and empowered base of locals.

In Aspen, the elements that make up its place-based class culture contain complexity and contradiction; this derives, in large part, from the fact that local government and other stakeholders recognize that the "three communities" that make up Aspen—year-round residents, visitors, and part-year residents—are critical stakeholders in the Aspen brand. It is a place where well-educated, relatively privileged locals are the beneficiaries of redistributive policies that enhance their quality of life, and where they vote, more often than not, to preserve a political structure that honors the town's storied egalitarianism. It is also a place where developers, visitors, and part-year residents pay extensive taxes and mitigations.

While these affluent parties could develop their projects or buy a second home in Vail, Colorado, or Park City, Utah, for much less, they do not, nor do they form an active lobby to oppose these fees. Instead, they seem to understand that the benefits associated with buying into Aspen inevitably come with some costs.

As I show throughout this book, the fates of Aspen's "three communities" are intertwined and largely interdependent. Whereas working locals depend on revenues generated by affluent visitors and part-year residents, affluent visitors and part-year residents benefit from the character and place-making expertise that working locals contribute. Increasingly, these communities—or at least factions of them—appear to be in conflict, stimulated, in part, by a new influx of global capital. The next two chapters capture the recent anxieties that have emerged over class and place in Aspen. The next chapter peers into the ways that working locals understand and navigate the class disparities in their communities. In chapter 3, I show how growing anxieties over class prompted a building moratorium and a push to rewrite the land use codes. Each subsequent chapter examines how, during the yearlong building moratorium, local government sought to use the land use code to resolve these tensions and preserve deeply held convictions over what Aspen is and who it is for.

2 Living the "Aspen Dream"? Redefining and Realizing the Good Life

I have sometimes wondered why anyone would choose to live in Aspen. Scratch that. Given all the natural beauty, it is immediately evident why someone would *want* to live in Aspen. What is less clear is why someone with skills and options would choose to live in this town, year after year, given the punishing housing market and unique and sometimes uniquely constraining job market. I have seen small-business owners get priced out of their livelihoods, forced to move down valley where commercial real estate is more affordable, or retool their professional identities and aspirations so that they can remain closer to Aspen. I have seen friends and family members get displaced from their residences, with rental agreements falling through as condo owners convert units with longer-term leases to more lucrative short-term vacation rentals. Things have certainly changed since the "class-less" vibe of the 1970s, when young folks couch-surfed their way through Aspen, sometimes for years, eventually earning enough to buy a modest home in the "free market."[1] Over wine and conversation at L'Hostaria, an Italian restaurant that simultaneously caters to working locals and elites, architect Heidi Hartmann summarized it best: "The lifestyle is phenomenal, but living is difficult."

Although place-makers in Aspen had, since the 1970s, worked to balance class interests and create opportunities for locals to live and work in this upscale mountain town, today, many residents confront challenges in realizing the American Dream. With the fairly narrow economic base of the town, where jobs are concentrated in real estate and tourism, residents struggle to climb job ladders and achieve career success. Despite the extensive affordable housing program, many working locals are unable to find stable housing, let alone become homeowners. Each year, some portion of these residents give up the fight: they reach the end of their economic rope, get tired of the grind, and leave Aspen to seek a career, home, or family in a more forgiving locale. Yet others keep on coming, and plenty of locals dig in, committed to the hustle of finding workable housing or, ideally, grateful that they have won a unit in the affordable housing lottery.[2] Despite the efforts of local government to protect the interests of year-round locals, broader market forces still exert their power on this town, resulting in constrained economic opportunities. This chapter examines the experiences of working locals, situating them within the context of *lifestyle migration,* and shows how Aspen's unique place-based class culture provides both challenges and opportunities to these residents' way of life. These analyses serve as a foundation for the chapters to follow, which focus on how elected officials and place-makers use the tools of urban planning to balance and institutionalize class interests. Yet before examining place-making efforts, it is important to understand why people move to Aspen and the Roaring Fork Valley and how they experience the community with respect to social class.

Many people migrate to Aspen or continue living there primarily because of the *lifestyle* opportunities it provides; unlike the Latino migrants who live down valley, they are not there principally because the employment conditions are better than what they find in their home countries or even elsewhere in the United States. In fact, many Aspen residents could, ostensibly, earn more and experience more career mobility if they lived in cities like Denver, Austin, or Chicago. Because these analyses focus on those who are *pursuing Aspen,* rather than those pursuing a job or better work opportunities, these voices represent the largely White, middle- and upper-middle-class working locals. Cognizant of their constrained economic opportunities, many of them substitute the "Aspen Dream" for the "American Dream." Whereas material success and homeownership typically define the American Dream, the Aspen Dream is measured in "quality-of-life dividends." This mental substitution is necessary, in part, because incomes are not sufficient to purchase a home in the free market. Those who live the Aspen Dream assert that the symbolic and lifestyle benefits associated with living in Aspen outweigh the economic costs. Rather than continued career growth or salary increases, they claim that living in Aspen provides nonmaterial work and lifestyle benefits. Accomplishments are quantified not in terms of salary or promotions, but in terms of how many days of skiing one can amass. Locals typically invoked access to nature and the ability to hike or ski on lunch breaks as the essential perks of living in Aspen. Others praised the easy access to world-class culture, whether volunteering at the legendary Food and Wine Festival or taking in a concert for free while sitting in the garden-like atmosphere of the Music Festival. Being surrounded by interesting people was similarly mentioned as a lifestyle premium, made possible by Aspen's ability to attract worldly, well-educated, and quirky characters. While many of these experiences are consistent with the phenomenon of lifestyle migration more broadly, what makes the experiences of Aspen's working locals noteworthy, and potentially mitigates their feelings of deprivation compared to the affluent visitors and part-year residents they are surrounded by, is how the local place-based class culture both validates and facilitates their pursuit of these lifestyle dividends.

LIFESTYLE MIGRATION AND THE PURSUIT OF THE GOOD LIFE

Recent decades have seen an increase in lifestyle migration and, with it, scholarly attention devoted to understanding the phenomenon. For British scholars Michaela Benson and Karen O'Reilly, lifestyle migration is an umbrella term that refers to geographic moves motivated by pursuit of "the good life."[3] For some, the good life means moving to an area with ample access to nature and recreation or opportunities for cultural enrichment.

This subtype is called amenity migration.[4] For others, the emphasis is therapeutic or spiritual in nature, where movers seek to reconnect with themselves or build community with others. Many scholars, including anthropologist Brian A. Hoey, attach a moral valence to lifestyle migration. His profile of migrants to the lakeside idyll of Traverse City, Michigan, shows movers wanting to fashion a better, more authentic version of one's self.[5] In almost all its forms, lifestyle migration and pursuit of "the good life" means rejecting fast-paced careers, long commutes, and the sense of detachment that typifies middle- and upper-middle-class existence in late capitalism.

Geographic migration itself is nothing new. Indeed, humans have been on the move for millennia, pushed and pulled in various directions seeking better political and economic opportunities. Lifestyle migration is different in that people do not pursue it out of material or economic necessity. Rather, it is a mobility of choice. As Karen O'Reilly and Michaela Benson note, a host of social and economic transformations have given rise to the ability to make this choice, including globalization, technological advancements that provide flexibility in working lives, ease of movement, and the emphasis on self-actualization.[6] "Freed from its primordial grip," Leonard Nevarez writes, "place can now be categorized, strategized, and used to achieve social concerns, values, and identities."[7] With late capitalism meeting our basic daily needs, Nevarez suggests, affluent individuals can now pursue health, intimacy, community attachment, and emotional well-being.

The complex intertwining of technology, economic forces, and an emphasis on quality of life enables yet another subtype of lifestyle migration: *lifestyle mobilities.* Here, moves are not intended to be permanent or year-round, but are part of a broader pattern of mobility, where work and leisure are intimately interconnected. As Scott Cohen and his coauthors note, with the affluence that late capitalism affords, the "binary divide between work and leisure may be collapsed."[8] In many cases, the migration of the relatively affluent is made possible by the asymmetry between their own lives and the lives and of those in the receiving communities, who largely lack an ability to move. This is especially evident among affluent residents of the United States and Great Britain, who have flocked to places like Costa Rica, Spain, and Portugal's Algarve region, where they are able to downshift because their money goes farther there and local economies depend on their demand for services. Collectively, the scholarship on lifestyle migration situates this phenomenon within a particular time and place, and among a select demographic, where relatively affluent and often older adults are able to pull up roots and move to places where their dollars go farther, thereby facilitating their pursuit of the good life.

Yet scholars have not fully explored what happens when the economic and non-economic aspects of the good life stand in tension to one another. The case of Aspen, Colorado, provides the opportunity to ask such questions, impacted as it is, by a wave of supergentrification. While the motivations to move to Aspen resemble those found in existing studies of lifestyle migration, and the individuals involved are similarly privileged, differences also exist. Unlike European movers to Bali or American expats in Panama, lifestyle migrants to Aspen are not uniformly more affluent than the members of the surrounding community, nor are they able to find housing that would be considered a bargain back home. In fact, the housing market is quite tight, and the cost of living offers only the wealthiest migrants the opportunity to downshift their careers. For the majority of local residents, maintaining a full-time job is not optional, and yet the pursuit of a traditional career trajectory is made difficult by the narrow scope of the economy. Given these tensions, it is worth asking: What happens when residents' pursuit of the good life butts up against economic constraints? How do they weigh their material challenges and sacrifices against the nonmaterial benefits they receive? Conversations with locals show that achieving the Aspen Dream involves ongoing negotiations, satisficing, and substitution, more so than sacrifice, all within the context of a place-based class culture that both idealizes and institutionalizes egalitarian class relations.

"I'M GOING WEST": OF PRIVILEGE AND POSSIBILITY IN THE MOVE TO ASPEN

The notion of the "freshman class" is embedded in Aspen lore. It captures the footloose-and-fancy free attitude that brings many young people to town each year, and inspires many to try to make it their home. The vitality and excitement of these young adults is so palpable that in 1975, Marc Demming and Al Pendorf founded Aspen State Teacher's College, with the motto: "The no-credit, fun college of the Rockies." Aspen State Teacher's College is not a real college; rather, it was an extended satire and marketing gimmick that likened the town to a party school, with new workers in the resort industry as the "freshman class" and longer-term locals as the "faculty." It maintained a "student union" in the downtown core, which functioned as a gathering place and headquarters for planning school events, like "homecoming," and sold the "school's" newspaper, pennants, and other paraphernalia. Even today, locals share stories of their own "freshman class," and use their date of arrival and tenure in town as a form of currency. My conversations with locals, ranging from twenty-five to seventy-five years old, echoed and illustrated these themes— stories of young adults adrift who sought Aspen as a place of refuge and relaxation, and managed to make it their home.

Many of those who live in Aspen came as post-college drifters, armed with degrees from good colleges, but not quite ready to settle into a nine-to-five existence. Such feelings of restlessness brought many young adults to Aspen in the late-1960s and early-1970s, amid protests against the war in Vietnam and other social agitations. Having visited Aspen for family ski vacations as a child, and then later hearing about the antics of gonzo journalist Hunter S. Thompson, former mayor John Bennett described Aspen as "an extraordinarily exciting, fun, cool place back then." Traveling the country in a van after graduating from Yale, he said that "a bunch of us fell in love with it and never left. . . . There was no intention [of making the move permanent]; we were floating around and this seemed like a cool place to plant ourselves for a time." The same context and intentions characterized Jesse Hanks's move to Aspen. An Ivy League graduate who has worked as a journalist and a restaurant owner, Hanks described his arrival this way:

> I graduated from college in 1970 and spent the next two years banging around the country on a hippie school bus, putting on light shows. In 1972, a college friend got in touch with a few of us from that group and said, "Hey, come on out to Aspen, I got a great project for us to work on." The project [laughs], given our hippie days, was to build a geodesic dome as a performing arts center. Well, that fell apart almost immediately, but I looked around

town and though that this was just about the nicest place that I had ever seen and I've been here ever since.

Finding themselves in a small but growing town, with still relatively accessible housing options, these well-educated and counterculturally inclined migrants were able to put their imprint on the town and durably influence its progressive social and political institutions.

Over the decades, the appeal of Aspen has continued to pull in a freshman class. Without a firm job offer or intent to make a permanent life, many of these moves are made possible by friends and family members who ease the way and provide housing within an expensive market. Having left college and bounced from San Francisco to New York, renaissance man André Lewandowski landed in Aspen in 1993. What first struck him when he visited friends was "the friendliness, the willingness to lend a hand, the trust, making actual quality friendships"—which he had not experienced in bigger cities. Having crashed on a friend's couch during one of these visits, André describes the moment he decided to move to Aspen and make it his home: "I woke up the next morning, my friend comes in the room, he says, 'Hey what do you wanna do today? We could go hiking, biking, play golf, go whitewater rafting, hot-air ballooning, horseback riding,' and on and on. I was like, 'What?' He was like, 'I'm serious, you just gotta tell me what you wanna do. I gotta call somebody and let him know we're coming.' And I was like, 'I wanna move here! That's what I wanna do.'" That summer, André found his own housing and the first in a series of restaurant jobs. Twenty-five years later, he typically works three jobs at a time and has dedicated himself to public service. His trajectory has been different from the ideal-type lifestyle migrants who move to paradise in their forties or fifties after burning out in their careers, and perhaps better matches lifestyle mobilities described by Scott Cohen and his coauthors, where younger migrants integrate work and leisure, and enjoy off-season sojourns to other locales.

Like other lifestyle migrants, movers to Aspen describe the gravitational pull of the surrounding nature, not just in terms of it providing opportunities for recreation, but for how it facilitates self-actualization. Whereas migrants in the 1960s described the psychic pull to a place that allowed the expression of their countercultural ethos, recent arrivals like

Kimberly Chase described a more individualistic, spiritual pursuit. After graduating from college, she was "a little lost." Looking back a decade later, she said: "I was depressed. I had some issues of my own and anxiety. I really went through a rocky time where life for me was just about managing. . . . I was making good money, working in the restaurant industry, but also having an eating disorder. I was definitely living in the moment and not really sure about what I wanted to do. I think I was clouded by insecurities and just not knowing who I was as a person." Without clear direction, Kimberly did what many of those I spoke to did: accepted an invitation from family members—in her case, an aunt and uncle—to relocate. She describes the transformative moment when she decided to commit herself to this place: "I remember going over Independence Pass . . . and I was like, 'Wow,' like just to see mountains like go on and on and on; it was just glorious. Aspen was like my Walden. . . . It was just like this sacred place to me where I felt alive." Like Ralph Waldo Emerson's Walden Pond, Aspen has allowed Kimberly to commune with nature in ways that are meditative and therapeutic. Since her early days in town, she has completed a master's degree in counseling and set up a successful practice and foundation. For Kimberly and others, migration is used, in the words of Michela Benson and Karen O' Reilly, as a way "of overcoming trauma . . . taking control of their lives, releasing them from ties and enabling them to live lives more 'true' to themselves."[9] Whether seeking refuge or recreation, often on a whim and with temporary intentions, many of those I spoke to accepted the invitations of friends and family members to come explore the area.

Alongside those who arrived with a college degree but without clear plans to use it to build a career are those who explicitly sought Aspen as a destination to pursue their professional goals. This meant "papering" the ski towns of the West with job applications in the hopes of receiving an offer, somewhere. For these individuals, migration was less about Aspen, per se, and more about finding a place that offered the opportunity to combine work and a love of the outdoors. Journalist Ce Ce Catalano, for example, sent resumes to new outlets across Colorado and Montana, eventually landing a job in Aspen via phone interview. Ten years later, at thirty-four, Ce Ce has worked at many of the town's newspapers and glossy magazines, making ends meet by combining jobs there with marketing gigs. The day I interviewed her, she had just learned that she and her husband would be closing on a mobile home in Aspen's "Smuggler Park," a mobile home park with *resident occupancy* restrictions to prevent units from being converted into luxury vacation rentals. "It's ridiculous," she told me, "to be so excited about buying a trailer and living in a mobile home park. But that is the Aspen Dream." With price tags in excess of $1 million, buying a home in a model home park is no small feat.

Aesthetically, Aspen is not just any old town, and its aesthetic and cultural qualities, as much as its natural beauty, can attract migrants. Raised in the Midwest and trained as an architect on the East Coast, Clark Demming was drawn to Aspen's association with modern design. While the Victorian architecture of the late-1800s and the Alpine motifs that sprang up during Aspen's rebirth in the 1940s are two of its signature aesthetic features, tucked away in a corner of town is the Aspen Institute, where the clean lines of Modernism flourish. Founded by Chicago industrialist Walter Paepcke as a place of study and contemplation, many of the buildings and outdoor art installations that dot the Institute's campus were designed by Herbert Bayer, an Austrian who trained at Germany's Bauhaus. The fact that "the guy who proceeded a lot of the thinking that grew into Modernism was based here in Aspen" brought the quirky and cerebral Demming to town in the 1990s. What he discovered upon arrival, however, was quite different: "What I found when I got here was that I was very naive about the public embrace of Modernism. They had this crown jewel of International European architecture, the examples are just some of the best in the world, which truly is not an exaggeration, and no one cared." The style known as Aspen Modern is, in fact, protected by the town's Historic Preservation codes, but Demming felt that the public and the Institute failed to fully appreciate this resource. Thirty years on, Demming operates a successful architecture practice and has stayed in Aspen due to the extensive opportunities for high-end residential work and public projects like libraries, parks, and transit facilities, where big budgets and a knowledgeable clientele make the work especially gratifying.

A handful of those I met told stories resembling those found in the literature on lifestyle migration, of relatively established adults who came to Aspen in their thirties, forties, and fifties, and used lifestyle migration to hit the reset button. With a successful career in marketing, Kathryn

Henderson had tired of the long commutes and lack of community she experienced in Atlanta. Feeling a "little itchy" and ready for a change, she began making her way to Los Angeles, first stopping to stay with her parents—themselves lifestyle migrants from the East Coast—in the town of Basalt, right outside of Aspen. Although she had not intended to stay, things quickly changed: "I was offered a place to live, which is very hard here, in exchange for cat sitting for a month. And then three days after I moved here, I was just walking around town and someone offered me a job doing what I loved to do [in marketing], so I said, 'Let me just finish out the season and then I can move [to L.A.] with even more.' I just kept changing the parameters for that, saying 'I'm gonna stay another six months' and 'I'm gonna stay another six months.'" Kathryn's move farther west never materialized. Like many people who move to Aspen, she told me, "You just come for a winter and you stay for a longer time for that. You get sucked in because the winter is why you come, but then you stay for the summers because it's the most beautiful place in the world." Doug Donaldson's move to Aspen shares points of commonality with Kathryn's, as does Jess Adams's. Whereas Doug came to Aspen in his sixties to serve as an interim pastor and Jess came in her late forties with husband and child seeking refuge from a fast-paced life in L.A., each move was made possible by immediate access to housing. In Doug's case, his parish provided a residence, while Jess and her family found a temporary landing spot with her in-laws, themselves lifestyle migrants.

Like other studies of lifestyle migration, privilege is at the center of these stories.[10] First, these migrants to Aspen have enough economic and human capital that they are able to delay the start of a career after graduating from college or leave a career in which they have built up earning power and expertise. These resources offset the risk they are taking, providing both a financial cushion that facilitates the move and a safety net than can mitigate questions of "What if . . . ?" Second, the role of social capital is instrumental in their experiences. Many of these inhabitants were drawn to Aspen and the surrounding area with the encouragement of friends or family members—people who were already established in the community and could offer a temporary place to stay, along with connections to housing and employment. A remarkable number of these people had grandparents, parents, and aunts and uncles who themselves had the resources to move to Aspen as lifestyle migrants. Yet *coming to Aspen* and *remaining in Aspen* are two entirely different things. Despite these initial resources, unique features of the housing and job markets make it difficult for many—even those with college degrees and financial safety nets—to make Aspen a permanent place of habitation. How people respond to these challenges, and how the local place-based class culture shapes their navigation of life in Aspen, is the subject of the remainder of the chapter.

OF SACRIFICES AND SATISFICING

> It's been difficult. I have had several great relationships here,
> but they have not gone further. I think that's been one
> [sacrifice of living in Aspen]. Career, you know, money
> and maybe that "American Dream" lifestyle is something
> I gave up.
> —André Lewandowski, renaissance man

Lifestyle migrants typically leave a more conventional life to pursue the good life, but in Aspen, achieving the good life can be hard. Working locals described the sacrifices they made to live in Aspen, sometimes lamenting and sometimes merely acknowledging that if they had chosen to live elsewhere, there is a greater likelihood they would have gotten married, had children, and purchased a home. Many locals mentioned threats to one's mental health as something they had struggled with, as well as a serious issue facing the community. Despite its reputation as "Disneyland for adults," living in Aspen can take its toll. Kimberly Chase, the mental health professional who described Aspen as her Walden, was especially attuned to these risks. "It may look like fairytale land, but it's not. If you choose to live in this town, with its economic realities and materialistic aspects, and try to be a ski bum, you will struggle." These struggles can be all the more challenging, she said, because of Aspen's beauty and reputation as a place for mindfulness: if people are not happy there, they wonder what is wrong with them. To make it in Aspen, you have to be a "survivor," said marketing professional Kathryn Henderson. In addition to being resilient and resourceful, she suggested, and figuring out "how to get through the lean off-season and how to crash the best party on the high season," you become a survivor if you "don't get sucked in by the drugs or the lifestyle." With thirty years in Aspen, Clint Jones, a personal chef, had seen this happen many times, where people who cannot figure out how to effectively balance the town's harsh financial realities with its bountiful social opportunities "become broke or a mess," and have family members come to town to bring them home.

For those who remain in Aspen—whether for a year or numerous decades—life is made possible by a number of strategies. In the realm of career and economic considerations, migration to Aspen requires *satisficing*. First coined by the American economist Herbert Simon in the 1940s, satisficing describes a decision-making strategy that aims for a satisfactory or adequate result, rather than the optimal solution. It is the portmanteau of *satisfactory* and *sufficient*.[11] Whereas Simon used this term to explain how people respond when they do not have complete information or where seeking additional information would be onerous, I use *satisficing* to refer to a situation where options may be known but one seeks a suboptimal financial outcome by valuing other attributes of one's job. In Aspen, many working locals had the credentials and aspirations to ascend a career ladder in accounting, marketing, sales, journalism, or what have you, but soon realized that the range of occupational sectors in Aspen is quite narrow, and you "quickly run out of runway," according to forty-something Kathryn Henderson. In this context, satisficing means altering one's aspirations and recognizing that while an optimal career solution may exist somewhere, a viable career can be built in Aspen by hustling, periodic retooling, and embracing unique opportunities.

People in Aspen work hard. A common description of Aspen is that it is a place where the people who visit have three houses while the people who live there have three jobs. Having lived in Aspen for forty years, New York native Julie Kane quickly enumerated all the jobs she has "cobbled together": "I have a full-time job in a retail store. I also sell radio ads part-time. I also have a singing telegram company. I sing at church, and around 2008 I said, 'Is there any chance you guys could pay me?' I started getting paid to sing at church. I sing at lots of wakes, lots of weddings. . . . I'm part of a multilevel company and I sell essential oils—even though I probably give away more essential oils than I sell." While the typical Aspenite has a primary full-time job, they often have numerous "side-hustles": many earn their real estate license, just in case they have a personal connection where this would come in handy, and others earn money by catering, dog walking, housesitting, doing small construction jobs, or working the gates at the airport (for which employees receive generous travel benefits). The result is that during the summer and winter high seasons, many locals work seventy hours a week and may go weeks without a day off.

With thirty years in the Roaring Fork Valley, Clint Jones illustrates what the Aspen hustle looks like. Holding a primary job in the summer guiding visitors in outdoor sporting activities and a primary job in winter as a private chef, Clint has supplemented his income by working as a private driver, an entertainer, an art consultant, and a construction worker. Describing the seasonality of his work and, therefore, the difficulty of assembling something like a "career," Clint told me: "We have six months where there's nothing going on; like you have to dig for something. Restaurants are closed, stores are closed, no one is here. . . . It's never going to be consistent year-round. I've never had a job that's been year-round here, ever. So I've had to piece together careers, and I think that you're probably going to find that a lot of people have done that." Every season is a gamble, as he waits to see which private clients return and which decide that they no longer want to host dinner parties. He knows he is a "luxury item," even in this town, so demand for his services ebbs and flows with broader economic conditions and with fluctuations in taste. "I've cooked for the same families for up to ten years," he told me, "and all of a sudden, they're like, 'You know, we want Thai food, do you do Thai food?' I'm not an expert in Thai food, so they'll find someone who is." Because of the high level of talent in town, and the relatively small and tight social networks, he has been able to expand his interests, becoming an artist and presenting his work at gallery shows. Here, he describes how he has benefitted from Aspen's embrace of the arts and its notorious sense of class egalitarianism and interconnectedness:

> If you have a bit of ambition, this valley can peel away a lot of layers. . . . You can come up here and just kind of like bypass a lot of steps that you'd have to take in a city to build a reputation. Let's just take the art thing for me. The fact that I can get a show up here gives me validity at a city gallery, without going through all the steps of trying to get a city thing. . . . If you can meet

the demands of the people that live here, and you build a reputation because of that, the economic pay-off is massive, versus working for wealthy people in Denver, where you're only in that circle; you're not part of an umbrella.

By being part of Aspen's national, if not global network of wealth, Clint has flown across the country to work as a private chef for clients he met in his home base; his art now adorns their homes. Despite these unique opportunities, he has also experienced the limitations of honing his skill set in Aspen. As he has transitioned to living off-season elsewhere, Clint has discovered that finding work in more mundane, conventional job markets is a challenge, given the eclectic array of talents he has assembled by working in this unique, high-end market.

Many other locals echoed the theme that they are willing to satisfice within their careers—whether by enduring the endless hustle, facing heightened competition, or downshifting their ultimate goals—because of the town's unique opportunities. While the career runways may be short—limiting the ability to take off—many working locals told me that Aspen allows newcomers to establish themselves as big fish in a small pond. For interior designer Oksana Baldwin, the taste level and extensive budgets of the local clientele make the Roaring Fork Valley an attractive place to work. Mental health professional Kimberly Chase similarly noted that the extensive wealth in the community had allowed her to make more of a difference locally than would have been possible back East, given the publicity she has received in the local media and the subsequent financial support for her foundation. Architect Woody Bateman, having worked in the Valley for nearly three decades, had recently thought about moving his firm elsewhere, given the tight competition he faces among firms producing high-end work. The area's physical landscape, however, has kept him in the Roaring Fork Valley. "The beauty about doing projects here," he told me, "is that the sites are always incredible, meaning they're always unique in some way. We have incredible weather patterns, and the views!" For Woody Bateman, the challenges and rewards of working in a setting with beauty and wealth outweighed the possibility that he may have been able to earn more money and establish a distinctive reputation in a place like Denver.

For many of those living in Aspen, especially in the early stages of their careers, the ability to professionally satisfice often meant trading financial remuneration for other work-related benefits. Having come to Aspen from Eastern Europe, Nadia Telpiz rented a bedroom in a mobile home and lamented the fact that as a thirty-something, she was not allowed to invite friends over to entertain. Not unlike New York City, living and working in Aspen is fun, and many young professionals sacrifice nice apartments for other social and cultural benefits. Given the many events in town, as well as the carefree attitude brought by visitors, Nadia said, "You feel yourself on vacation; you feel yourself as a tourist, but at the same time you're living here." For her, one of the greatest forms of capital came from her job at an international luxury retailer, and what kept her in town despite the financial challenges was the ability to acquire cultural capital. By being in a community with wealthy people, interacting with them socially and at work, Nadia said, "You learn their habits, how to become one of them. I'm looking forward to implementing them in my own life." Like Pierre Bourdieu, who coined the term, Nadia understood the subtlety and non-explicit nature of these cultural codes.[12] She described her acquisition of this knowledge—whether how to order wine or structure one's investments—as a "book you keep on reading, page after page, but nobody is just giving you right away the whole book, like, 'Here you go.'"

In Aspen, the short occupational runways may be offset by the unique opportunities presented by those jobs. A Colorado native who returned to the state after college in Boston, Sarah Peters believed she would "definitely get paid more" if she lived elsewhere, and would experience "more opportunities for advancement," like increased compensation. This communications professional, however, remained in Aspen because of the "fun" opportunities presented by her jobs. Working as a writer and marketing associate for a local glossy lifestyle magazine, she compared her work in Aspen to what it might be like in New York or L.A.: "I don't think it would be as much fun. Because we are a small team, we get to do more. I mean, [working elsewhere] I would still be very busy, but here, I get to go to more events; I get trusted with more things 'cause there's not as much of a hierarchy. I think it would be less fulfilling [elsewhere]. I think it would feel more like I couldn't escape." For Sarah, the novelty of the work and the ability to cross-train across reporting, marketing, and technical positions, makes her job enjoyable, where it otherwise could feel limiting. Holding a similar position and arriving in Aspen through a similar trajectory, Ce Ce Catalano made an almost identical point, this time providing concrete examples:

> My first week in town, I covered X-Games [ESPN's signature winter sports event]. It was crazy. I had come from [another market] and as a reporter I hadn't covered anything like that before. My first couple weeks were like the X-Games, major music artists, and politicians and state heads coming to town. I just remember being sort of wowed by that. I thought it would be a basic ski town, where I would cover county meetings, and there is definitely that, but the access to a lot of the stories that you would get in big cities happened right away for me.

Whether for the ability to move between positions, as noted by Sarah, or for the quality of the stories, as noted by Ce Ce, many locals recognized that while they may not be able to ascend career ladders in traditional ways, they at least experience interesting work along the way.

Having been in Aspen for just a year, journalist Mason Ward had similar experiences, but was starting to sour on the town's appeal. An intellectual to the core, he had become somewhat cynical about the Aspen Idea, the embrace of *mind, body, and spirit.* As opposed to an authentic sense of inquiry and engagement, he began to see the wealthy women who grocery shop with their Aspen Idea's Fest tote bags—given for attending the Aspen Institute's annual festival, where registration fees approach $4,000—as the commodification of the town's driving ethos. Chatting at a picnic table where a rundown flop house with a Domino's Pizza on the ground floor and $10 million townhomes sit orthogonally to one another, Mason saw these contradictions among his professional peers, as well. "I think that access is what people like [about working in Aspen] and I think has fueled them to stay here and has convinced them that they have important kind of jobs. And I think that gives them the justification of, 'I'm gonna keep living here because my voice matters a little bit more and because I'm in this sought-after community,' and not move to a city and getting a bigger, better job." Yet for Mason, the aesthetic appeal of interviewing *New York Times* journalist David Brooks, former secretary of state Madeline Albright, or Supreme Court justice Ruth Bader Ginsburg did not make up for the fact that for most of the year, local journalists work on relatively mundane projects. His critique gains poignancy, moreover, when one learns that he previously covered an African community recovering from war and he generally aspired to write about issues he thought were more meaningful, like environmental justice and immigration reform. Whereas the allure of "access" had come to feel a bit hollow to Mason, other professionals in Aspen embraced it and other nonmonetary aspects of their jobs as they satisficed their way through their careers.

SUBSTITUTION: TRADING CAREER FOR LIFESTYLE

> I don't know if I will ever have something I can call a career,
> and I really don't care. I'd rather have a life.
> —Kara Mason, gallerist

Like the lifestyle migrants described in the literature, people move to Aspen in pursuit of the good life. Yet, phasing into retirement or downshifting one's career was not an option for these migrants, in large part because of the high cost of living, but also because many moved to Aspen at a relatively young age. They managed to stay in Aspen by continually substituting symbolic lifestyle rewards for the monetary benefits that might come with career advancement elsewhere. In contrast to the satisficing described above, which emphasizes nonmonetary benefits gained at work, the substitutions described in this section involve benefits gained outside of work; where access to nature and world-class cultural events trump the ability to achieve the conventional markers of the American Dream, such as homeownership. According to historian Hal Rothman, this pattern has a long history, dating back to the 1950s when young adults "were willing to stay in relatively low-paying jobs to remain in the town where they had invested their identity."[13] The benefits provided by these jobs dovetail with the local place-based class culture, so to the extent that these individuals are able to participate in Aspen's exceptionalism—attending cultural events and communing with nature—they gain full membership in the community, despite their relative economic limitations.

Nature dividends were a commonly cited benefit of living and working in Aspen; like many migrants to California, who accept payment in "sunshine dollars" to offset the high cost of living, these migrants placed great value on the accessibility of nature. Indeed, Aspen is unique, even among other mountain resort towns: hiking trails and the ski lift literally abut the town's main streets. For people who live and work downtown, accessing the mountain does not require a schlep in a car or bus or other cumbersome logistics; one can literally walk out the door of their workplace and be on the mountain within five minutes. When architect Mitch Nelson moved to town in the mid-2000s, he was offered several jobs, but accepted an offer from the one "closest to the gondola"—the enclosed lift that ferries skiers to the top of Aspen Mountain. Numerous professionals similarly appreciated the flexibility and proximity afforded by their jobs. Whereas Ce Ce Catalano lamented the fact that "there's not a lot of traditional ladder climbing" in the local economy, she was happy to have "a lot more freedom," so that "if it's a powder day, I can come in late. That doesn't exist in the city." Fellow journalist Sarah Peters echoed this point: "There is kind of mentality, especially in our office, that's just like, 'We're here for a reason. We live in Aspen for a reason. And if you want to take an hour break during the day and go ski a couple of runs, go do it. As long as you're getting your stuff done, just go.' [Peers in New York] just don't understand that because they just—it's not their lifestyle. Like if I say, 'I'm sorry, I was out skiing,' they're like, 'What?'" In the summer months, these same individuals can enjoy hiking, a mountain bike ride, or lunch next to the Roaring Fork River. Not merely physical proximity to the mountain, the Aspen Idea of mind, body, and spirit has become institutionalized within the workplace culture; employers routinely provide flexibility in work schedules, along with ski passes, which facilitates working locals' participation in the town's sense of exceptionalism.

As young adults at the beginning of their careers, these individuals had yet to confront some of the major dilemmas that Aspen sometimes presents to its working locals. As they move through their forties and fifties, and especially if they have families or are seeking to create families, working locals may be confronted with a longing for those things they had given up. When comparing the professional peers that he and his wife went to graduate school with, and who now live in cities like Denver and Houston, financial professional Donald Ranstead offered this observation: "Some of those people would look at us and think we made huge sacrifices with our careers. Most of our peer group from the big accounting firm ended up in

CFO positions with big successful companies and they have big salaries and perks and huge houses and country club memberships and, you know, economically they're very successful. . . . And they would look at us and say, 'We're happy, we're rich, we're somewhat famous, and you sacrificed that.' And to that I would say, 'Meh.'" When asked what he got that his peers in bigger cities with bigger firms did not, this native Aspenite replied: "Just a small town and skiing at lunchtime and, you know, riding my bike on a nice trail from my doorstep. A roof over my head, food on the table, my kids have clothes . . . that's all I need."

Beyond the *body* component of the Aspen Idea, working locals also substituted conventional markers of success for opportunities to attend to their *mind* and *spirit*. Sixty-something Midwest native Greg Clendenning had continually reinvented himself in Aspen, working first as an entertainer and then as a beverage sales person, after the local dinner theater closed. Referring to himself as a "working-class person" who was "eking out a living," he recognized the sacrifice in not being able to build a traditional career or land "a great paying job." He and his wife remained in Aspen, however, in large part because they could pursue their love of the outdoors, along with "all of the opportunities to see world-class music, dance, theater." Having come to town with a degree in music, "he latched onto that right away," and still regularly takes in events at the Music Festival, Theater Aspen, and other venues.

Thirty years his junior, and similarly working in beverage sales, Colorado-native Scott Bailey came to Aspen with a degree from a highly ranked liberal arts college. Growing up in a lower-middle-class family in a Colorado ranching community, he said that "the extreme wealth wears on you sometimes," as he struggled to find things in common with other young professionals, whom he perceived as "trust-funders." Like many I spoke to, Scott "hates driving" and greatly appreciates that within his primary job, he "get[s] to walk around town all day, saying hi to people and tasting wine." When asked how it felt to be heading into his late thirties and not have a career in his field of study (economics and international relations), he replied, "I really don't care." Elaborating, Scott explained: "I'm a liberal arts guy. I enjoy, you know, reading my magazines and keeping up with what I consider good journalism, like *Mother Jones*, or *Harper's*, or something like that. That's what I enjoy out of life; not work. . . .

I'm not really focused on what I'm doing for a career. I'm focused more on what I do for enjoyment outdoors, my friends, what I'm learning." In Aspen, working locals can substitute nonmaterial lifestyle benefits like cultural and intellectual engagement for pay and promotions.

Having lived in Aspen for more than a decade, forty-something marketing professional Kathryn Henderson continually negotiated sacrifices and substitutions to make her life work. She chose to pay more to rent in Aspen and share a small apartment with roommates, for example, rather than live in a condo she owned down valley. "If you're out late singing karaoke," she explained, "you can just walk home," whereas living down valley you have to drive or depend on the bus schedule and cannot be as spontaneous as you can living in town. For her, that's "worth the extra couple hundred bucks or even more" she pays to rent in Aspen. Like many working locals, having an interesting social life and living in a safe community was a form of currency with its own precious value. Asked how it felt to downshift in her career, Kathryn emphasized the lifestyle dividends paid out by living and working in Aspen: "I've traveled more than I ever have, and I couldn't do that in a nine-to-five job. There, you get your two weeks off; you get a couple long weekends for holidays. I've taken like four or five weeks off every year, consistently. And that's something—again, money can't buy time, and you gotta make that time because otherwise you have no memories in your life." Despite these lifestyle benefits, Kathryn recommended that everyone who moves to town have "an exit strategy." Yet, in a town that fosters a Peter Pan lifestyle ("I won't grow up!"), this can be hard. According to Kathryn, "Nobody is ever going to say to you, 'Hey, you want to stop doing happy hour?'" Surviving Aspen requires internal discipline. "It takes a strong person," she told me, "to be like 'I'm going to put up with all of these things here—I'm gonna live in a studio at the age of fifty and I'm going to be single for the rest of my life. I'm going to not work a job that I went to school for. I'm going to settle for less'" As she herself approached fifty, Kathryn decided to take a break from Aspen: first, with an off-season trip to Spain for several months and then to contemplate moving elsewhere to settle into a more traditional career. Should she decide to return, she still owns a small apartment in Basalt. While many working locals successfully substitute lifestyle benefits for conventional markers of occupational success, and did so for many years, the grind can wear you down, eventuating the need for an exit strategy. In the meantime, locals effectively substitute cultural benefits for economic benefits, and do so in ways that reflect and legitimate Aspen's sense of exceptionalism.

SEGMENTED ASSIMILATION AMID ASPEN EGALITARIANISM

> I get to live other people's vacation.
> —Mitch Nelson, thirty-something architect

Given the high cost of living, it is reasonable that migrants to Aspen would feel incredibly alienated living in town. With few boutiques selling garments below $300, few restaurants serving entrees below $35, and plentiful social and cultural events with high-priced admissions, working locals could feel displaced from the social and cultural amenities that make Aspen such a great place to live. Yet Aspen's place-based class culture accommodates and eases some of these tensions and the potential for alienation. Claims to egalitarianism, while more evident within earlier iterations of Aspen's history, are not mere discourses. They are sustained by day-to-day practices that facilitate cross-class mixing. In a number of instances, these interactions are made possible by efforts to institutionalize working locals' access to the good life. These discourses and modes of institutionalization result in a form of *segmented inclusion*: situations where working locals and more affluent visitors and part-year residents share the same spaces and same experiences, albeit in different ways. This pattern of cross-class interaction shares some similarities with the notion of *segregated inclusion*, coined by scholars of culture Fabien Accominatti, Shamus Khan, and Adam Storer.[14] In their analysis of cross-class interactions among new and old money during New York City's Gilded Age, they discovered that as new money elites gained access to august cultural institutions like the New York Philharmonic, older money elites engaged in practices that reaffirmed their position, such as monopolizing seating patterns—preserving social closure—within the concert hall. In so doing, newer elites gained social access while older elites reasserted their dominance. A similar sharing of space happens in Aspen, yet locals' understandings of these spaces complicates hierarchical dynamics, resulting in patterns of segmented inclusion more than segregated inclusion.

Numerous local businesses, including restaurants, bars, hotels, and recreational outfitters, have institutionalized benefits for working locals, permitting access to Aspen's cultural and natural amenities. Many coffee shops and lunch restaurants, for example, offer a "locals' discount," which deducts 15 to 20 percent from their purchase price. Newcomers can sample their first class at yoga and fitness studios across town for free, simply by showing an ID or a local address. Outdoor adventure companies similarly offer a tiered-pricing scheme, where locals can enjoy activities like whitewater rafting at a discounted rate. The Aspen Art Museum offers free admissions to visitors and locals alike, each day it is open. Even Aspen's cannabis dispensaries offer locals' discounts, which makes getting high a bit more accessible. Yet perhaps no benefit was more beloved among locals than the "bar menu" offered at many high-end restaurants. While not explicitly designed to accommodate locals, bar menus have that effect. With a separate menu that applies only in the bar area, locals can enjoy drinks, appetizers, and smaller entrees at a reduced price. At Jimmy's, for example, the bar menu features flat iron steaks and braised short ribs for $15, while the cheapest steak in the dining room—served a la carte—sets diners back $46. A plate of pasta carbonara at L'Hosteria goes for less than $15 in the bar, but more than twice that in the dining room. Importantly, sitting in the bar area was not considered *less than* among locals; indeed, bar areas often felt more convivial than the formal dining rooms, allowing for a see-and-be-seen kind of vibe, and are often inhabited by those waiting for a table in the dining room. On top of all of this, sitting in the bar offers locals the opportunity to socialize with friends who may work in these establishments. The icing on the cake is what marketing professional Kathryn Henderson called "the law of getting things for free." The longer you live in Aspen, the more people you know, the more likely you are to be treated by service professionals to a free round of drinks, appetizers, and other extras that just show up at the table, and happy hour drink prices routinely extend beyond the happy hour time frame. Through both formal and informal mechanisms, many

Figure 5. Aspen egalitarianism on display at the music tent. Photo by Jenny Stuber.

Aspen establishments offer working locals the opportunity to share spaces and enjoy the same lifestyle that attracts many visitors to town.

Cultural events—which draw many residents to town in the first place—were similarly within reach of many locals. The Aspen Music Festival's annual summer concert series offers ticket holders the opportunity to see world-class jazz and classical music for about $75, seated inside a tent designed by Finnish modernist architect Eero Saarinen. Yet locals and even some high-brow visitors choose to sit on the lawn outside the tent, where they can enjoy the same music for free (see figure 5). Reclining on a blanket and staring at the quaking Aspen trees or raising a glass of rosé, many locals thought this experience was better than, not lesser than, being seated inside the tent. Although this sentiment could be considered sour grapes or some other kind of compensating mechanism, it is more likely an authentic assessment, given the town's embrace of unpretentious luxury and the fact that enjoying music and nature at the same time has more local value than enjoying music, alone.

In addition to the music festival, the summer season offers many opportunities to attend cultural and intellectual events, with tickets ranging anywhere from $50 to $4,000. Although working locals sometimes found it difficult, in the context of working three jobs and every day of the week during the summer season, to take full advantage of the town's busy event schedule, many managed some level of involvement. Some volunteered, for example, at the Aspen Ideas Festival or the Food and Wine Classic, where in exchange for working a twelve-hour shift, participants could enjoy the event's offerings, like a wine tasting or lecture by former secretary of state Madeline Albright. Over time, however, locals learned that they need not volunteer in order to receive these benefits and that free passes were likely to come their way. A one-day VIP ticket to the Labor Day weekend concert series—which featured artists like Maroon 5, Stevie Wonder, Duran Duran, and Stevie Nicks—sells for about $800. Yet "because I'm a long-term local," Kathryn Henderson told me, "I got three calls one day, offering free tickets, and the last call was like, 'I have a VIP for you; you don't have to pay for it.'" Such stories were far from unusual, as locals variously received invitations to attend fundraisers and galas to complete a table that one of their more affluent friends or work associates sponsored. Meanwhile, during June's Food and Wine Classic—the event that kicks off the summer season—locals make a game of finding their way into the best "after parties," where liquor companies like Veuve Clicquot or Campari take over a space, like a yoga studio, and offer free food and drinks and dancing. Claiming you are "on the list" or making refence to the person who owns the commercial space hosting the event seem to work surprisingly well. Despite these strategies, many locals knew that the only way to gain access to the most fantastic private parties was to be part of a catering crew. In that case, segmented inclusion breaks down and class hierarchies become more clearly drawn.

Despite their access to Aspen's dining scene and signature culture events, increasing anxieties characterized locals' feelings about their place in the community. As I discuss in chapter 6, the ability to shop locally was a near impossibility, and were it not for secondhand stores and online shopping, working members of the community would experience significant challenges in purchasing ordinary clothing and houseware items. In some cases, this caused them to feel displaced from the local retail scene, lamenting the loss of the Gap. Although the affordable housing program serves as a stop gap for residential displacement, some worried that more locals would be pushed down valley due to the conversion of condominiums to short-term rentals, and that new affordable housing units would be built on parcels further out of town, thereby resulting in a level of residential segregation not yet seen in Aspen. Yet when asked why they remain in town, given these increasingly difficult economic times, many locals simply pointed to the mountain, the view of which was never far from where we were seated, and access to which seemed enshrined. Some locals, in fact, seemed relatively oblivious to the upscaling of local boutiques and restaurants. They asserted that as long the mountain remains, these other changes to local character are superficial and irrelevant to what brought them to town and what remains its heart and soul. In the words of beverage distributor Scott Bailey, "I don't consider not having a single-family home a sacrifice at all, when you live around this"—by which he meant access to nature. Elaborating, he said: "I never once cared about money. As long as I can make $70,000 a year, or whatever I need to pay my bills, that's fine by me. . . . At the end of the day, I ski the same mountain that billionaires ski. Their home's nicer, yeah, but I eat at same restaurants they do—and for cheaper than they do. My lifestyle here is good. That's probably why I can't leave." Twelve years on, this thirty-something with a master's degree from an Ivy League university, two jobs, and a one-bedroom apartment, continues to make Aspen his home, owing in large part to its beauty and the fact that he can live a lifestyle that bears a resemblance to the town's affluent visitors.

Making a similar claim, but in a more cerebral manner was Karl Paulsen, an author and educator who had lived in Colorado for more than thirty years. Raised in Chicago's affluent northern suburbs, this seventy-something described his obsessions with wealth growing up. During high school, Karl said, he would "wander around the ruined estates" of Chicago industrialists like Cyrus McCormick and Marshall Field, "wondering what life was like for these exalted beings of American capitalism." In the early-1970s, during a hiatus from college, Karl got a job at Chicago's Mercantile Exchange, what he envisioned would be a first step in his own journey toward spectacular material success: "I used to ride the subway from the suburbs. I would drive to the station, smoke part of a joint, and then I would get on the train. And it was like an amusement park ride for me—the train plunged underground and rumbled and rattled and the lights flashed, and I never knew who was going to get on the train or who would get off." All of this, he hoped, would lead him to be "rich and wealthy and have things and wear cool clothes and go to country clubs and dance to jazz bands and sip champagne." During the late-1970s, however, Karl moved to Colorado, where his "deep values evolved into a very earth-based sensitivity to environment and ecology." After more than twenty years in Aspen, Karl "no longer [has] a sense of envy for them because I feel like I live a richer life than most people do." Living in a rural cabin, what he calls his "sanctuary," he reflects on how a life in nature has been not only the great equalizer, but a godsend. The uber-wealthy, whom he once aspired to join, are: "Searching desperately for, 'Where's that place that's going to touch me? Where's the place that's going to enliven my soul and spirit? Where can I be a fully engaged and fulfilled human being?' They touchdown here and there, but they don't have a genuine niche because they don't allow themselves to root into it." Using *niche* in an ecological sense, describing the phenomenon in which the seeds and spores that circulate in the jet steam ultimately land, but can thrive only within specific environments, Karl shows how his one-time American Dream has come to fruition as the Aspen Dream, where access to nature is the ultimate currency.

CONCLUSION

Since the late 1950s, newcomers have arrived in Aspen and the Roaring Fork Valley, seeking an idyllic lifestyle. In the early days of Aspen's renaissance, a desire to retreat from materialism marked many of these moves; in more recent decades, Aspen's culture of intellectualism and recreation has attracted a new generation of migrants. A desire to commune with nature, however, serves as a point of continuity in why people move to these mountains. As with many desirable places, upscaling and the uptick in socioeconomic inequality have followed. These analyses show how lifestyle migrants manage the economic pressures they have felt in this community; pressures that become more palpable as those seeking a post-college respite move into their thirties and contend with aspirations to climb the career ladder, buy a home, and start a family. Absent in these stories are the voices of those who have left. Although Kathryn Henderson hinted that she was on the precipice of enacting her exit strategy, and Clint Jones described the angst he's experienced in finding meaningful employment in his off-season home, I gained little insight into how people decide to pull up stakes and leave town, and whether they experience more fulfillment elsewhere.

These analyses complicate existing understandings of lifestyle migration. In contrast to older adults with a degree of financial security who move to communities where their dollar stretches farther, these stories highlight the experiences of younger migrants who move to an area with complicated class dynamics and an exorbitant cost of living. The financial challenges that come with living in Aspen and the Roaring Fork Valley are many, but the local place-based class culture shows why and how lifestyle migrants make it work. Within the context of their jobs, they engage in satisficing, whereby the kind of work they do offsets the truncated career ladders they climb. Outside of their jobs, working locals substitute economic rewards for access to unique cultural and recreational opportunities. Finally, they experience a form of segmented assimilation wherein at restaurants and cultural events and on the mountain itself, they gain access to the same things that draw visitors and part-year residents to town. In these settings, working locals show that by tapping into Aspen's sense of exceptionalism and egalitarianism, they achieve membership in the community. Much of this is made possible, moreover, by the fact that even if they do not resemble one another with respect to economic capital, many of those who are drawn to the area have shared cultural capital, so distinctions may blur as locals and visitors alike careen down the mountain or gaze at the Aspen trees while listening to internationally known classical musicians.

Even though working locals feel incredibly attached to Aspen and are able to construct a meaningful existence amid the hustle, they are not naive to the struggles. Mental health counselor Kimberly Chase asserted that the notion that Aspen is "fairytale land" is an illusion; one that masks considerable mental health problems beneath the surface. Four-decade local Julie Kane described living in Aspen as "trial by fire," and hit on one of the troubling contradictions embedded within lifestyle migration: "A lot of people come here after a major life change: they've just got divorced or they just became widowed or something like that, and they come here because it looks beautiful, they think, 'My life here will be beautiful.' But that's misleading because in that suitcase, no matter how light you travel, you pack up your problems. I mean, not to get philosophical on you, but I think people are troubled by that and surprised by that." It was this contrast between what Aspen presents on the surface and what one may experience on the inside that, both she and Kimberly speculated, partially accounts for the area's high suicide rate. For others, "keeping up with the Joneses" can be just as hard as the financial struggles. Yet in Aspen, "the Joneses" are those who accumulate the highest number of days skiing during the winter or the most miles mountain biking in the summer. In the words of journalist Mason Ward, "The athletic culture here is overwhelming." With just one year living and working in Aspen, he has become frustrated by the fact that "all everyone ever fucking talks about is skiing." Although he's had "a lot of fun" in between these "really inane conversations," he's come to "feel that it's sort of lonely and, at times, I wonder, is this really enough for everybody else?" Despite the claims to mind, body, and spirit, the town may fail to deliver those elements in equal measure, leading to a sense of emptiness.

Finally, although some Aspenites recognized the troubling contradictions of their town and brought a sharpened class lens to their experiences, they rarely presented a racial or ethnic critique. Marketing professional Kathryn Henderson, for example, likened Aspen to the post-apocalyptic class-divided world depicted in the science fiction movie *Elysium*, but neither she nor others spontaneously commented on the stark racial divides that mark the community. This is somewhat surprising, given the fact that Aspen proper is less than 10 percent Hispanic (and less than 3 percent Black), but the nearby community of Carbondale is 48 percent Hispanic. Hispanic laborers, moreover, form the backbone of the tourist economy. In a rare instance of addressing the community's racial dynamics, Skippy Mesirow, a young entrepreneur and community activist (elected to city council in 2018), made these comments on his podcast:

> There is a bizarre political inversion that happens in small mountain towns, where the more liberal you are and identify yourself nationally with a liberal ideology, the more conservative you are locally. Like, "I am staunchly pro-immigration, but please don't come and move here." Or "We want to make sure that things are affordable so there can be diversity of opportunity, but

let's make sure all our mitigations are so high that there's no way anyone of color can spend time in our community for more than a shift doing dishes.". . . If that's the town you want to live in, that's fine, but to sort of claim this righteous mantle, but then act in so many ways that actually inhibit that from happening, [pause] it's really unfortunate.

Plenty of Latinos reside in the Roaring Fork Valley, but they commute to work in Aspen, and only a small percentage lives there. White, working locals acknowledge the critical contributions of Latino workers, local governments have declared themselves sanctuary cities and made other efforts to ensure that Latinos live and work peaceably, and Latinos themselves described the community as safe and accepting. Yet race and the politics of Whiteness are surely relevant to how social class and the politics of redistribution work in Aspen. As suggested by Louise Seamster, it is not a coincidence that liberal, low-growth cities are often overwhelmingly White.[15] In Aspen, Whiteness operates not so much as a force that actively excludes others, but as a factor that facilitates cohesion and allows class solidarities to congeal. These class solidarities, then, provide support for extractive and redistributive policies—which might not be possible if the community were more racially and ethnically diverse. Whiteness, in this sense, is one more factor that facilitates the transformation of the American Dream into the Aspen Dream. In chapter 7, I more fully document the combination of pushes and pulls that lead to them living down valley, drawn by cheaper housing, larger plots of land, and closer proximity to churches and businesses serving their needs.

3 Steadying the Pendulum

The apocryphal story of the Aspen City Council's decision to declare a land use moratorium in March of 2016 harkens back to an early winter day, four months prior. "I was walking around with my daughter last November, on one of the pedestrian malls," council member Adam Frisch recounted to me, "it must have been the afternoon, after school, or something like that, and the sun was starting to go down, and all of a sudden some of the sun was disappearing on the streetscape." In a typical city, with a downtown corridor of tall buildings, this would be an unremarkable occurrence. But this is Aspen, a place where sun exposure and views of the mountain are sacrosanct. "I'm not sure of the exact heights of the buildings on that part of the mall," Frisch continued, "but I think they're only twenty feet or something like that. And I'm thinking, we already have this twenty-eight-foot limitation on buildings on one side of the street, but maybe twenty-eight feet is too tall for some of these places."[1] Reflecting further, Frisch said, he looked around and noticed that the "funky nook-and-cranny spaces" that allow Aspen locals to establish locally serving business were becoming an "endangered species": victims of a building code that encouraged not an array of shapes but maximization of every allowable inch of square footage. On this fateful walk, council member Frisch reckoned with the fear that Aspen's small-town character and beloved sense of "messy vitality" was disappearing. In Aspen, "messy vitality" and the mixing of old, funky spaces and slick, modern spaces is not merely an aesthetic; it is an aesthetic preference that reflects underlying assumptions about who Aspen is for and how class relations operate there, and it facilitates those relations.

Over the next several months, Adam Frisch began a quiet crusade, talking to fellow elected officials and members of the city planning staff about their concerns with the evolution of Aspen's place-character and how the current land use codes were out of sync with the lofty progressive goals professed in the Aspen Area Community Plan. This crusade operated under the radar, as Frisch built support for a move that could potentially disrupt local real estate markets and cause further real estate speculation if discovered. Property owners tend not to like it when new restrictions are passed that potentially limit their property rights. And so, after months of careful strategizing, in March of 2016, the Aspen City Council declared an emergency ordinance that put a halt on all new building applications, so that they could begin the yearlong task of revising the land use code that shapes how Aspen looks and feels and also shapes class interests.

This chapter explores the social, political, and economic context in which Aspen's city council declared the 2016 land use moratorium. This revision of the land use code provides a window into the place-making process. The process of urban planning, as one prong of place-making, can be characterized as a pendulum swing—a swing that eventuates the need for changes in the land use code. The pendulum is typically set in motion by changing global or local market forces, like supergentrification or periods of economic boom and bust, or the unintended consequences associated with earlier policy provisions. In this chapter I show that the 2016 land use moratorium emerged as an effort to steady the pendulum and address growing anxieties over the question, "Aspen for whom?" In the years leading up to it, locals increasingly expressed concern that city officials were providing too many concessions to developers—variances to the existing code that reduced their responsibility to fund affordable housing, for example. With these concessions, many locals worried that the city council was complicit in remaking the town in the image of affluent outside forces rather than preserving "messy vitality" or protecting locals' interests, as inscribed in the Aspen Area Community Plan. Increasingly, citizens threatened to go to the ballot box to vote down projects that they believed threatened community character, acting as a check on the council's decision-making. Their efforts were motivated by an effort to protect local character, as well as their "right to the city," though it should be noted that local Aspenites have more power and legitimacy than the dispossessed urban residents and activists profiled by Henri Lefebvre.[2] While previously elected councils were responsible for some of the decisions causing the community angst, the current city council members had concerns of their own. In particular, they were concerned that recent building codes had led to the "sterilization" of the downtown core: as affluent outsiders bought up penthouse apartments situated on the third floor of commercial developments, the bottom two floors of retail and office space remained empty, devitalizing the streetscape. With the price-tag of $20 million, the cash deals for these penthouses allowed the bottom floor spaces to remain vacant while still providing profit to the developers. The council's problems with this building model were myriad, but they generally reflected the sentiment that luxury condos in the downtown core compromised working locals' ability to live and do business as they chose, in the place they called home.

Responding to these anxieties, the Aspen City Council—in conjunction with consultants, business owners, community members, and other local stakeholders—embarked upon a year of place-making in an attempt to steady the pendulum, a pendulum whose momentum gained strength from global economic processes and easy access to capital. Using the "police powers" that allow municipal bodies to declare an emergency ordinance in order to protect the health and safety of the communities, on March 15, 2016, the council voted unanimously to halt all new building applications so that zoning regulations could be rewritten. For the city council, the mandate was clear: Align the land use code to better reflect the aspirations and values that are spelled out in the town's comprehensive plan, the Aspen Area Community Plan.[3] Efforts would focus on Aspen's five commercial zone districts (residential and lodge zone districts were excluded), with the mandate to address how the town looks, namely in terms of commercial design guidelines, public amenity spaces, and view plane restrictions, as well as how the town functions, in terms of use mix (balance of housing and commercial and the creation of commercial spaces that serve

Aspen's diverse economic constituencies), affordable housing mitigations, and off-street parking. This process illustrates an interesting case, one in which community leaders sought to balance and intertwine the progressive, low-growth history that has characterized the local political landscape with the aggressive global headwinds brought about by financial deregulation and neoliberal market forces. The response and outcome, shaped by Aspen's unique place-based class cultures, contrasts with British scholar Rowland Atkinson's model of the plutocratic city, where money rules and the affluent imprint their interests on the city. London's affluent boroughs of Kensington and Chelsea are ideal examples, where middle-class residents are squeezed out, and the provision of services like public housing is diminished.[4] Here, elected leaders, representatives from the business community, and community leaders sought to preserve Aspen's charm and value, while creating opportunities for local residents.

RESURRECTING AND REINSCRIBING
THE ASPEN AREA COMMUNITY PLAN

Every five to six years, almost like clock-work, the pendulum swing of local development in Aspen sets off a predicable process that involves the halting of development, followed by community-wide psychoanalysis and yet another effort to revise the zoning laws or the municipal planning document that serves as a centerpiece for place-making. In part, this is a regular part of any city's urban planning responsibilities; in this case, it also reflects just how intimately tied global market trends are to Aspen, and how much the town is impacted by fluctuations of global capital. In 2016, the community, yet again, had come to feel that the pendulum had swung too far—too far, in this case, from fulfilling the promises of the Aspen Area Community Plan. Most recently revised in 2012, this one-hundred-page document provides "a vision, a map and a plan of action for achieving community goals."[5] Organized around topics like housing, economic development, historic preservation, and transportation, the AACP articulates community values and specifies the loose policy goals that city council and its appointed boards and commissions should work toward. With respect to the concept of place-based class cultures, the community plan is both the articulation of local cultures, including class cultures, and the tool by which those cultures get institutionalized in policy and the built environment.

While providing a roadmap for the future, the AACP is also mindful of the "historical context and underlying values that define our community," and notes that in order to move forward, one must pay homage to the past.[6] It reminds readers of the epic "downzoning" of the county that progressive low-growth politicians passed in the 1970s, which changed zoning laws throughout Pitkin County from those that allowed fifty-five residential units per acre, to allowing just one residential unit per ten acres. This move institutionalized the sacredness of open space in Aspen, and the ethic that mountain views and access to nature are primary values. The AACP also celebrates the town's history of "messy vitality." Quoting the 1993 AACP, the 2012 version states: "Aspen as a community should avoid an environment that is too structured, too perfect, and that eliminates the funkiness that once characterized this town." In part, this funkiness is captured by Jane Jacobs's notion that what makes for a vibrant community is a mix of uses, a mix of people, and a mix of styles. Yet the "kind of vitality brought to Aspen by its full-time residents," the document warned, "is being seriously diluted" by a dramatic increase in property values.[7] Aesthetically, that meant that a funky, dilapidated miner's cabin sitting adjacent to an alpine-style structure was becoming a thing of the past, with older buildings being cleaned up and restyled in ways that attempted to retain their period character, but ended up looking too polished (see figure 6). With locals being priced out of their beloved community, global market forces now challenge Aspen's progressive approach to politics and its claim to being a place that appreciates unpretentious luxury and the mixing of social classes.

In order to re-center or preserve the progressive values that are foundational to Aspen's social and political aspirations, the Aspen Area Community Plan called for "more aggressive measures to ensure the needs of the community are met, and to preserve our unique community character."[8] Within the commercial sector, the plan suggests that policies should "encourage a commercial mix that is balanced, diverse and vital and meets the needs of year-round residents and visitors," and facilitate "the sustainability of essential businesses that provide basic community needs."[9] In Aspen, some community activists were perennially afraid that grocery store

Figure 6. This $16 million renovated home shows the integration of Aspen's "messy vitality" and authentic exclusivity. Photo by Jenny Stuber.

parking lots would be lost, victims to the notion that the land's "highest and best use"—its greatest potential for profit—is not accommodating the cars of grocery store shoppers, but building the lodging or retail that might draw more visitors and produce more revenue. In a town where even the Gap, Banana Republic, and J. Crew are endangered species, this fear is not unfounded. The AACP calls for housing policies that "bolster our economic and social diversity, reinforce variety, and enhance our sense of community by integrating affordable housing into the fabric of our town."[10] In Aspen, having middle-class locals living in town represents a core value and supports notions of what makes it a unique community. "A healthy social balance includes all income ranges and types of people," the document goes on to say, so that future development "should endeavor to further that mix and to avoid segregation of economic and social classes."[11] The ideal of class integration, however, was increasingly compromised by the conversion of locally owned homes into second homes—often renovated into spectacular vacation properties—which drove up the price of real estate and reduced supply, which in turn displaced locals to communities down valley. To that end, the AACP calls for a critical mass of working residents living in Aspen and affordable housing mitigation to be paid by developers whose projects increase the need for workers. Ultimately, the AACP claimed, a stable affordable housing program for locals would create a "better visitor experience, including an appreciation of our genuine, lights-on community."[12] The emphasis on a critical-mass of local year-round residents reflects both the reality that workers who are stressed from long commutes do little to enhance the relaxed feel of a resort town, and the unique belief that Aspen's locals are interesting and of interest to affluent visitors.

When published in 2012, the most recent version of the Aspen Area Community Plan was already responding to concerns about the changing community character and displacement of long-term locals. These concerns were exacerbated by land use codes that were passed in 2000, which play out alongside the global economic downturn stemming from the 9/11 attacks and the bursting of the dot-com bubble. These events set the pendulum swing in motion, prompting the Aspen City Council to protect their community through "infill" legislation that would create more density in the downtown core and take advantage of existing infrastructure, thus limiting the burdens eventuated by sprawl.[13] These infill codes resulted in taller buildings (soaring as high as forty-six feet, or four stories) with greater mass and scale—changes that created heights and densities that later came to be viewed as an assault on Aspen's unique "small-town character." Several years later, these revisions collided with a global economic boom. This sent the pendulum swing in motion, once again, as the Republican administration under George W. Bush further loosened financial regulations, stimulating the flow of capital and leading to rampant real estate speculation. Mayor Steven Skadron recounted that with looser economic policies, "Money got cheap and it had to land someplace." During the mid-2000s, Aspen became a desirable location for that money to land, leading to a building boom of luxury properties and disappearance of locally serving businesses like Aspen Drug.

Although city officials began rolling back the infill-era land use codes in 2006, focusing primarily on reducing building heights and sizes, both the legislative and physical vestiges of that period lingered. When the moratorium was declared in 2016, the city council and many other community stakeholders felt that the Aspen Area Community Plan and the existing land use codes were fundamentally at odds with one another. On the one hand, the AACP pledged to preserve funkiness and small-town character, encourage a viable year-round economy with locally serving businesses, and extract mitigations from developers to protect the affordable housing program. The land use code, on the other hand, was producing boxy buildings that made use of every inch of allowable square footage and compromised the viability of locally serving businesses (e.g., watch repair, barbers, dry cleaners, pharmacies). The council was also accused of bargaining away mitigations for affordable housing. Simultaneously, in order to reduce their mitigation costs and comply with the land use code, some builders built smaller buildings. As a consequence, new development in Aspen reduced the supply of real estate and drove up prices, so that only Prada, Gucci, and their ilk could afford the $225-per-square-foot rents. As a consequence, this reduced contributions to affordable housing, given that smaller buildings create fewer new employees, which is the basis upon which mitigations are calculated. "I think we're losing the ability to be measured," Mayor Steve Skadron told his colleagues, as the conversations about revising the land use code got underway. Reflecting on transformations in the town's class culture, he said, "I think we're more inaccessible and exclusive, and we're moving there at an accelerating rate." Feeling that the land use code was no longer serving the interests of working locals or protecting messy vitality, the city council declared a building moratorium in 2016 to align the land use code with the AACP.

THE PROBLEM WITH PENTHOUSES

Perhaps more than any other factor, the 2016 land use moratorium was eventuated by one very pernicious side effect of earlier land use codes: the boom of third-floor luxury penthouses atop commercial buildings in Aspen's small downtown core. These luxury penthouses were a visual reminder of how the local class culture had changed. Some of the issues posed by third-floor penthouses seemed to be drawn from the stories of "Lifestyles of the Rich and Famous." For example, in 2014, purchasers of a $16 million penthouse bought the "air rights" to the property next door. That is, the owner of the adjacent building sold to the penthouse owner the open-air space above their two-story building, which guaranteed that no vertical development would occur on that parcel, thereby ensuring that the penthouse owners would have a clear view of Aspen Mountain in perpetuity. The broader problems caused by Aspen's penthouses can be captured in a single word: sterilization. Planners in Aspen used this term in a functional sense, not an aesthetic sense. Urban landscapes became sterilized when the streetscapes were devoid of pedestrian activity or commercial vitality. Once again emerging from the global expansion of capital and real estate speculation, Aspen developers seized upon a new building model in the mid-2000s: they developed properties that took advantage of the three-story building heights, designing them to be filled by restaurants or retail on the first floor, offices and locally serving businesses on the second, and penthouse apartments on the third. Yet with price tags in the vicinity of $20 million, builders could recoup a substantial part of their investment through the sale of the third-floor penthouse alone. "The real money was up above," council member Art Daily recounted in a city council work session that set the stage of the moratorium. "With those units selling for $25 million, you didn't worry about what you leased the remaining space for." Flagging these concerns at a meeting four months prior to the moratorium, Mayor Skadron said that what "horrifies [him] right now is the red building, with the penthouse that sold for $30 million." Officially known as the Aspen Core building, he worried that the "ground floor spaces will sit vacant, because the owners have no urgency to fill [them]." What concerned Jessica Garrow, Aspen's lead city planner, about this development is that an active streetscape is the centerpiece of virtually any vibrant urban community. With penthouse apartments occupied only part of the year, and vacant ground floor spaces, Aspen's downtown core was becoming sterilized. It was becoming devoid of the kind of activity that had made it a vibrant "lights-on community" and promoted opportunities for locals and visitors to mingle with one another. Ms. Garrow worried that this type of sterilization was now creeping out from the commercial core into other areas of town.

Concerns about Aspen's penthouse boom did not emerge sui generis in 2015. They were evident as early as 2012, when then mayor Mick Ireland (2007–2013) referred to this new wave of development as "penthouses on stilts," where the two floors below the residential units served merely as structural supports for the real money-making venture up above. Yet what firmly put this building form on the map and in the consciousness of locals was a couple that lived in Aspen for part of the year, often referred to in the newspapers and public conversations as "the Ukrainians." Two years after purchasing and then combining two condo spaces in Aspen's city center, owners Michael Sedoy and Natalia Shvachko (a one-time Miss Ukraine), could no longer take the trials and tribulations of living on Aspen's lively "Restaurant Row." Throughout 2013, they lodged more than thirty noise complaints with the city, alleging that the music flowing from nearby businesses like the Aspen Brewing Company and Boosty Bellows, a nightclub, interfered with sleep and even caused health issues. During an eventual court proceeding, they described this as "noise harassment and torture of our family." That same year, the city sued the couple, alleging that the couple had claimed for their exclusive use an elevator designed to provide access to the entire building, in compliance with the Americans with Disabilities Act. Frequent reporting about these activities and the eventual court trials appeared in Aspen's two free daily papers, generating awareness and angst across the community. It was a great relief to locals that the couple lost their noise complaint case against Aspen Brewing Company and then failed in their quest to monopolize the shared elevator.

Despite their defeat, many locals were concerned that newcomers like "the Ukrainians" had become the new normal in Aspen. They took offense to the notion that wealthy part-year residents would dictate the terms and conditions under which local businesses operate. Coverage in the *Denver Post* reported that Aspen restaurant owners characterized the couple as buying a condo "in a vibrant nightlife district and now [wanting] to turn it into a bedroom community."[14] *Aspen Times* columnist Meredith Carroll mockingly suggested that the community "break out a tiny violin" for the couple, finding their complaints of wafting smoke and drunken revelry to be too rich, especially after the couple commented that they chose this location to replicate the vibrant urban lifestyle they were accustomed to in New York.[15] A key difference, of course, is that New York penthouses soar many stories above the vibrancy below; height limitations in Aspen, however, make these relations more intimate, potentially exposing residents to more annoyances (e.g., garbage collection and early-morning deliveries to adjacent restaurants). Aspen business owners felt threatened by the possibility that wealthy vacation home owners—who could purchase any number of properties in quiet surrounding neighborhoods or ranch lands—would seek to limit the rights of local businesses to offer entertainment consistent with the vibe of a resort town (and who still had to adhere to decibel limits dictated by code). Quoted in the *Aspen Times*, Trenton Allen, musician and booker of live music acts in town, said, "You shouldn't sacrifice the vitality of the downtown community, a commercial area, for one or two residents who complain." And Jimmy Yeager, owner of one of Aspen's most successful restaurants, suggested that the aggrieved couple "join the party or move to Starwood," a more isolated luxury development outside of town.[16]

Using Ryan Centner's framework, Aspen's affluent newcomers came to possess increasing quantities of *spatial capital*: as they gradually took up more space in the community, they threatened to remake the space through their demand for more upscale experiences and their quotidian practices.[17] Yet, while plutocrats are part of the Aspen community, their ability to fashion the plutocratic city, one subtly shaped in their images and responsive to their preferences, has remained somewhat muted. In 2017, the city council responded to locals' concerns and attached for the first time a "no-complaining clause" to a permit for renovation of a mixed-use building on Aspen's vibrant pedestrian mall. The goal was to protect the property rights of existing businesses, whose livelihoods were threatened by newcomers.[18] In each of these cases, local business owners prevailed, as did those who sought to protect the fun, casual atmosphere of downtown. Yet these mounting complaints seemed to inflict psychic costs on locals, who worried about being residentially and socially displaced. These incidents also ratcheted up questions among the city council and the Community Development staff about whether mixed-use buildings—ones that combine residential and commercial uses—have a place in Aspen's downtown core.

WHEN BAD BUILDINGS LEAVE A BAD TASTE

As the Aspen City Council embarked upon their rewrite of the land use codes, a number of recent building projects hung over the proceedings, serving as object lessons in why this moratorium was needed. These buildings offended for reasons that both reflect and constitute Aspen's unique place-based class culture: first, they violated the deeply held value of *small mountain town character*; second, these buildings came into being through processes that locals saw as contrary to the notions of progressive decision-making that are institutionalized into Aspen's political fabric.

Rising forty-seven feet from the corner of Spring and Hyman is a building like no other in Aspen. Opened in 2014 and designed by Pritzker Prize (architecture's biggest prize) recipient Shigeru Ban, the Aspen Art Museum declares its presence in a downtown filled with modest buildings and a handful of significant historical structures. Housing a thirty-three-thousand-square-foot interior, its woven-wood edifice rises like an improbable giant basket that protects a world-class art museum. In designing the building, Shigeru Ban said: "I wanted to create a site-specific sequence that took into account the mountain views and the building's purpose as an art museum, and to open the building to the outside so visitors could appreciate the beauty of Aspen from inside the building."[19] An eastern-facing wall of glass allows visitors to peer out through the basket-weave; up top, the third-floor café—which is accessible to the general public as part of the project's *public amenity* requirement for meetings, reading, and relaxation—opens to majestic views of Aspen Mountain.

Locals called it "horrible," "deplorable," and "disgusting," and asked the council not just if they would put a halt to new developments, but whether they would be willing to go so far as to tear down a few existing buildings. Public outreach during the nearly year-long moratorium revealed the museum to be the most disliked building in town. For many, the most immediate objection to the Art Museum was aesthetic. Local beverage dealer and avid mountain biker Greg Clendening called it "ugly as hell." In a town of two-story, twenty-eight-foot building heights, the blocky forty-seven-foot structure boldly declared itself, offending further by obscuring views of the mountain from the street. While some locals appreciated the architecture, and could imagine it elsewhere, they felt it was out of place in downtown Aspen. Toni Wilson, a real estate agent and polo enthusiast, said, "It would have been fine out by the music tent"—home to buildings in the mid-century Aspen Modern style—"but not in the heart of town. We no longer have a historic center of town." In fact, many locals mourned the loss of the building that was knocked down to make room for the Art Museum.

Although the Historic Preservation Commission did not deem the Weiner-stube restaurant to be of historic significance, which would have prevented it from being demolished, it was a beloved institution for many locals, both for its quaint chalet-style architecture and the affordable breakfasts and "joiners table" that facilitated community engagement. Instead of places that bring diverse people together, Toni Wilson saw "more opportunities to make everything bigger, bigger, and bigger. And better, better and better. Not necessarily better to most of us. But bigger, grander." For her and others, the Art Museum was "the tipping point," after which she lamented, "Now we're lost."

Intertwined with the aesthetic objections to the Art Museum were objections to the process by which the structure got built. Law enforcement officer Willie Dayton described this process quite simply: It was "shoved on us." When the Aspen Art Museum opened in 2014, it did so after an eight-year battle that wound its way through the Planning and Zoning Commission (P&Z), City Hall, the Pitkin County Courthouse, and many lawyers' offices. It was, in fact, under pressure from an impending lawsuit in 2010, ushering it through an expedited review process. The lawsuit was brought against the city by major local developer Nikos Hecht, who owned the parcel of land upon which the Weinerstube once sat and would one day host the museum. Hecht had submitted a proposal for a mixed-use project spanning two lots on that block, rising to forty-two feet and comprised of 47,000 square feet (one-third the size of a typical Target store). At the time, the museum was not part of this proposal, and museum director Heidi Zuckerman looked elsewhere for an appropriate building site. Although Hecht's proposed building met the existing land use code, the city council rejected the application. Drawing on the 2000 Aspen Area Community Plan, the council deemed the building too tall and too boxy for the site, violating the commitment to small-town character. Thus, while the proposed building met the letter of the law (the land use code), it violated the spirit of the law (as captured by the AACP). In 2008, Nikos Hecht sued the Aspen City Council based on their decision, arguing that they had abused their discretion. In 2009, District Court Judge Gail Nichols sided with the city, arguing that it had properly exercised its authority when it rejected a proposal that they felt "would adversely affect the future development of surrounding areas."[20]

Figure 7. Two disliked buildings: The Aspen Art Museum (left) and Hecht's Victorian Square. Photo by Jenny Stuber.

While he publicly threatened to appeal the case and take it to a higher court, Nikos Hecht privately moved back and forth between members of the city council and Heidi Zuckerman, who had withdrawn her proposal to develop the art museum in an alternate location. In 2010, under the threat of lawsuit, all three parties agreed to a settlement where the Shigeru Ban–designed art museum would anchor the corner of the block, and a smaller version of Hecht's original mixed-use project—whose height was now reduced to 38.5 feet—would sit in the space adjacent (see figure 7). City Planner Ben Gagnon contextualized city staff's support of the project in a written memo: the fact that the Art Museum rises above adjacent buildings and has a blockier façade "reinforces the civic and public nature of the structure." Alas, in addition to the fact that the museum was approved largely behind closed doors and outside of the normal land use process, the public was outraged by one more processual element: as an essential public facility, it was deemed exempt from affordable housing mitigations and other fees. The fact that museum director Heidi Zuckerman's compensation package was $600,000 at the time made the "civic good" argument a bit disingenuous for many community members.

Reflecting back on the event in 2016, community member Greg Clendenning called Nikos Hecht a "bully" and accused the city of "rolling over" and giving the developers "more and more and more"—waiving parking requirements, housing mitigations, height allowances, and density restrictions. At a city council meeting during the moratorium, Phyllis Bronson, a local political gadfly stated, "People felt very disempowered by that process. The fact that the Art Museum came into existence by threat of a lawsuit . . . created an energy that a lot of this is reactive to." The very existence of the moratorium, she said, was reflective of this angst. "The feeling of needing to put a halt on things is causing the pendulum to swing in the opposite way because people are so concerned about things that happened a few years ago." John Whipple, a member of the Historic Preservation Commission (HPC) made a similar statement in one of the commission's official meetings: "We're now faced with knee-jerk reactions"; the proposed revisions to the land use code seem to "reflect the vibe that the goal is now to make up for someone else's bad work"—bad in terms of aesthetics or process. Reflecting on the question of whether there should be residential units in the commercial core, as prompted by "the Ukrainians," architect Mitch Nelson lamented: "One bad apple is spoiling an entire community because they think that every building will eventually be sterilized . . . one bad thing happens in the core and now we can't have anybody live there."

One block from the Aspen Art Museum, one more building left an enduring bad taste in locals' mouths. Built according to the land use code of the time, but similarly offending both taste and process, the Aspen Core building was referred to by council member Bert Myrin as "the Tangerine Monster." Many locals referred to it as the "Lego Building," a moniker inspired by the building's reflective, orange-y surface and simple, modular design (see figure 8). The sheer mass and scale of the building, in addition to its bright color, offended many Aspenites. Speaking in a fall 2016 P&Z meeting, Community Development Director Jessica Garrow described the external tiles as "utterly inappropriate in Aspen," adding that the material "does not relate to anything in Aspen's history." Amy Simon, director of the city's Historic Preservation division, described it as "an eyesore," and went on to say she was "embarrassed by it." The building resulted from a "horse trading" process in 2012 that

Figure 8. Aspen's most hated building: The Aspen Core, a.k.a. "The Tangerine Monster." Photo by Jenny Stuber.

similarly offended local sensibilities. As owners of three lots at the corner of Hyman and Hunter, Nikos Hecht and his son Andy proposed a mixed-use development spanning these lots. The sticking point, however, was that one of the soon-to-be demolished buildings was Little Annie's, a beloved affordably priced restaurant, and the other was the Benton Building, the former studio of Tom Benton, an Aspen modern artist who conjured the gonzo spirit and progressive politics of the early 1970s. In exchange for agreeing to preserve these adjacent historic structures, the city granted the Hechts approvals for a mixed-use building (commercial and third-floor penthouse) on the corner and waived the millions of dollars' worth of affordable housing mitigations generated by the project. Over the next several years, lingering disgust over the mass and scale of some buildings, as well as the feeling that the city was selling its soul to developers, increased anxieties and placed pressure on the city council to rewrite the land use codes to better preserve Aspen's small-town feel and deliver on its informal motto, "Development Pays Its Own Way," which would protect the interests of working locals.

REFERENDUM 1: THE TIPPING POINT

Perhaps the tipping point for declaring the moratorium came from Referendum 1, a cri de coeur in defense of locals' rights and reflective of Aspen's tradition of citizen action. If passed, Referendum 1 would amend Aspen's Home Rule Charter so that any commercial project that was approved by the council with "variances"—deviations from the land use code— would require final approval from the voters. The citizen-activists behind Ref 1—as it was called—were sick and tired of developers receiving breaks from the size limits, parking obligations, and contributions to the affordable housing program required under the code. In a March 2015 town hall meeting, Michael Behrendt, former council member and owner of one of Aspen's most affordable lodges, the St. Moritz, explained his support accordingly: "It's always too big; it's way too big and it's happening way too fast. Those are the people who live here, and I think they have a right to their say, and my belief is that the council has listened to the developers and they have not listened to the people, again and again." Under the banner of "Keep Aspen, Aspen," he and other activists went to work trying to hold city council accountable to the building rules they themselves adopted, and deliver to the city and its citizens the *community values*— especially access to affordable housing—inscribed in the land use code.

Not surprisingly, members of the Aspen City Council were largely opposed to Referendum 1. Although they understood and shared some of the community's anxieties over recent development patterns, they saw it as a dangerous challenge to representative democracy, one that could potentially undermine both the authority and the responsibility of elected officials. Council member and landscape architect Ann Mullins got out in front on this issue, speaking against it in council chambers and a local town hall meeting. In our one-on-one conversation, she explained her opposition to the proposed amendment this way:

> The one thing you never want to say to anybody is, "You're not as smart as me or you can't understand those issues." But in reality, when I'm at work, spending twenty hours a week on city business, whether it's land use, water issues, sidewalk paving . . . you learn about all these things and you are able to put these things together; you're looking at one issue and you're pulling information from here and from here. And you work with all the city

[planning] staff and you can call them and say, "What's the deal with this?" So, when an issue comes up, they are so complex, it's my job to understand all this stuff, and you do need access to all this stuff that we are looking at weekly to understand it.

For Mullins, taking development projects to a public vote places them in the hands of people who may not have access to essential information. "We [the city council] need to take the lead and make decisions that seem best for the community," Mullins said, "not shove it down the line and say, 'Okay, we can't decide; you guys vote.'"

Nuance and complexity also characterized the opposition to the amendment by Bill Stirling, a former four-term mayor (1983–1991). A progressive champion in his own right, who fought to preserve locally serving businesses while in office, Stirling saw the use of variances as an important planning tool; one that recognizes that urban planning is not a one-size-fits-all science, but one that occasionally requires the use of variances in extenuating circumstances. At the March 2015 town hall meeting he said, "If you lock in those four specific aspects to every application—height, mass, parking, and housing—you lose the opportunity to reshape an application; to make it more effective, make it more successful, make it more responsive." Under some circumstances, variances can "add character of the town," Stirling continued. In conversation with me, he further stated that deviating from the code is something elected officials should do "only it if it is absolutely necessary to make something better happen or is in the long-term interest of the community." Several recent lodging projects, for example, had been given breaks on parking requirements or size limitations because the council applauded their plans to increase the number of affordable lodge units in town—thereby helping make Aspen accessible to a larger demographic. Stirling said that the exercise of authority and subjectivity is part of the "the fun of what it is to be an elected official." Legislation like Referendum 1, however, "handcuffs council, so that it is no longer representative democracy. It's more mob rule."

Other former mayors had different stances on Referendum 1. Whereas Bill Stirling considered the community benefits of flexible land use planning tools, four-term mayor Mick Ireland (2007–2013) worried about the

long-term economic impacts of variances. "Doesn't the granting of variances on a consistent basis encourage speculation in real estate, with the
result that the realtor or the owner of the property comes before council
and says, 'I paid extra for this property. I expected to have a variance;
without that variance I may have to leave . . . an unbuilt project.'" From
Ireland's perspective, the council's willingness to make concessions,
whether by allowing larger buildings or waiving mitigation requirements,
pushes the market value of many commercial properties above what they
would be worth had the code been regularly enforced. As a consequence,
commercial real estate prices continue to escalate, undermining another
community value inscribed into the Aspen Area Community Plan, namely
opportunities for locally owned and locally serving businesses.

   In a community that takes great pride in their progressive, smart-
growth politics dating back to the early 1970s, many locals felt adrift
in their own community. Lodge owner and key supporter of Referendum 1, Michael Behrendt, called this a crisis of "co-optation . . . which
has occurred with every council we've had during my time in Aspen."
Although he bristled at the suggestion that he or his peers had been co-
opted, council member Adam Frisch similarly saw this as the confluence
of broader political and economic issues; the larger issue, in his analysis,
is that Aspen voters continuously elect what they believe are slow-growth
councils, yet the town continues to grow in ways they do not like.[21] For
him, secular market forces posed a problem that even the most progressive of councils would struggle to address. Speaking softly but delivering a
very pointed message at a town hall meeting, Terry Murray described the
"citizen disgust" in the community, motivated by frustration over the fact
that elected officials do not live up to their constituents' desires: "You guys
just can't fight anymore, so, we're taking the hard issues away from you."

   Soon thereafter, Terry Murray's prediction came true. On May 5, 2015,
Aspen voters passed Referendum 1 with 53 percent of the vote. The fact
that it did not pass by a landslide suggests that many locals continued to
have faith in the city council, worried over the possibility of tyranny of
the majority and saw some danger in chilling the climate of real estate
development. In a statement that would come to fruition nearly one year
later to the date, citizen-activist Marcia Goshorn weighed in at the town
hall meeting, addressing the sentiments that motivated Referendum 1,

and its logical conclusion: "The one thing I think this ballot question has done is force the council to look at the land use codes—which have desperately needed to be rewritten for a number of years. . . . I want the land use codes to be written in clear enough language so they [council members] can understand exactly what's allowed, because now, they're open to interpretation. Even two projects coming in within months of each other can be given two different interpretations of exactly the same land use code, and that concerns me." This type of concern captured many underlying anxieties, as discussed throughout this chapter: anxieties over the growing power of developers, the inability of council to make good on their promises, the loss of community character, and the selling out of community benefits to development projects (e.g., contributions to affordable housing). Together, these dynamics captured a frustration over how class is done in Aspen.

After its passage in the spring of 2015, Referendum 1 continued to reverberate throughout the community. Just one month later, chief champion Bert Myrin won a run-off election for a council seat against former mayor Mick Ireland, signaling the electorate's hunger for a candidate who would push back against development. Then, in the fall of 2015, Referendum 1 faced its first test, when Mark Hunt's proposal for a small lodge known as Base2 was put up for a vote. A Midwesterner with deep business ties to Chicago—just like the founders of modern Aspen, Walter and Elizabeth Paepcke and the Crown family, current owners of the Ski Company—Mark Hunt had quickly become one of Aspen's largest owners of commercial real estate and was alternately credited with and condemned for giving a facelift to the downtown core. One of his most noteworthy projects stood on Galena Street—Aspen's Rodeo Drive—where he renovated the building that once housed the Gap and replaced it with a Dolce & Gabbana. In the process, he transformed a parcel of real estate that was valued at $8.8 million in 2012 and turned it into one valued at nearly $32 million after renovation.[22] In the years following, locals frequently lamented the loss of the Gap, one of the retailers where they could buy clothing basics for the entire family.

Yet Mark Hunt aspired to do more than cater to Aspen's luxury crowd. With his Base2 hotel proposal, he sought to develop a small, thirty-seven-room "affordable" lodge whose units would rent for $200 per night (in contrast to the city-wide average of nearly $450 and a state average of nearly $150).[23] In order to make the project "pencil out"—that is, earn a return in investment—Hunt's project exceeded the allowable floor area and provided minimal "setbacks." In other words, the project was bigger and blockier than allowed by code (more than twice as big, in fact), filling the space with a lot-line to lot-line footprint. Recognizing the community value of making Aspen accessible to visitors from a wider range of demographic groups, the city council approved this project with the variances mentioned above. Although Hunt's project was approved prior to the passage of Referendum 1, months of legal wrangling resulted in the conclusion that it was, in fact, susceptible to a citizen's vote, per this legislation. As the campaign mounted to gain signatures to put Base2 to a community-wide vote, Hunt said, "I truly set out to do something to make a difference with affordable lodging. I'm proud of it and was actually really excited to bring it to the community."[24]

Alas, the voters were not ready for Base2, despite Hunt's pledge to democratize the Aspen experience. On November 3, 2015, they rejected the development application with 63 percent of the vote—a wider margin than Referendum 1 had won by in the first place. Mark Hunt outspent the opposition by a 5–1 margin, yet money could not overcome the sentiment that the city council was giving away the community to developers and that outsiders were remaking the town in ways that were antithetical to local character. A year and a half later, Ward Hauenstein, one of the chief opponents of Base2, won a seat on the council, further illustrating the community's desire for a voice against development. Yet none of these efforts seemed to dampen Mark Hunt's development strategy. He continued to submit proposals to remodel his properties, mixing within them high-end retail that would pay the bills and smaller projects he hoped would satisfy local community needs. Reflecting on his loss, Hunt called the Aspen electorate a "tough crowd." Reporting by the *Aspen Daily News*'s Curtis Wackerle quoted Hunt as saying that the "barrier of entry" to develop in Aspen is high, but that's ultimately a good thing.[25] His comment hints at the irony and contradiction that is at the heart of this town: the intense regulatory environment and community engagement that characterize local politics are a fundamental part of what makes Aspen so attractive to visitors and so lucrative for investors.

CONCLUSION

Every six years or so, Aspen city council, the planning department, and its citizens seemed to go back to the drawing board. In semi-predictable cycles, sometimes through emergency ordinances, they stop the pendulum swing and rewrite the land use codes to ensure that Aspen retain its small-town character and serve the needs of locals and visitors alike. The rewriting of the land use code to better align with the Aspen Area Community Plan represents a clear and concerted effort at place-making—one that is cyclical and persistent, given pressures from global economic forces and cultural and technological trends.

While every municipality has its complexities and contradictions, those in Aspen seem to pose thorny, if not intractable, challenges. There, the realization and institutionalization of the AACP is made especially difficult by the complex constellation of people who make up the community. As the AACP states, "We are dependent on our commuting workforce, second homeowners, tourists, and those who live here full time."[26] Yet, to acknowledge the diversity of people who make up Aspen and to implement policies that balance their seemingly disparate interests are two different things. These constituent groups differ first and foremost in their class positions and material resources. Therefore, they differ in terms of their access to housing and their ability to satisfy basic daily needs, such as groceries, clothing, and household items. Second, they differ in terms of their stake within the community: whether they vote locally, how much they pay in taxes, and whether they have family members with vested interests in the town's school system or social services. As such, key stakeholders in the community have legitimate differences of opinion about whether free-market penthouses should exist in the urban core, whether a world-class art museum increases the town's caché as an art destination or constitutes an eye sore, and how to extract mitigations from developers in ways that best suit the needs of year-round locals. Balancing the needs of these disparate groups and making "Aspen work as a community and as a resort," as the AACP states, is a cyclically Sisyphean task.[27]

Further complicating the task of place-making in Aspen is the fact that local political forces and global economic forces operate according to different logics, and in Aspen they appear both fundamentally linked and hopelessly oppositional. On the one hand, the success of Aspen is dependent on the town's ability to attract wealthy visitors, residents, and investors. On the other hand, the presence of these constituencies seems to push the town farther out of reach of many year-round locals. As the city council endeavored to "stop the pendulum swing once and for all" and deliver a land use code that would, in the words of Mayor Steve Skadron, "endure for fifty years," not the usual six years, fellow council member Adam Frisch commented on the challenge of this task, saying, "I feel like we're trying to rewrite the US Constitution, Bill of Rights, *and* the Tax Code." As a former Wall Street banker, he had perhaps a better understanding than most of the global economic pressures bearing down on Aspen, and the ability of the town's political leaders to push back. Despite the town's considerable intellectual and financial resources, the need to revise the land use code seemed to reemerge, like clockwork. "We're trying to hold onto this small town," Frisch said during a 2015 meeting that laid the foundation for the moratorium, "and the forces out there are a tremendous amount of money, and a very small amount of space [in this town] to put the money. The town of Aspen is only becoming more desirable. We're growing farther ahead of our peers with desirability and development pressures." About these pressures, Frisch asked, "Are we facing a bazooka fight, but we're showing up with a BB gun?" With these concerns in mind, the Aspen City Council declared a land use moratorium in March of 2016, hoping to transform its land use code into a city planning bazooka that would effectively "push back" against global economic forces and reassert the values expressed in the Aspen Area Community Plan. The next chapter details these efforts, focusing specifically on restoring small-town character and locals' access to recreational and economic opportunity.

4 Place-Making and the Construction of "Small-Town Character"

On March 13, 2016, on the eve of declaring an emergency ordinance that would freeze development and allow the city to revise the land use code, council member Adam Frisch used his colorful way with words to capture the challenge facing the city: "One of the key economic drivers of our community is the small-town, pedestrian-friendly built environment. Anyone who has any economic interest in our community—free-market or affordable housing owner, business owner or developer, with anything more than a short-term goal—will need to make sure we do not kill the golden goose that allows Aspen to not only provide, the built environment we want as full-time residents, but that attracts the level of tourism that provides the tax coffers that are the envy of every resort community in the world." With these words in mind, the city council and the Community Development Department (the professional staff of planners who guide the process, also known as Comm Dev) set to work, identifying those aspects of the community most in need of attention, and the land use tools best suited to addressing those needs. With the overarching goal of protecting small-town character and sense of place, while at the same time balancing the needs of working locals and affluent visitors, the city council focused their attention on the land use code. The land use code is the body of regulations that establishes the look, feel, and function of a place. It does not merely concern itself with a municipality's aesthetics or logistical operations; it also structures the social relations and narratives that shape its place-based class cultures. According to geographers James S. Duncan and Nancy G. Duncan, the land use code facilitates "[c]ollective memories, narratives of community, [and] invented traditions," which are "repeated, performed, occasionally contested, but more often stabilized" as artifacts of place.[1] The land use code, then, is one of the settings in which class relations become institutionalized. In this chapter and the next, I explore how the Aspen City Council and its urban planning staff, in conversation with locals and the development community, revised the land use code with careful attention to the question: What is Aspen and who is it for?

During this year-long period, the Aspen City Council zeroed-in on three technical issues. First, in response to the Aspen Area Community Plan's call for policies that "maintain Aspen's small-town character," they considered *commercial design standards* and issues related to *mass and scale*.[2] By addressing what buildings look like, how large they are, and how they are situated within the built environment, the council sought to restore the aesthetics of authenticity and preserve the sense of place that makes Aspen a valuable global "brand." Second, in recognition of the AACP's call for policies that "encourage a commercial mix that is balanced, diverse, and meets the needs of year-round residents and visitors," they focused on *use mix* regulations.[3] These regulations dictate where specific types of uses (commercial, residential, industrial, and so forth) can be situated. They were embraced as a tool for restoring vitality and reinvigorating the kinds of cross-class interactions that Aspen prides itself on. Finally, in recognition of the AACP declaration that "a strong and diverse year-round community and a viable and healthy local workforce are fundamental cornerstones for the sustainability of the" local community,[4] the council responded to the concern that developers were getting breaks on their affordable housing responsibilities and explored the possibility of increasing mitigation rates. The contentious debate surrounding this question, and how it revealed fault lines and contradictions in the land use code, is the topic of chapter 6.

In the end, the moratorium ushered in a series of code amendments that substantially "downzoned" Aspen, resulting in smaller buildings, more open space for outdoor enjoyment, retail spaces designed to better meet the needs of locals, and higher affordable housing mitigations. These revised policies have two important consequences for how class is done in Aspen. First, by limiting building sizes and strengthening aesthetic guidelines, the land use code provides a hedge for developers, investors, and vacation home owners who may be looking for a good place to invest. Second, by increasing affordable housing mitigations and forcing developers to create second-tier spaces—a design solution meant to attract businesses serving daily needs—and "public amenity space," the land use code re-centers the needs of working locals, enhancing opportunities for them to live, work, and recreate in Aspen. These findings make two important contributions to scholarly understandings of place. First, they provide a ground-level view of place-making. Places emerge over time, in the accretion of small decisions and actions, but they are also made in more protracted engagements, through the activation of discourses, the building of consensus, and the institutionalization of these understandings in code. These analyses provide insight into such moments. Second, this chapter shows that in some cases, a place's use value and exchange value are not fundamentally opposed to one another, as Logan and Molotch's theories of the growth machine would suggest. In crafting a sense of authenticity and reinforcing Aspen's small-town character, the city council and other stakeholders enhanced its exchange value. They instantiated a sense of authenticity in contrast to less-authentic mountain towns and the cities and suburbs inhabited by Aspen's elite visitors and investors. Yet, Aspen's city council and other key players did so not merely to brand it and sell it as a product. Rather, they crafted these regulations with simultaneous attention to Aspen's use value, to ensure that it provides a quality of life for locals, whose presence in turn enhances the town's brand.

REINVIGORATING SMALL-TOWN CHARACTER

Invoking the importance of "small-town character" is one thing; inscribing it onto a community, and making if feel authentic, is quite another. As the Aspen City Council began their revisions of the land use code, their overarching goal was to implement policies that would restore the mountain-town character of the place. With respect to the model of place-based class cultures, notions of Aspen exceptionalism informed these conversations, the goal of which was the reinstitutionalization of its distinctiveness and preservation of the legitimacy of calling Aspen an authentic place. But as Maggie Carson, a city employee with knowledge of the planning process, told me: "Small-town character means something different to everyone, and so it doesn't have a definition at all. . . . It's a loaded term." With the potential to mean all things to all people and, therefore, have no practical operationalization, the 2012 Aspen Area Community Plan provided a definition for this seemingly elusive quality: "Our built environment respects historical context while allowing for innovation. We have welcoming, non-exclusive and casual gathering places that promote interaction among locals and visitors. Our lively and diverse downtown is an important asset that contributes to our overall character."[5] With both aesthetics and social interactions in mind, the Aspen City Council and its advisory boards (Historic Preservation Commission and Planning and Zoning), the Community Development Department ("Comm Dev"), and a cadre of consultants set about tweaking the *commercial design standards* to ensure authenticity in the built environment and facilitate Aspen's treasured cross-class interactions.

With its high-end real estate market, Aspen has no shortage of *place professionals*, a term used by Tom Gieryn to describe the technical and aesthetic experts who use their expertise to mediate relationships between economic, political, and other interests, who can translate "small-town character" into the land use code.[6] In aligning the code with the Aspen Area Community Plan, these parties were tasked with reproducing Aspen's historical charm and its vaunted "messy vitality," a term that first appeared in the 1993 iteration of the AACP. This ethos states that "Aspen as a community should avoid an environment that is too structured, too perfect, and that eliminates the funkiness that once characterized this town."[7] Rather than the uniform "Little Tyrolia" aesthetic of Vail, Aspen grounds its aesthetic value in the mix of historical structures dating from the 1870s mining days, the chalet-style and Aspen Modern buildings of the 1950s, and more recent flirtations with postmodernism. The challenge, though, is to draft code regulations that capture the local mountain flavor, without being hokey or contrived, and strike the right balance between prescriptiveness, which ensures that high-quality standards are followed and design disasters are averted, and innovation, which has made Aspen famous.

PRESERVING THE BEST OF THE WEST THROUGH COMMERCIAL DESIGN GUIDELINES

The goal of revising Aspen's Commercial Design Guidelines was to "preserve the character and history of existing development and foster consistency and cohesiveness between neighboring developments."[8] These guidelines structure the look and feel of Aspen, providing detailed requirements for building design (e.g., roof shapes and window types), landscape, site layout, materials, and so forth. Whereas some municipalities may prescribe Spanish tiles or gabled roofs for the entire town, Aspen's guidelines vary across its seven "character areas," spelling out distinctions, for example, between an area made up of lodges that hug the mountain base and one populated by civic buildings. With these guidelines, "The City does not intend to limit creativity in the built environment but to promote architecture and site design that creates cohesive neighborhoods that are walkable, interesting, and vibrant."[9] Much of the process surrounding these revisions focused on striking the right balance between being too prescriptive and allowing too much freedom. When responding to the proposal to specify guidelines for each of Aspen's seven character areas, Skippy Mesirow, a member of the Planning and Zoning (P&Z) Commission asked, "Is there the danger of over-segmentation, and getting rid of the natural messiness? We don't want it to be like EPCOT, where there's China here and Norway there." Mesirow reminded the commission of the importance of creating opportunities for "messy vitality," and avoiding the strict guidelines and artificiality of Disney's EPCOT, which takes visitors on a tour of different countries and cultures, or even a purpose-built resort like Vail. In a conversation about preferred and allowable paint colors, Mesirow echoed this theme and signaled Aspen's antipathy toward Vail and other tightly crafted environments. He worried that a prescriptive, "dumbed down" set of guidelines that express a simple preference for "natural colors" could turn Aspen into a "beige-ified Disneyland"—which would be utterly boring and predicable.

The comparison to Disneyland is perhaps quite apt, from the standpoint of geographer David Harvey. From his standpoint, in the postmodern era, capitalism remakes place and extracts monopoly rents by transforming places into spectacles. Although Aspen may seem like a restrained, humble, former mining town, the creation of spectacle need not be ostentatious or in-your-face. It can, according to Harvey, manifest as global capital's search for the distinctive, and the "valuation of uniqueness, authenticity, particularity"—in contrast to the homogeneity that visitors and part-year residents experience elsewhere.[10] Thus, even if the city strove to avoid becoming a "beige-ified Disneyland," it still faced the challenge of finding a balance that would protect its collective symbolic capital and keep drawing monied interests.

With the tensions between discernable character and banal predictability in mind, council members and commissioners time and again asked the question: "How do you write a code that regulates 'sometimes'?" Such a code would allow for predictable aesthetic guidelines while also allowing for spontaneity and innovation. Questions about the firmness of guidelines was especially evident when discussing building materials. The freedom to push aesthetic boundaries had perhaps gotten too loose in recent years, and many city officials felt that a correction was in order. Nowhere was this possibility more visible than in the object lesson of "the Tangerine Monster." The Aspen Core building, sometimes called "the Lego Building," rivaled the Art Museum as the town's "most hated building." While the most vocal objection was to its blocky mass and scale, many found the shiny terracotta tiles covering the exterior equally offensive. Comm Dev director Jessica Garrow thought the tiles were out of step because, as she said, "they don't relate visually or historically to anything else in Aspen." Some stakeholders in this process wanted to pass guidelines that would never again allow such an abomination. Yet Gretchen Greenwood, architect and member of Historic Preservation Commission, disagreed, arguing that simply banning terracotta tiles would be an excessively blunt move. "I have some terracotta tiles in my office," she offered during a commission meeting. "They're textured; they would be great. A traditional pattern and application would work." She wanted greater nuance and more room for design creativity in the proposed guidelines. Spencer McKnight of the Planning and Zoning Commission similarly favored a looser interpretation of allowable materials. "I like having guidelines," he said during a P&Z meeting, "but there are examples of things that get built, and at first it's like, 'This is crazy,' but then it becomes a favorite building." Fellow commissioner Brian McNellis agreed, saying "We don't want to stymie creativity." Despite the desire for innovation and creativity, all supported guidelines that would discourage applicants from proposing projects that used offensive materials, whether reflective or "tacky," or non-native and lacking connection to the local context.

The boundary between innovation in design and locally appropriate aesthetics emerged repeatedly throughout these conversations. Another discussion asked whether materials other than wood or brick could be used in the Main Street Historic Area. The Main Street Historic district, which is dotted with stately Victorian homes and smaller miners' cabins, is the first glimpse of Aspen that many experience on their way into town. According to Director of Historic Preservation Amy Simon, the renewed preference for a narrow palette of materials partially reflected objections to the Jewish Community Center, a contemporary two-story building that incorporated limestone "that's not from around here." Although public outreach revealed some distaste for this building, architect Willis Pember pushed back, arguing that aesthetic "concessions should be made" for religious institutions, knowing that such buildings often become architectural landmarks. Gretchen Greenwood disagreed, again pointing to the importance of honoring the local: "That's not a historic material. What we want to do with these guidelines is prevent someone from coming before us with limestone." Indeed, the need to tighten up on design "standards"—which *required* particular elements, as opposed to guidelines, which named them as *preferences*—had become increasingly popular as developers based outside of Aspen brought their aesthetic styles to their building projects. "Locals know the context and what is appropriate," Bob Blaich, architect and HPC member noted, "but we have one developer who keeps using architects from Illinois, who have a different point of view." Blaich referred to Chicago developer Mark Hunt, who having quickly purchased upwards of fifteen buildings in town, was viewed with suspicion. Although the Aspen Core building was not part of Hunt's portfolio, he had converted "the Gap building" into a Dolce and Gabbana, bringing to Aspen a retailer that does not serve working locals, along with architecture—excessively large windows and non-native limestone—that some saw as incongruous with the local vernacular. This left a bad taste in many people's mouths and motivated the desire to establish standards that reinforced the Aspen brand and, ostensibly, signaled the value of local people and materials.

The revision of Aspen's Commercial Design Standards allowed local place professionals to draw symbolic boundaries not just between Aspen and other, less authentic resorts, but between Aspen and the cities from which many visitors come. Debate over the size of materiality of shop windows, especially their "glazing," illustrates this point. In an October 2016, meeting of the Historic Preservation Commission, the orange-tinted Aspen Core building once again emerged as an illustration of what the new guidelines should ward against. In addition to the mass and scale of the building, Gretchen Greenwood objected to its nearly floor-to-ceiling windows. While they may be appropriate for New York or Chicago, she argued, they are not appropriate in Aspen because "we're not a shopping mecca." Whether Aspen qualifies as a shopping mecca was a matter of debate, as detailed in chapter 6, yet Greenwood further explained why large windows in retail locations are not suitable in Aspen: "Those windows are more typical of the glazing used in high-traffic areas, where you're riding the bus and you quickly want to see what the latest is at the GAP. That's completely out of context here, and is a breakdown of the local character of the pedestrian mall and our commercial core." With a stronger respect for modernism and postmodernism, and a greater willingness to question the orthodoxy of the western vernacular, Willis Pember asked, "Is there is such a thing as too much glass?" In response, Greenwood doubled down on the distinction between Aspen and elsewhere: "The windows at [Mark Hunt's renovated Gap building] just scream out"—using spotlights in the window displays to draw attention to opulent Dolce and Gabbana outfits and the minimalist fashions at Theory, another high-end retailer, next door. "We just approved another Mark Hunt project," she lamented, "and it's all glass . . . which may be fine for an urban setting or a restaurant, but not retail in Aspen." While Greenwood did not argue that large windows are tacky, she favored tighter regulations around window design so that buildings reflect Aspen's unique history. "I want to make sure that a [building] project has a sense of place, a connection to the community I am in. That often gets lost. Too often they're monuments to *people*"—rather than to Aspen's history and sense of place, ostensibly a dig at Mark Hunt and other developers.

With place professionals trained in well-regarded academic programs and used to working on expensive and innovative design projects, debates over Aspen's built environment and its aesthetics were often amusing and highly technical. It is a place where buildings are taken seriously, and where there are plenty of locals with a vocabulary that allows them to parse seemingly trivial aesthetic distinctions. In the end, to affirm a sense of place, the revised design guidelines clarified that building materials should be composed of "brick, stone, metal and wood," and that "color and finish" should "reference other materials traditionally found downtown." Shiny or glossy surfaces were explicitly forbidden. Further reinforcing the importance of place, council and commission members reaffirmed prohibitions on corporate branding on building facades. In one meeting of the Historic Preservation Commission, director Amy Simon reminded the group of a recent application that had "lululemon" (a chain yoga gear retailer) "all over it and was with the exact same materials used at the mall." Her reminder highlighted local disdain and disapproval for the homogeneity represented by the iconic American shopping mall. Echoing and extending this statement, Gretchen Greenwood referred to another problematic application where HPC forbade large external branding and pink accent colors on what was expected to house a nationally known cupcake store, stating, "It should be about Aspen, not the brand."

If Aspen place-makers were keen on reinforcing the Aspen brand, it might stand to reason that they would rewrite the commercial design guidelines to foreground its Victorian roots and Western mining vernacular. Yet this, too, was a matter of debate. In Aspen, about two hundred buildings, or 15 percent of local structures, are designated as historically significant. Seven downtown buildings from the Victorian era are considered so significant that they have protected view planes, preventing any structure from being built that would impede views of the mountain from their front steps. It was within this context that the city council, its planning boards, and its citizens debated the degree to which western-style arcades, chamfered corners, and other features should be listed as *guidelines* or *standards* in the design manual. In principle, virtually

Figure 9. A western-style arcade painted in Aspen's signature Beyer Blue. Photo by Don Stuber.

everyone agreed with HPC member Jim DeFrancia, a cowboy boot–wearing developer with multigenerational ties to Aspen, who opined that the revised codes should "reflect the mining heritage" of the town, preserving this essential character while not seeking to replicate this look; putting this ethos into code language, however, required debate.

In several meetings, Mayor Steve Skadron argued that guidelines should be written to encourage the building of arcades or covered walkways (see figure 9). "I like the wood and the western vernacular and I love the character it brings," he told council and Comm Dev staff. "If an arcade can speak to that tradition of Aspen's personality, the western tradition, I support an arcade being allowed as a pedestrian amenity" (a developer's requirement to contribute to the street scape). In a rare instance of comparing other towns favorably to Aspen, he added: "I became sensitive to that after spending time in Jackson Hole [Wyoming] and Ketchum

[Idaho]. It's so western and so authentic." Council member Bert Myrin objected to this justification, responding, "I spent some years in Jackson Hole, and I don't want to copy them. I want us to be Aspen." Insistence on the Aspen vernacular was also evident in the response of council member Ann Mullins, a landscape architect: "I remember one application from Mark Hunt, and he had this Spanish-style arcade thing. It looked like Stanford University, and it was so inappropriate. You may want to be strict with the design, mandating *western* references." That said, Mullins favored a measured, but not a prescriptive approach, like the one that tightly guides architectural development in some municipal areas and universities, including Stanford. "Arcades are a fun way to shape the pedestrian experience," she continued, "but you don't want them all over. When you discover it every couple of blocks, it works." To that end, the city council and its advisory boards amended the guidelines to encourage arcades to add vitality to the pedestrian experience, but limited their frequency to prevent them from becoming too predictable; too much like Vail or other self-consciously designed places.

Trained as a sociologist and not as an architect, I sometimes had to google technical terms while sitting in municipal meetings. "What the heck is a chamfered corner," I asked myself, "and why are these people so invested in whether this design feature should be a standard or a guideline?" I soon discovered the answer to the first question: a chamfer is a beveled cut-away that blunts right angles in architectural design (see figure 10). They can be used to soften or merely adorn the edifice of an otherwise large, imposing building. At a meeting on a cold December evening, I began to get an answer to the second question when former council member Torre (a one-name persona, elected mayor in 2018) voiced his thoughts on the matter. "This is a big reason why I'm here tonight," he declared during the public commentary period, "I support having chamfers added as a requirement." Justin Barker, a member of the Comm Dev team, noted that chamfered corners were quite common in the Victorian period when Aspen's civic and commercial buildings were erected. Sara Adams, a planner in private practice who worked as a consultant during the moratorium, contributed her two cents: treating it as a design requirement, she said, "starts to reduce how special the historic buildings are." With this in mind, the council called for a study to determine how

Figure 10. A Victorian-era chamfered corner. Photo by Don Stuber.

many chamfers might be added if they were listed as a requirement, and whether that might lead to chamfer overkill.

One month later, Torre returned to the council meeting to press his point, arguing for guidelines that reinforce Aspen's historic character. "Living downtown and walking around as much as I do," he said, "you can't have too much of a good thing when it comes to history." He saw chamfers as an alteration to the built environment and the pedestrian experience that is "a benefit to everybody." Council member Ann Mullins, however, was unmoved, arguing that "variety is the spice of life," and that it actually "becomes more interesting if you don't see it every time, and that it's the surprise around the next corner." Council members Myrin and Daily expressed a desire to make chamfers "more frequent rather than less," once again grappling with the question, "How do you regulate a desire for 'sometimes'?" These debates, again, highlight the attention to aesthetics in this town and the vocabulary for talking about them, even among people like

Torre, who was not trained in architecture. Granted these were hearings on architectural design, it is also important to recognize that what constitutes a problem or a flashpoint is different in Aspen than it is in many munici- palities. Ultimately, the council decided to treat chamfered corners as a guideline, and not a required standard. That said, conventional wisdom among council members and the Community Development staff was that including a chamfer in a development proposal would speed the process of approval; given the general preference for them.

With its revised Commercial Design Guidelines, Aspen's Urban Plan- ning Department, with guidance from the council, tightened up the aes- thetic considerations that shape the town's sense of place. The goal was to provide developers with clear guidance on how to operationalize small- town character. The resulting document is one that attempts to strike a balance between predictability and innovation and foregrounds the value of historic building patterns and locally relevant materials. It recognizes that stylistic features, like chamfered corners, are a symbolic resource; a positional good that communities can use to enhance their identity and value.[11] By arguing against what Aspen is not, and by resisting design con- ventions seen as either too urban or too contrived, the city council rein- forced Aspen's uniqueness and strengthened Aspen's brand.

RESTORING THE "SMALL" IN SMALL-TOWN CHARACTER

In both its commercial and residential markets, Aspen has some of the most expensive real estate in the country. Conventional notions of supply and demand suggest that expanding the amount of real estate would reduce the cost of real estate in Aspen, opening the way for locals to start a business or buy a home. Yet in Aspen, the idea of expanding the built environment to achieve community goals flies in the face of other treasured values— namely, protecting small-town character, the "golden goose" that generates plentiful revenues and creates a rich quality of life. When the morato- rium was declared in March 2016, it was council member Adam Frisch's lamentation of lost mountain views that led him and his peers to under- take their work. Central in this work were discussions over "right-sizing" Aspen's buildings to protect small-town character, while protecting other community goals. Ultimately, after nearly a year of deliberation, Aspen's revised land use codes significantly *downzoned* the built environment—paving the way for smaller, less boxy buildings and lower population densities. This accomplishment was in part a reaction to the *infill codes* of the 2000s. The infill codes, which allowed more density and taller buildings, were a logical reaction to market stagnation after the burst of the dot-com bubble; they were implemented with the goal of lowering real estate prices and stimulating economic development. As time went on, however, many came to view them as overly friendly to developers, allowing too many "variances" and resulting in projects that were out of step with the AACP. "Infill" became a dirty word, according to Mayor Steve Skadron, because "it undermined the principle of small-town character," allowing buildings that reached upwards of forty-two feet (four stories), and cast "shadows on the street and blocked the sunshine."

Central to the goal of restoring small-town character was debate over how to reduce the mass and scale of the built environment. Consistent with more gradual efforts that had been underway since 2012, conversation turned to the possibility of capping all new buildings at twenty-eight feet.[12] But why twenty-eight? Some of the most visible and historically relevant properties in downtown Aspen soar as high as four stories, including the classic red stone edifices of the Wheeler Opera House, the Hotel Jerome, and the Elks Building. It was not historic precedent that set the bar at twenty-eight feet. When asked by Planning and Zoning Commissioner Jesse Morris if "there is any science on this," Community Development Director Jessica Garrow indicated that the desire for twenty-eight feet has some historic grounding, as it "is the minimum for a two-story building with a higher first floor." The style she described was typical of Victorian-era buildings where saloons, banks, and other commercial entities occupied a more majestic first floor—with tall windows and pressed tin ceilings—and second floors were more modestly scaled, housing small offices and residences. Moreover, with many landmarked buildings achieving heights in excess of forty-two feet, restricting buildings to lower heights sets the historic buildings apart and ensures that new buildings do not compete with them.

For council member Adam Frisch, support for twenty-eight-foot buildings boiled down to how they contribute to a "sense of place"—one of his stock phrases. Paraphrasing Winston Churchill, he told me, "People build the buildings and then the buildings build us," so that "the shape of the buildings shapes the town and the community." Mayor Skadron agreed, referring to modestly sized buildings as Aspen's "competitive advantage," setting it apart from ski resorts like Vail and Beaver Creek, where buildings soar above seven stories. According to Maggie Carson, an employee in the planning department, "Whether we end up at twenty-six, twenty-eight, or thirty feet, I just want the buildings to make sense together and contribute to the historic values of the community." Although questions periodically rose about the specificity of twenty-eight feet, virtually no one within city government, either appointed or elected, questioned the general desire to limit building heights. Gretchen Greenwood, an architect on the Historic Preservation Commission, was one of the few who voiced opposition to twenty-eight-foot heights, arguing that a third floor in the commercial core allows for "more varied uses, like affordable housing." Unfortunately, although the topic appeared on the agenda at numerous city council, Planning and Zoning, and Historic Preservation meetings, the beauty and value of two-story buildings received little debate, and, therefore, elicited little insight into either the unquestioned appeal of twenty-eight-foot buildings or the consequences of mandating them.

Where debate did exist over buildings heights was in the exact execution. As with chamfered corners and western arcades, committee members argued that some variation in building heights is preferred because uniformity can produce monotony and work against the goal of "messy vitality." Planning and Zoning Commissioner Brian McNellis argued that "we need some flexibility to allow for variation," and Historic Preservation Commission Director Amy Simon worried that a fixed building height would be "blah." Allowing slight variations up to thirty-two feet, however, was a nonstarter. In the years leading up to the moratorium, as local government tried to steady the pendulum swing set in motion during the infill years, architects and developers routinely submitted proposals built to maximum allowable heights, given that the code permitted structures up to forty feet, if deemed "exceptional." Yet the city council no longer had much appetite for horse trading or subjectivity, so to allow room for both clarity of regulations and nuance in design, they agreed to a hard limit of twenty-eight feet, with allowances up to eighteen inches for decorative features like cornices, parapets, or false façades.

Amid the orthodoxy of small-is-beautiful, remarkably little discussion emerged with regard to how smaller buildings might impact the real estate market. My field notes contain no record of anyone asking, *How will twenty-eight-foot buildings affect real estate prices?* Over lunch at the iconic Little Nell Hotel, however, Jim DeFrancia, a long-time Aspen developer and HPC member, expressed an economic truism:

> Any regulatory constraint has an impact on the community in the sense of constraining development, therefore reducing supply, therefore increasing values for demand. If you can't go out, right, then you want to go up. If you can't go up, then you can't go anywhere. . . . In the meantime, you're faced with demand and you've constrained supply that drives values up. If you're already in and you're a property owner, that's fine. If you're not, that's a huge barrier to entry and ultimately it also impacts the broader community in the sense of affordability.

Yet members of the Aspen City Council were either oblivious to this possibility, rejected the premise outright, or discussed it only in settings to which I was not privy. But as the moratorium wound down and the revised land use codes began to take shape, questions began to emerge about the intended and unintended consequences of this downzoning. Committed to the initial goal of restoring small-town character, Adam Frisch defended the decision, arguing that, while the council has the ability to shape the aesthetic contours of the built environment, there is virtually nothing they can do to affect affordability, given market forces: "We cannot build enough commercial space to create $10 [per square foot], Grand Junction [Colorado] warehouse pricing. . . . If we thought we could go from twenty-eight to thirty-two feet [buildings] and the rents would drop, we would be having an interesting discussion. But history has shown and everything else has shown that it's going to be really expensive to be here, so how much humility can we add to think we can tweak something?" Given the desirability of Aspen, coupled with extensive fees for development, it was a foregone conclusion that real estate prices would remain at stratospheric levels. It would require "fifty thousand new homes" to bring prices within reach, Frisch speculated, at which point "the whole town would go to hell and it wouldn't matter anyway" because unbridled sprawl would spell the end of authenticity and small-town character. With this reasoning, which was not contested by other city officials, it is perhaps not surprising that twenty-eight-foot buildings heights were endorsed by the city's advisory commissions and sailed to approval by the council.

One additional way in which the council downzoned Aspen and staked out a strategy for restoring vitality and local character was through the expansion of pedestrian amenity spaces. Within urban design, pedestrian amenities (sometimes called public amenities) are features of the built environment that enhance vitality and promote public safety. They do so by creating spaces—like courtyards, seating areas, and features with visual interest—that inspire people to linger. Within urban design theory, vibrant public spaces enhance safety because they facilitate, in Jane Jacobs's famous phrase, "eyes on the street": an active presence to both detect and diminish uncivil behavior.[13] By drawing people into urban spaces, pedestrian amenities may also encourage spontaneous spending. Perhaps starting with William H. Whyte's *The Social Life of Small Urban Spaces* and later with the urban designers he inspired—including Fred Kent and Jan Gehl—many have engaged the question of how to engineer public spaces to attract people and promote social interaction.[14] More recently, Benjamin Shephard and Gregory Smithsimon show that access to and use of public space is central to the exercise of democracy, yet within many neoliberal cities, public spaces have been increasingly privatized and brought under elite control.[15] A desire to counteract this trend guided the council's revision of the land use codes and aligned them with the AACP goal of "facilitating an interesting, vital and walkable downtown and fostering a sense of small-town character."[16]

At the heart of the council's conversations around pedestrian amenity space were two key questions: How much space is appropriate, and what kinds of spaces best promote vitality? Prior to the moratorium, development projects were technically required to devote 25 percent of their overall lot size to public amenity uses. Yet many properties were built prior to this mandate, so that the real impact on the town was less than desired. The presumption guiding these conversations was that the council would adopt a hard percentage for pedestrian amenity space, giving developers clear and transparent guidelines and giving the community "an interesting, vital, and walkable downtown and a sense of small town character."[17]

In a town where bringing nature into the built environment is a default design proposition, few in city government questioned the value of devoting 25 percent of each lot to public use. Only Adam Frisch questioned the fundamental economics, noting that "public amenity space is a zero-sum game with net leasable," so that tradeoffs between the two would affect both revenue generation and the price of real estate. Even if other council members seemed reticent to consider the economic implications of their decisions, the Aspen Chamber and Resort Association (ACRA) was not. As the revision of the land use codes came into sharper focus, it began to voice objections to the proposed code changes. In one of the final council meetings prior to adopting the new code amendments, local lawyer and ACRA board member Maria Marrow outlined a number of the business community's concerns. With respect to pedestrian amenity she stated: "The pedestrian amenity requirement, while it sounds nice, is too high. . . . Requiring an owner to give the public 25 percent of their lot area to provide nice angles hurts the supply of affordable square footage. You are diminishing the supply, period. Anything we do to make buildings smaller drives up rent. You're going to drive out the local's choice bologna sandwich [a special at a beloved deli] and what you're going to get instead is Barton Perreira [a high-end optical store], where you can buy $900 eyeglasses that are $700 for locals in the off season." For ACRA, which represents small business owners like accountants, lawyers, and lodge and boutique owners, the new code would tip the balance in favor of mere aesthetic considerations, when the public could be better served by implementing policies that drive down the price of rents and create opportunities for local business owners and businesses serving daily needs.

In lieu of questions regarding whether 25 percent was too much, the city council and its appointed boards debated how to best design and "activate" pedestrian amenity spaces. That is, to make them meaningful rather than merely decorative. Conversations focused, for example, on whether an arcade or covered walkway truly met the definition of a pedestrian amenity, ultimately yielding the consensus that it does, given that it provides visual interest as well as protection from the elements when needed. Additionally, commission members asked whether an amenity must be outside, or whether a developer could create an internal courtyard allowing folks to bring take-out or a bagged lunch from home. "I'm concerned about the privatization of public spaces," said Mayor Steven Skadron. A prime example of this was a high-end restaurant that satisfied their amenity requirement with a roof-top bar area, which technically met the definition because members of the public could access the space and use the outdoor tables. This space effectively ended up being privatized because the public was unaware of this space. The "gray areas" in pedestrian amenity also emerged in reference to Peach's Corner, a beloved coffee and lunch spot, which had an attractive outdoor patio. Like a few other restaurants in town, most of the tables fell within the official lot line, but a few sat beyond, dotting the adjacent sidewalk. Identical in style, with bright orange umbrellas, these tables satisfied the pedestrian requirement, and could be enjoyed by the public at large, without becoming a customer of Peach's. Visually, however, this was not obvious; it was also unclear whether the public was "free" simply to sit there and take in the scene, or whether they could bring their own lunch and occupy this space without supporting the adjacent business. Many locals did, however, seem to know that the pool at the Sky Hotel was designated a public amenity, and made great use of it during its advertised "Sunday Funday" activities (see figure 11). The council sought clarity on these issues and advocated for policies that made these spaces genuinely accessible to the public.

Conversations about pedestrian amenity spaces reveals deeply held beliefs about what Aspen is like, how visitors and locals interact, and how to institutionalize these beliefs. Aspen's unique place-based class culture was something I learned about as a seven-year old, when my dad convinced me that local hotel swimming pools were generally open to the public, and that anyone could dive in and make it their own. I spent considerable time pool hopping as a child—most memorably during a magical snow shower—so I accepted it on faith when people told me that locals are free to use the pool at the St. Regis or the fitness center at the Viceroy Hotel. This is one of the early ways I absorbed the lore of cross-class interactions and the rights of working locals. While my days of pool hopping remained a vestige of my fancy-free Aspen childhood, the essence of the public-private pool lore was confirmed when I learned that the rooftop pool and lounge area at the Sky Residences—a swanky property owned by

Figure 11. "Sunday Funday" at one of Aspen's public amenity spaces (the former Sky Hotel). Photo by Jenny Stuber.

W Hotels—would, as part of its redevelopment agreement, be open to the public when it reopened in 2019 after extensive renovation.

The idea that Aspen had democratized luxury spaces through policies that open them up to the public was entirely consistent with my socialization into Aspen and with how, as a researcher, I came to understand localized ways of doing class. Indeed, Aspen's approach to pedestrian amenity space stands in contrast to locales that have used public spaces as a means of social control and exclusion. Some plazas that ground commercial buildings in urban areas, for example, are built as public-private partnerships that substitute for public parks, but are designed in ways—with high walls or accessible only through interior space, for example—that discourage public use and effectively privatize the spaces. In other cases, social control is more direct, with open-space projects that incorporate design features that explicitly discourage use, such as divided benches that make it difficult for homeless individuals to sleep on them.[18] When it comes to pedestrian amenity space, Mayor Skadron stated that his guiding assumption was that such spaces are designed "*not* primarily for the benefit of users of that building"—meaning its official users—but for the public at large. The primary purpose of amenity space, for Skadron and his colleagues, was promoting civic engagement and community vitality.

In light of these presumptions, the city council passed new pedestrian amenity requirements, reflecting the view that "frequent opportunities to dwell outdoors is of utmost importance."[19] In conjunction with their architectural consultants, the council passed guidelines that provide flexibility in form and design across each character area, so that visitors and residents can have a variety of experiences throughout town. Options included covered arcades; interior, exterior, and sunken courtyards; and midblock walkways that create "breathing room" in the streetscape. To ensure that spaces are meaningful and usable, guidelines specified that they must be open to public view, not have permanently enclosed walls, and encourage "good solar access, mountain views, and seating."[20] To hedge against an architect cleverly designing the area to avoid sacrificing leasable space, the council mandated that no single segment of the space can be smaller than one-third of the total requirement (at least 300 sq. ft, if the total obligation is 1,000 sq. ft). A key theme of the council's debate was that in order for these spaces to be meaningful, they must be "activated"—that is, visible and usable. Some members of the Planning and Zoning Commission even recommended that the City of Aspen implement a system of wayfinding that clearly communicates the presence of publicly accessible interior courtyard and roof-top patio spaces. This suggestion was not embraced, however, given concerns about not wanting to "junk up" the exterior of the building with extraneous signage.

Taken together, these code amendments downzoned Aspen's built environment. They shrunk building heights and used pedestrian amenity requirements as a tool for allowing "nature to bleed" into urban spaces. Council also adopted new "view plane" regulations that tightened and clarified prohibitions on structures that would block views of the mountain from the front steps of seven of the city's historically designated buildings. All of these measures were explicitly aimed at aligning the land use codes with the Aspen Area Community Plan, which calls for a built environment that reflects Aspen's Victorian heritage and protects its small-town character. As written, the regulations were designed to strike a balance between creativity and prescriptiveness, thereby reinscribing opportunities for messy vitality and ensuring that Aspen does not fall victim to the contrived predictability of other resort towns. With respect to understandings about what Aspen is, these regulations protect the Aspen brand and its sense of unpretentious luxury while shoring up its attractiveness to investors. Implicitly, these regulations protect the Aspen brand in another way: they further restrict the supply of space for development. Given Aspen's desirability, reducing the supply of real estate and space available for leasable uses only increases its price. Although local officials acknowledged this, they also balked at it, suggesting that only extreme, pro-growth measures would ever successfully bring down real estate prices. Adam Frisch even argued that a degree of honesty and humility is necessary when assessing the complicated tradeoffs of Aspen's real estate market and the land use code. "It's not meant to be a joke," he remarked at a city council meeting, "but 99 percent of what we do increases the cost of doing business in town, and that's just a trade-off the community has made." The council's decisions, while intending to stop the pendulum swing of development and protect the local community, may yet again produce seemingly unintended consequences if escalating real estate prices further undermine locals' access to housing and businesses serving their daily needs.

PROTECTING LOCAL CHARACTER WHILE PROMOTING LOCALS' RIGHTS

Aspen City Council members were far from oblivious to the needs of locals. In fact, another important goal of the moratorium was to implement the Aspen Area Community Plan's call for "more aggressive measures to ensure the needs of the community," given that high rents have displaced affordable, locally serving businesses and have "resulted in a continuing shift towards exclusivity."[21] "Use mix" refers to the part of the land use code that encourages desirable uses and discourages less-desirable uses. It answers questions like, "Where should we place factories and toxic waste sites in relation to where people live?" Revising the "Use Mix" ordinance aimed at re-centering the daily needs of locals, and affirming their civic importance, by creating opportunities to live in Aspen and operate businesses that contribute to "local character." Yet how to do this in light of market forces that price the vast majority of locals out of the real estate market was a matter of debate. Given their commitment to reducing the scale of the built environment, the council sought other ways to reset the pendulum and create zoning solutions that would allow businesses to provide basic necessities while balancing Aspen's market realities against a progressive political history that has foregrounded the needs of locals.

Throughout the moratorium process, one of the most persistent topics of discussion was: how can we ensure that the daily needs of working locals are met? When prime commercial real estate in the downtown core rents for $200 per square foot, it is nearly impossible for stores selling socks, underwear, or almost any apparel priced at less than $200 per garment to make it. Services like dry cleaning, barbering, and watch repair were similarly priced out. In the context of supergentrification, Aspen lacked restaurants that served working families and places for back-to-school shopping. As they kicked off the "use mix" conversation, Mark White and Alan Richman, two planning consultants hired to provide advice during this process, presented the council with an array of options for how they might use the land use code to address the community's daily needs. *Regulatory options* included limiting chains and luxury retailers by setting size caps on stores, which would make them less attractive to businesses that have a standard model built around a large footprint. They could also establish a *quota system*, allowing a limited number of stores selling handbags, furs, jewelry, and art. Alternatively, an *incentive-based approach* would give developers a break in mitigations if they agreed to charge lower rents to locally serving businesses. Another approach would subsidize *legacy businesses* that contribute to community character. At the center of this debate was the question of how much the council was willing to tinker with the free market in crafting its solutions. In thinking through these options, Mayor Steve Skadron said, "Whatever checklist we come up with, I'd like it to lead us to a massive ecosystem of cool hangouts. These predictably gritty, cool places that we don't seem to have anymore, that seem to have been sterilized." This notion of "predictably gritty" served as a synonym for "messy vitality," and harkened back to the days when the bar at the Hotel Jerome was a hot bed of cross-class interactions and other shenanigans.

Despite a forty-year history of tinkering with the housing market, the city council seemed reticent to tinker with commercial real estate in the same way. Adam Frisch, in particular, had no appetite for casting the city into the role of picking winners and losers within the business realm. He expressed concern that subsidizing individual businesses would generate animosity among business owners in ways not evident within the housing program, which was generally viewed as fair and beneficial to the community at large. More generally, council was wary of any regulatory approach that would require excessive oversight, having to monitor, for example, the price point of goods and services or the percentage of sales generated by locals. After a decade of bargaining away housing mitigations, the council was similarly uninterested in any scheme that would use trade-offs—like reductions in affordable housing mitigations—as a tool to incentivize developers to create spaces with lower rents that might house businesses serving daily needs.

Given these proclivities, the council and its cadre of city planners seized upon a *design-based approach* to the problem of locally serving businesses. At the first meeting devoted to the topic of "use mix," council member Frisch said, "I think the number one thing that has allowed [locally serving] businesses to succeed, that we've liked, and what's now driving them away, are the nooks and crannies of the downtown core." By nooks and crannies, he meant the oddly shaped and harder-to-find spaces that make up many mixed-used buildings, whether below ground, toward the back of the building, or occupying a second floor. These "second-tier spaces" stand in contrast to prime spaces, which are the spacious, ground-floor units with street-level visibility—spaces that many retailers prefer and, therefore, command higher rents. Second-tier spaces had become almost nonexistent, as developers built properties to take advantage of the demand for prime real estate and to conform to infill-era codes that encouraged blocky structures extending from lot-line to lot-line. Where infill spelled the death of "messy vitality," the council was trying to bring it back through a revised land use code.

In a town replete with nostalgia, some council members early on endorsed a legacy business approach. Such a measure was passed by San Francisco voters in 2015, providing ten years of grant funds to businesses that had operated for thirty years or more and had meaningfully contributed to neighborhood character. Council member Ann Mullins repeatedly voiced support for this option but was unable to rally others. Some council members questioned the usefulness of the tool, pointing out that Aspen had lost some longtime, treasured business due to their owners' retirement, not because they were priced out of the market. While virtually all the city council members agreed that the lack of locally owned and locally serving businesses was problematic, this issue seems to have found the Aspen City Council in a somewhat uncharacteristic nonregulatory mood. Capturing this sentiment, Adam Frisch stated: "To get into a legal definition—which is what the land code use does—of what *high end* is and what *locally serving* is, would require a CPA audit, and that gives me the heebie-jeebies." "We need to be very careful and not get into all that gobbledygook," he said at a meeting one month later, adding, "I don't want to get into central planning. China's getting out of central planning, Cuba's getting out of central planning." Although social engineering was part of Aspen's political legacy, this was not an area they sought to regulate.

Over time, council support grew for a design-based approach that required the building of "nook-and-cranny" or "second-tier spaces." Under this approach, new projects and significant remodels would be required to devote a percentage of floor area to "second-tier space": space that is below grade, upstairs, or off an alleyway. These spaces could accommodate an office supply store, a kids' clothing store, or a juice bar. Under this mandate, architects would need to find clever solutions that both fulfill this requirement and maximize leasable space while also producing the innovative, high-end buildings Aspen is known for. The virtue of this approach, Frisch said, is that the city government would not "need to get into regulating them; by definition, they will end up being non-desirable by the brand standards that national chains need to have," and will therefore command lower rents. The belief was, in his words, that "Nook-and-cranny spaces will create nook-and-cranny businesses."

Yet not everyone got on board with this solution. Ann Mullins was slow to endorse this approach and worried that imposing this requirement would kill creativity and diversity in design, so that "these interesting spaces that catch you by surprise" become commonplace and lose their ability to enchant. High-profile developer Mark Hunt strongly objected to these spaces. Although he was sometimes admired for his efforts to balance the community's needs with his own financial bottom line, Hunt never lost sight of the fact that as a developer, he needs to generate a profit. He worried that the council was gung-ho on passing something they had not fully investigated. "What if there isn't demand for these spaces?" he asked, "What if they remain vacant, but the developer has already built them?" In a clever verbal maneuver during one of council's final public meetings, Hunt stated: "We use the term 'messy vitality' a lot, and that sounds really sexy, which is so Aspen, but we could get something that is all messy and no vitality, because the buildings are sitting empty." He implored the council not "to regulate so much that buildings remain vacant" and asked them to write the ordinance that would allow developers to upgrade aging commercial spaces without triggering a new requirements or regulations.

In the end, the council embraced these "nook-and-cranny" spaces and passed an ordinance requiring new developments and significant remodels (those that demolish more than 40 percent of an existing structure) to devote 20 to 35 percent of their floor area to second-tier space, depending on zone district. Less-substantial remodels would be required to maintain existing percentages of second-tier space. Jessica Garrow, the Community Development director who shepherded the revision of these land use codes, was a fan of this approach: "I think this speaks to Aspen as a real town, with a real history, that we have these nooks and crannies . . . and through the land use code [we can] encourage these things to continue." With this move, council implemented a policy that they hoped would stem the tide of high-end retail displacing residents' daily needs. They stopped short, however, of implementing a regulatory approach that would explicitly protect locally owned and locally serving businesses. As such, the council sought to institutionalize the interests of middle-class locals, but perhaps not as aggressively as some wished. As I show in chapter 6, a group of locals emerged during this process to press council members to move more forcefully on this issue, and more fully defend the economic interests of locals.

PUTTING AN END TO THE PENTHOUSE PROBLEM

Addressing the precise mix of uses (residential, service, commercial) allowed under the land use code involved not just finding ways to encourage uses that promote local character and the well-being of residents; it also involved finding ways to minimize "undesirable uses." In the wake of Aspen's penthouse proliferation, the topic of chapter 3, the question of whether residential uses should be permitted within the commercial zones was foremost on the council's mind. In part, this question reflected the desire to pass feel-good legislation that would take a stand on the place of wealthy outsiders within Aspen's class culture. It was an opportunity to reinforce the message that purchasers of high-end penthouses cannot impose their lifestyle preferences on local ways of life. Relatedly, this question reflected concerns about how to maintain a vibrant downtown. Although the council banned free-market housing in the two main commercial zone districts in 2012, in 2016 they were concerned, in the words of Community Development Director Jessica Garrow, "that what we saw in the core, with free-market residential uses killing the vitality of commercial spaces, was now bleeding out into other zone districts." A quiet downtown, where seasonally occupied penthouses "crowd out other uses" and even make it unnecessary for landlords to lease the retail spaces below, was not something the council could abide. This debate also engaged practical considerations: in a town where locals benefit so significantly from tax revenues, how can *use mix* be designed to maximize the taxes and fees that trickle down and fund social programs? All of these questions, but particularly the last, speak to how Aspen sought to institutionalize small-town character and class interests through the land use code.

Although many on the council agreed that luxury penthouses led to supergentrified real estate prices and vacancies in commercial spaces, not everyone agreed that banning residential uses was the answer. Indeed, several council members repeatedly reminded their colleagues that segregating residential and commercial uses goes against decades of urban planning wisdom. From Jane Jacobs to the new urbanist movement, planners have presumed that economic and social vitality depend on old funky buildings being physically integrated with newer buildings, with residential and commercial uses brushing up against one another. Drawing on this theory, Ann Mullins, a landscape architect, repeatedly told her council peers that it would be "a mistake to ban residential" in town. Former mayor Mick Ireland (2007–2013) agreed. During one public commentary period he stated, "The presence of people in the community, in downtown, is integrally related to the desired goal of creating vitality of uses. You have to have *users* to have *uses*." Council member Frisch reinforced these points: "The live-above-where-you-work model has worked well for centuries in a lot of societies." He sought a solution that would honor this tradition, and protect local character: "I can see Main Street having some smaller apartments, with locals living above commercial spaces. Maybe we could impose some restrictions, so that you have to live there [year-round], to deal with this entitlement issue, of feeling like you own the whole building, rather than just one part of it." The council, however, was concerned that even small units with occupancy restrictions would slowly be taken over and transformed into tiny luxury condos.

Public outreach revealed that fully 80 percent of the community favored residential uses in the downtown core. The disconnect between council and community gave some stakeholders pause. Caught between the council's vision and her background as an urban planner, Jessica Garrow reasoned, "Planning 101 is that mixed uses are great and they add vitality. But Aspen is not Planning 101. We have different economics here, different realities than many communities, even resort communities." As explained by former community development director Alan Richman, the luxury and status of downtown penthouses attracts "a person who should really be buying a house on Red Mountain, who wants peace and quiet, and distance from their neighbors, but now they're in a mixed-use building." Confronted with these realities, the council had to consider how to craft a vibrant and functional community where local dynamics fly in the face of orthodox planning wisdom.

One factor that shaped opposition to housing—especially free-market housing—in Aspen's commercial core emerged from the town's rigorous anti-sprawl measures. Passed in 1993, the urban growth boundary prevents commercial uses from being built outside this line of demarcation. In limiting sprawl, the city limited the amount of land available for development, thereby driving up prices. This decision has powerful implications for tax revenues: because retail sales taxes outpace property taxes (Colorado has one of the lowest millage rates in the United States), the city faces crucial decisions on how to allocate residential and commercial uses. Although real estate transactions generate a one-time transfer tax, commercial uses generate ongoing tax revenues. In this low-growth context, any square footage devoted to lower-revenue-generating residential uses results in the loss of square footage of higher-revenue-generating commercial uses. Council member Bert Myrin, a low-growth activist who had a long history of organizing community-led ballot initiatives, raised this concern in several meetings: "The vitality that comes from having commercial rather than residential is enormous. The vitality of all of those people showing up [to work] in the morning and going out to lunch, and going out for business meetings, is much more vitality than one unit would be, or a couple units, if that was residential space." Further articulating his "zero tolerance" for free-market housing in any of the commercial zone districts, Myrin stated: "I used to think we should have mixed uses, and all of the textbooks say you should have, and everyone who comes out of planning school probably says that's the way you do it. But in Aspen, none of our zones are more than two or three blocks from residential. We're not isolating residential, or sterilizing where everyone has to move out." Given the compact nature of town, and the zero-sum relationship between commercial and residential uses, Myrin favored maximizing commercial uses in town, both for their tax revenues and their vitality.

With relative consensus on council's decision to ban free-market residential in downtown Aspen, debate turned to the appropriateness of affordable housing. Ever mindful of council's task to implement the Aspen Area Community Plan, Jessica Garrow reminded them that one of its explicit values states: "A strong and diverse year-round community and a viable and healthy local workforce are fundamental cornerstones for the sustainability of the Aspen Area community."[22] Given the expressed importance of being a 24/7, lights-on community, staff's recommendation was to continue allowing affordable housing, given the AACP's call for housing policies that "avoid segregation of economic and social classes."[23]

Peter Fornell, founder of an innovative public-private affordable housing program, opposed even affordable housing being built in commercial zones. Midway through the moratorium, he asked the council to consider his point, reminding them that "the city of Aspen is a machine, and the machine runs on money." Given the town's extensive social programs and high-quality infrastructure, consideration of tax revenues is synonymous with promoting community values and the well-being of locals. Breaking down the math he said:

> A thousand square feet of residential generates $200 per year in property taxes, but a thousand square feet of commercial generates $7,000 per year in property taxes—that's thirty-five times more. Plus, they're paying sales taxes, property taxes, and the transfer taxes that get paid when these properties sell. Affordable housing never does any of those three things again. There's a lot of places we can go to build affordable housing, but there are limited places to build commercial. We need the [commercial zone districts] to be a profit center for our community, and the creation of affordable housing in the core is counterproductive to that goal.

A builder and supporter of affordable housing, Fornell noted that his properties are still within walking distance of the commercial core and easily able to contribute to the town's vitality.

In the end, the city council defied conventional planning wisdom and implemented a solution that landed a feel-good blow against wealthy penthouse owners while keeping in mind the importance of that same constituency for generating tax revenues. Expanding the decision initially made in 2012, the council banned free-market housing from future developments in each commercial zone district. Under advisement of Community Development and the support of a minority of council members, they decided to allow affordable housing, but only as an "accessory use," defined as any use that is subordinate to a development's primary use in terms of floor area and/or economic significance.

CONCLUSION

In a move that paid homage to its progressive, low-growth politics of the 1970s, in 2017 the city council significantly downzoned Aspen's built environment. They did this through land use ordinances that addressed the aesthetics of buildings and their mass and scale; that carved up the built environment to make way for protected view planes and more meaningful pedestrian amenity spaces; and that banished free-market residences and promoted "nook-and-cranny" commercial spaces. These efforts both reflect and reproduce Aspen's place-based class culture. In their place-making work, the council and other stakeholders invoked place narratives about what Aspen is. In debating the proposed policies, council members and their advisory boards, citizens, and members of the community pressed for policies that would restore small-town character and a sense of exceptionalism. Their efforts showed respect for Aspen's Victorian mining history and the importance of locally relevant forms and materials, but warned against the oversupply of these design motifs, arguing that the line demarcating "authentic" and "hokey" can be vanishingly thin.

In revising the land use codes, stakeholders marshalled discourses about how class is done in Aspen. Especially in consideration of use mix, council members and other key players sought to implement wording in the Aspen Area Community Plan that foregrounds the needs of locals—whether in affordable housing, the opportunity to own a business, or the ability to have daily consumer needs met—and that simultaneously results in not just a vital town center, but one that fosters social-class mixing. At times these discourses felt a bit muted, especially for a community seen as having egalitarian roots and where a history of cross-class interactions sometimes takes on mythic proportions. On occasion, Community Development Director Jessica Garrow had to remind the council of wording in the AACP that calls for affordable housing projects to be built downtown, as part of a mixed-use project. Questions about how a smaller built environment might impact commercial rents were not publicly discussed. Instead of considering ways to use regulatory measures to promote ways for locals to open businesses and shop for daily needs, a majority of the council opted for design-based solutions (in the form of nook-and-cranny space) and stepped back from endorsing the kind of social engineering that produced Aspen's extensive affordable housing program. While the AACP still expressed a value for class integration, the discourses used to consider various policy options, as well as the resulting code amendments, tilted in the direction of free-market solutions, in some cases backed by the sentiment that market forces in Aspen may be beyond regulatory reproach.

Place-based class cultures involve the ways in which class relations and class opportunities are institutionalized, which gains expression in these revised land use codes. As drafted, these revised ordinances strike a blow against aspiring penthouse dwellers and those wealthy constituencies that might seek to impose their own less-vibrant ways of doing class in Aspen. They also strive to create urban vitality and cross-class mixing through policies that require meaningful pedestrian amenities and space for nook-and-cranny businesses. Yet none of these things come cheap, and with new development projects limited to just two stories, it should come as no surprise if the cost of Aspen's prime retail space soars ever higher. Indeed, within urban planning, the pendulum swing that necessitates revisions to the land use code is set in motion through the unintended consequences of well-intentioned policies. When it comes to the institutionalization of class interests, moments like these—moments that exist alongside slow, imperceptible, macro-level transformations—can alter how a place works and, in this case, the interests of the class constituencies that inhabit this place. Durable, place-based class cultures are not impervious to change. This policy debate sheds light on how this process works and how these changes may, over the long term, affect understandings of what Aspen *is* and how class is *done* in Aspen. Time will tell, then, whether these policies tilt in favor of landlords and developers and high-end consumers, who may benefit from escalating real estate prices, or middle-class locals, who may benefit from a built environment that acknowledges their presence. The ways in which all of these policy considerations intersect, and how Aspen's competing values collide, is the subject of the next chapter.

5 "But Does It Deliver Value?"

NEGOTIATING ASPEN'S LAND USE CODE

One night in January, during an especially contentious city council meeting with just one month remaining in the moratorium, council member Adam Frisch addressed his peers and the community, effectively summing up the challenges involved in aligning the land use code with the values statements embedded in the Aspen Area Community Plan: "As much as I love the AACP, and I truly do, there are huge, huge conflicts within it of epic proportions. It has to do with having the most restrictive land use code in the country, the highest mitigation rates in the country, and the huge desire for diversified retail, affordable retail, and cheap lodging. It is intellectually dishonest for the community to want to have all of those things in this one place, which we all love." Foregrounding the contradictions inherent in the Aspen Area Community Plan, Frisch stated that "some of our community values are in direct mathematical contradiction to one another." When implemented in the land use code, the goal of housing a large percentage of the workforce in town, providing for the needs of working locals while simultaneously creating an environment of exclusivity, and doing so within a community that allows limited area for development, where buildings must be architecturally significant, simply doesn't "pencil out."

In this chapter I explore how the Aspen City Council, along with stakeholders from the development and business communities, adjudicated between competing values and tried to make sense of the fact that when implemented in the land use code, the emerging policy recommendations would likely have both unintended and disparate impacts on Aspen's social class constituencies. As outlined in the previous chapter, a substantial portion of the council's work during the moratorium period focused on downzoning the built environment to foster small-town character and create more civic and retail spaces for people—especially locals—to enjoy a sense of community. As they approached the date when they would vote on the final code amendments, the council realized that these changes would likely increase the cost of doing business in Aspen. Asking developers to set aside space for public amenities and for "second-tier" commercial uses does not come cheap—especially in a town where that space might cost $200 per square foot in rent. Alongside these deliberations, the city council also discussed increasing affordable housing mitigations, which would help create more housing for locals; this move would both contribute to Aspen's exceptionalism by facilitating the authentic feel of a "lights-on community," while also institutionalizing the interests of working locals. Since the 1980s, developers in Aspen have paid substantial mitigation fees to help build affordable housing. Because free market housing had become increasingly out of reach for local workers, the community faced a widening gap between the demand for affordable housing and its supply. The lack of affordable housing was exacerbated by high-profile projects in which the council bargained away developers' housing mitigations in exchange for "architecturally significant" projects. In this context, the city council and its planning team contemplated increasing affordable housing mitigation rates. Collectively, these conversations forced the council and their partners to reckon with contradictions in the Aspen Area Community Plan and the harsh reality that trying to be all things to all classes might remain an elusive goal, even in a community as affluent, educated, and progressive as Aspen.

In the final month of the moratorium, these tensions and contradictions coalesced in the council's effort to find the sweet spot in affordable housing mitigation rates—an element of land use that links to almost every other element of the proposed code. If set too high, the rate could have a chilling effect on development: because new requirements for "nook-and-cranny" commercial spaces and increased pedestrian amenity space result in a reduction of leasable space, building costs would increase, potentially disincentivizing development. Not only would this fail to plug the hole in the amount of affordable housing, but with an aging stock of buildings, Aspen would risk losing its air of innovation and exclusivity; this, in turn, could deprive the town of much-needed tax revenues. Yet if the rate is set too low, Aspen would fall farther and farther behind in providing affordable housing and fulfilling its role in helping working locals achieve the American Dream. At the height of the moratorium, just prior to voting on the final code language, Mayor Steve Skadron recognized the complex interdependencies among the proposed policies and asked: "Does it deliver value?" He asked, in essence, whether all the land use code ordinances, when combined, would fulfill the promise of the AACP and, perhaps most importantly, serve the needs of working locals.

This chapter explores how the Aspen City Council attempted to find the mitigation rate that would extract the most benefit for locals without having a chilling effect on development. These deliberations show how one community attempted to reconcile competing community values and balance complicated class interests. I show that in the council's effort to create a unique sense of place, they sought solutions that would encourage new development and the upgrading of existing commercial spaces while at the same time requiring design solutions that would provide substantial benefits to the local, year-round community. This chapter makes an empirical contribution to understandings of place-making. These analyses show that places are not exclusively the product of the slow and steady accretion of abstract forces, whether local or global. While this is part of the process, it is also true that places are made in discrete moments; with careful attention we can see a community pivot, making a decision that may later be seen as a fundamental paradigm shift. Although the impact of these code changes remains to be seen, Aspen's trajectory toward greater exclusivity or toward protecting opportunities for locals can eventually be divined from the choices made at critical decision points, like the ones highlighted in this chapter.

ASPEN AND THE AMERICAN DREAM

Beyond climate change and the amount of snow produced for skiing, perhaps the biggest existential threat confronting Aspen and the Roaring Fork Valley is the challenge of housing the local workforce within one of the nation's most expensive real estate markets. With median household incomes around $73,000 and median home prices around $4 million, this existential threat has been managed by the area's affordable housing program. Mitigations paid by developers, with the goal of offsetting the demand for housing created by new development, have been implemented since the 1980s, when a 15 percent rate was assessed on new building projects. A 15 percent rate meant that developers were responsible for building new housing, often on site, for 15 percent of the workers that their developments—whether a hotel or retail complete—would generate. Over time, as the gap between locals' wages and the cost of housing expanded, the Aspen City Council raised the mitigation rate—first to 35 percent in the late 1980s, and then to 60 percent in 1993. At that time, Aspen's comprehensive plan established the goal of housing 60 percent of local workers within the county (as opposed to more affordable communities outside the county), which served as the justification for the mitigation rate. In reality, it is estimated that 40 percent of those who work in Aspen actually live within the boundaries of Pitkin County, thereby constituting a gap with the expressed policy. While some choose to live in towns like Basalt and Carbondale, because their money goes farther there and homes are allowed to appreciate at market value, many are involuntarily squeezed out, pushed farther away from their jobs.[1] One study estimates that as of 2019, the Roaring Fork Valley region faced an affordable housing shortage of more than three thousand units—which is equivalent to the number of units currently in Aspen Pitkin County Housing Authority's inventory.[2]

Because the Aspen Area Community Plan is not just an aspirational document, but also a document with legal force, the moratorium provided an occasion to revisit the question of whether current policies were aligned with the comprehensive plan. With respect to housing, the 2012 AACP states that policies should maintain an inventory of housing that "bolsters socioeconomic diversity" and provides a "visitor experience" that allows for an "appreciation of our genuine, lights-on community."[3] Given the increased inability of locals to find housing within the free-market sector, conversation turned to the question of whether to raise affordable housing mitigations and, if so, by how much. At various times in the past, local officials had considered increasing mitigation rates to 100 percent, meaning that developers would be required to create or fund enough new housing to accommodate 100 percent of the workers their projects generate. This could easily result in $5 million in fees for a significant commercial project (like a hotel or multiunit mixed-use building). Support for mitigations at this level never reached a critical mass among council members or Aspen's city planners, given concerns that such extensive fees would shock the system and freeze development activity. Although people sometimes joke that Aspen's motto could be "Development Pays Its Own Way," there was also an awareness that if set too high, mitigation rates could limit the creation of jobs and new affordable housing.

In the context of Aspen's unique place-based class culture, where locals are considered essential for contributing to Aspen's sense of authenticity, little disagreement existed over the value or necessity of affordable housing. Yet how to satisfy the demand for affordable housing, particularly through the land use code, was a matter for debate. While partially funded by the 1.5 percent Real Estate Transfer Tax (RETT), additional funds were generated by mitigations on development, which were intricately intertwined with other land use policies.[4] At one meeting, the director of community development, Jessica Garrow, reminded council of these linkages: "Individually, a lot of these policies [those proposed during the moratorium] make complete sense and are good policies. But when you put them together and have them implemented at the same time, that potentially impacts the amount of affordable housing created in a negative way. If we get no new development, that means no new affordable housing. We need to right-size the code to find that sweet spot." Throughout the moratorium, Garrow and her team proposed a variety of ways to use mitigations to meet the demand for affordable housing while at the same time balancing other goals of the AACP, namely creating spaces for businesses that serve daily needs. With Aspen's appetite for limiting growth and extracting fees from developers, one early proposal was to increase the rate to 80 percent across the board. Some council members and city officials worried, however, that a rate this high would result in legal challenges, with real estate owners alleging that the increase lacks a "rational nexus" and would constitute a retroactive tax, given that the properties they already own would be subjected to new mitigations rates in the event that they redevelop.[5] Another proposal was to increase the mitigation rate across the board, but then lower it on a case-by-case basis for developers who pledged to provide benefits to the community, such as lower rents for locally serving businesses. Some council members remained concerned, however, that bargaining away affordable housing mitigations to achieve other goals would further result in a housing deficit. One final proposal was a tiered rate, which would impose an 80 percent mitigation rate for "prime space" and a 40 percent for "non-prime space." In theory, this tiered-rate would incentivize developers to create projects with second floors, basements, or nook-and-cranny spaces—all non-prime commercial spaces—which would then attract businesses serving daily needs, instead of developments that attract only luxury retailers able to pay the high rents commanded by ground-floor spaces. The ability to satisfy the needs of both locals and lovers of luxury retail piqued the council's interest in the tiered-rate option.

With these options in mind, at an October council meeting midway through the moratorium, Mayor Skadron asked: "To increase or not? There's doing what feels good and doing what's right." By "doing what feels good," he presumably meant extracting money from developers and redistributing it to locals, thereby extending Aspen's time-honored tradition of institutionalizing the needs of less-affluent members of the community. "Doing what's right," by contrast, meant looking at the interconnected impacts of these policies and making sure they have the intended outcomes. "If providing housing is not doing what's right," council member Bert Myrin replied, "I don't know what is." Whereas Myrin operated with a low- to no-growth agenda that vigorously protected the needs of locals, Mayor Skadron encouraged his colleagues to look at the issue more holistically. "There's another half of the equation," he reminded them, "It's not just piling mitigations on. We have to be careful of the pendulum. At some point, we'll get nothing." In other words, if mitigations are set too high, development stops and the benefits to locals fail to trickle down. In weighing these proposals, council member Adam Frisch proposed an empirical approach, while still focusing on the needs of locals: "I want to make sure that the math makes sense in getting us what we think it might get us.

I think [the tiered rate] is worth exploring as a way to get a diversified retail mix, by putting rules and regulations in place that would incentivize second-tier spaces. But we need to do the math first to figure out where the tipping point is." With this request, Garrow's team was directed to conduct some analysis and return to the council with their findings. Their task was to explore the possible impact of a tiered mitigation rate on a number of hypothetical development projects, examining the degree to which the proposed land use policies would achieve the many goals articulated in the AACP—especially the goals of providing an attractive visitor experience while also satisfying the housing and consumer needs of working locals.

DOES IT DELIVER VALUE? UNVEILING THE SCENARIOS

With just one month remaining before the expiration of the moratorium, Community Development Director Jessica Garrow and her team of consultants returned to the council to answer Mayor Skadron's question: Does it deliver value? After nine months of thoughtful and high-minded discussions, council and the community were ready to receive concrete insight into how their well-intentioned efforts would impact development patterns in Aspen and, by consequence, the town's ability to both draw affluent visitors and provide for the needs of locals. To answer these questions, the team of consultants conducted "scenario work" on three existing buildings, examining how either a remodel or a complete renovation of the building would "pencil out," should the owner decide to redevelop.[6] In the parlance of planners and developers, a project "pencils out" if the return on investment justifies its costs. In Aspen, land costs are already exorbitant, but with new requirements for pedestrian amenity space, second-tier (nook-and-cranny) commercial space, and higher affordable housing mitigations, the scale could easily tip against development.

In prefacing the results of their analysis, hired consultant Jeremy Nelson stated, "Looking at the possible impacts of the code amendments, it's more Magic 8 Ball than crystal ball. This is more of a first cut," he continued, "to give you some direction." In this first cut, consultants calculated the increased costs associated with the new pedestrian amenity and second-tier commercial space requirements, as well as the costs associated with maintaining the current 60 percent affordable housing mitigation rate, compared to the proposed tiered-mitigation rate, which would impose 80 percent on prime spaces and 40 percent on second-tier spaces. For each of the three projects examined, each with different building footprints and different situations with previous mitigations and liabilities, analyses revealed that in none of these spaces would a full renovation pencil out. That is, the additional requirements and mitigations proposed under the new codes would be too costly for developers, thereby encouraging them either to execute a more modest remodel (which would not trigger these new requirements) or let their aging properties sit. While some degree of funkiness is valued in Aspen, both of these possibilities threatened the unique blend of funkiness and exclusivity that is Aspen's brand.

This discovery caused genuine consternation among the council. Curious about how a developer with a large portfolio might respond to the proposed code amendments, one of the projects selected for analysis was the "the old *Daily News* building," a strange postmodern structure that Mark Hunt had approval to redevelop under the pre-2017 code. Analyses suggested that under the proposed code, a developer like Mark Hunt would likely propose smaller, one-story buildings in an effort to avoid triggering the new building requirements. About this possibility, Mayor Skadron responded: "[The urban planning staff and consultants] have taken council's direction and written the code and applied it against Mark Hunt's application for this location. What you're telling us is that the code we're delivering may deliver a building that returns less commercial space, less affordable housing, and less second-tier space—all the things we're attempting to get—all because it's too costly and it doesn't make financial sense for the developer to do that." This would "return much less to the community," Skadron continued, in that there will be "less vibrancy to [the] town, less prime [retail] space *and* less non-prime space, and we lose affordable housing units." When combined, the proposed policies threatened to undermine the fundamental goals of the moratorium. One positive that could be conjured from this scenario is that the new code would likely result in a smaller, one-story building—which would partially accomplish the goal of restoring small-town character. Reflecting on these tensions, Alan Richman, a former director of planning for Aspen and now a consultant in private practice, summarized what he saw within the Magic 8 Ball: "If your primary goal is growth control, as it is for many people in the community, this is a strong policy. If that's not the primary motivation, and there's a desire for vitality and change, we're telling you that [these proposals] could have a significant dampening effect."

The discovery that the proposed changes to the land use code may not deliver all of the lofty goals that council had hoped for required them to weigh competing values against one another. The "conundrum," as expressed by council member Adam Frisch, "is the question of what is more important—that development pays its own way . . . or that we get the buildings and uses we want?" Council members had to consider, in other words, whether the value of housing a critical mass of working locals trumps the value of creating small-town character and an exciting visitor experience, while providing retail spaces that serve daily needs. The nature and specificity of this conundrum became clear when consultant Jeremy Nelson revealed that the biggest cost to developers, and therefore the biggest driver of developers' potential decision to remodel rather than redevelop, was not the cost to build second-tier commercial space or devote 25 percent of their property to pedestrian amenity space, but the higher tiered-mitigation rate, and especially the proposal to impose mitigations on buildings built prior to the mitigation era, should the current owners decide to redevelop. The city council was being forced to choose between affordable housing *or* commercial spaces designed to attract locally serving businesses. If they tried to get both, they might get neither. It is in moments like these that place is made; where Aspen has the opportunity to become ever more like Aspen —the Aspen that is known and beloved and enshrined in discourses—or become another kind of place, one that seemed to be causing increased anxiety for locals. This is a situation where the origins and shape of *place-based class cultures* can be seen most explicitly: in discourses that guide decision-making and where decisions become institutionalized in the land use code and likely have differential impacts on local class constituencies.

THE BUSINESS COMMUNITY RESPONDS

Although Aspen's city council and its cadre of planners played the most visible and consistent role in this yearlong process of place-making, the business community also played a role, sometimes behind the scenes in private meetings and other times more visibly in city council meetings. As Kee Warner and Harvey Molotch note in their comparison of the planning process and growth controls in three California communities, "People in the growth business find restrictions of any sort a pain in the neck, at best, and, at worst, a potential source of business crisis."[7] Right on cue, then, some of Aspen's biggest landlords and developers appeared at the council meeting, on the brink of crisis, pleading their case against the proposed code amendments. At the marathon six-hour-long council meeting in which these scenarios were unveiled, Karim Souki, partner in Ajax Holdings and son of energy magnate Charif Souki—at one time the highest-paid CEO in the United States—provided an inside look at how these new regulations might impact his business. Casually dressed in an army green sweater and a flat-billed cab-driver style hat, this thirty-something told council that if these regulations are passed, "we'll stop developing in town." Continuing, he laid out the financial realities of developing in Aspen:

> I can tell you that financial feasibility is a second-tier priority for us, because this is our home and community. We have more lucrative opportunities elsewhere, that are more open to development, and we can and will continue to allocate our capital there. But we have chosen to do a certain amount [of business] in Aspen because we do want to see Aspen thrive. We do, as a company, agree with the intent of the AACP and what you guys are trying to do, but this just goes too far. It takes everything that we're breaking even on and turns it into a hard loss. . . . Without any derogatory or ill feelings about this, I can just say, this will stop our development activities. We will still live here and contribute to the community . . . but it will stop our development opportunities.

Indeed, the three scenarios analyzed by the consultants revealed that the proposed regulations would add about $4 million to a project's development costs, on top of basic building costs (land, labor, materials, etc.). Because development is not philanthropy, these costs would be passed on to tenants, resulting in an estimated $50 increase, per square foot, in rents.[8] This would likely put rents in prime retail spaces in the vicinity of $250 per square-foot, further pushing Aspen's commercial spaces beyond the reach of locals wanting to start a business, stores serving daily needs, or even coffee shops and ice cream stores whose plazas and courtyards enliven the town's core. In Aspen, the ironic consequence of collecting impact fees from developers and redistributing them to meet the housing needs of locals is that rents escalate ever higher, pushing the town deeper into the territory of supergentrification.

Super-landlord Mark Hunt provided an additional perspective on how the council's efforts might impact developers like himself. While he did not threaten to stop developing in Aspen, he told the council that the new regulations would incentivize him to pursue a different development style. Seated at the table designated for those making public comment, Hunt addressed the room, making eye contact with community members, the planning team, and council members, to emphasize his point. With proposed regulations mandating second-tier and pedestrian amenity space, he told them: "You [developers] will lose money upstairs and downstairs. And it's just going to get more restrictive and more expensive to [redevelop], and you're just going to lose even more. If it were up to me, I would never build another second floor or a basement. Those [spaces] are subsidized by the ground floor. They simply do not work. By the time you pay for the cost of land, the cost to mitigate, you can't get enough rent [to justify those costs]. There isn't a market for that." Because the new numbers are unlikely to pencil out, Hunt told the council that his strategy moving forward would be to build a grand, one-story building. That way, he could fill a beautiful, ground-floor space with a high-rent tenant like Cartier or Tiffany, limit the amount required to build a second-tier commercial space, thereby reducing the total amount of square footage, which would, in turn, reduce the number of jobs created and the affordable housing mitigations associated with those jobs.

These potentialities clearly put the council in a bind, one that forced them to consider the economic realities behind their goal of fulfilling the grand aspirations spelled out in the Aspen Area Community Plan. Mayor Skadron, however, chafed at the suggestion that he should consider how the proposed changes to the land use code might impact developers' bottom line. After presenting the finding that the new regulations might cost a developer an additional $4 million to fully renovate a building (a "scrape-and-replace" in the language of planners and developers), Mayor Skadron told the team of land use consultants who had prepared this report: "It's important that we talk about this from the community perspective, not the development perspective. I'm interested in what the community gets, and who we are, and what we, as council, are delivering to satisfy that desire. I'm having trouble when you talk to me from the perspective of your clients." "Community," in this sense, centers the needs of working locals. Returning to the main theme of this meeting, consultant Jeremy Nelson responded, "That's a fair point, but I would argue that they're intertwined. . . . If the development feasibility is not there, none of the benefits are delivered to the community." Indeed, this comment points to the complicated intertwining of *use value* and *exchange value* in Aspen: the interests of developers need to be protected in order for locals to receive quality-of-life benefits.

At the same January meeting in which these tensions, costs, and contradictions were brought to light, Community Development Director Jessica Garrow reminded the council and others that "one of the broad themes of this plan [the AACP] is to manage long-term development so that it contributes to the long-term viability of a sustainable, demographically diverse community, with a visitor-based economy and a vital year-round community. If we win on the policy level, but get nothing, we're really not fulfilling the AACP. It's about finding that sweet spot." While the community could "win" in terms of policies that, on paper, promote small-town character and economic opportunities for locals, it might ultimately lose, should these policies have unanticipated consequences. With this recognition in mind, Garrow and her staff recommended to the city council that they stick with the existing 60 percent mitigation rate and not impose new mitigations on properties built prior to the introduction of affordable housing mitigations, in the event that the owners decide to remodel. They favored this 60 percent rate over both a slightly higher rate and over a tiered-rate that would apply a 40 percent for second-tier spaces and 80 percent on "prime" commercial space within a development. Although the council members agreed to Garrow's recommendation that older buildings would not be subject to new mitigations, they worried that a mitigation rate of 60 percent would fail to generate enough housing to accommodate working locals. As the meeting wrapped up, the council held off on making a final decision and asked Community Development to come back yet again with more research that would help them make a decision.

BAKING A CAKE THAT HAS A SWEET SPOT

With just one month remaining before the expiration of the moratorium, council member Adam Frisch summarized the process and the ordinances being proposed: "We have all of these ideas, a lot of great stuff being added to the cake, but are we really ready to make this cake? Once we bake it, we're stuck with it for ten years." With that in mind, he reminded his fellow council members that they have to be "really, really sure that's the cake you want to make." For Mayor Skadron, the central question was: "Are you willing to prioritize locally serving [businesses] over affordable housing?" especially given Frisch's repeated suggestion that "the town will never be able to build enough affordable housing to satisfy the demand out there." Signaling a possible shift in priorities, or at least a shift in how to rank the priorities that address locals' needs, Skadron suggested that "Maybe it's time to reconsider [our approach to housing mitigation rates]." The decision to prioritize locally serving businesses, he said, is "not an anti-affordable housing position, it's a community balancing position." In lieu of increasing affordable housing mitigations, Skadron suggested, the community would gain commercial spaces that allow locals to start a business and access retail spaces that satisfy daily needs. This insight made Skadron hesitant to raise affordable housing mitigations.

With the trade-offs between having diverse commercial spaces and a viable affordable housing program in mind, Jessica Garrow and the team of consultants returned to council chambers yet again with a number of proposals. Perhaps the most enthusiastically considered new option was taking the 80–40 tiered-rate and transforming it into an even more dramatically tiered system. The theory behind this proposal was that since developers have to build a ground floor anyway, "prime" space could be required to mitigate at a much higher rate, with a significant break given to "non-prime" spaces, which may incentivize the building of a second floor or basement. The building of a second floor or basement is crucial for fulfilling the AACP promise to provide a diverse commercial mix, given the reality that a barber shop or dry cleaners cannot reasonably afford the $200-per-square-foot rents commanded by Aspen's prime commercial spaces. Because earlier scenarios revealed that an 80–40 rate would accomplish none of the goals of the AACP, council member Bert Myrin suggested a rate structure that would extract a 100 percent mitigation rate for prime spaces and 0 percent for non-prime spaces. "We can go back and look at those numbers," Jessica Garrow told the council, but she was confident that the differential would have to be quite steep to incentivizing the building of second-tier spaces, and even in that case, she worried that such a rate would simply give a break to developers and constitute a retreat from one of the fundamentals goals of the AACP—namely, the belief that developers mitigate for the impacts of their development.

Other council members worried, too, that tinkering with these rates would not produce the intended outcomes. Mayor Skadron stated that "[Bert and I] share the concern that the community ultimately does not get what it was trying to get with these equations," so that even after the tinkering, "Maybe we get it [second-tier spaces], and maybe we don't." A key detail that cast doubt upon the ability of a tiered-rate to achieve desired outcomes emerged from additional testimony provided by local developers. Landlord Karim Souki told the council that "the developer doesn't care where that number is coming from"—whether one part is 80 percent and other part 40 percent. "It's just that blended rate"—a blended rate whose costs are passed on to the tenants. Long-range planner for the city Phillip Supino confirmed the developers' logic: "A number of industry professionals that we talked to noted that having the tiered rate was not going to be passed along in lower lease amounts for second-tier occupants. You'd still see the net increase in mitigation being passed on to all of the tenants in the entire building." Developer Mark Hunt added another gloss to this, warning the council of the policies' possible unintended consequences. He pointed out that developers do not currently own the properties in question, so that "the person who's ultimately going to pay for all of this is the current landlord." To illustrate, he returned to the example of the Butcher's Block building—an older, somewhat shoddy building on the edge of the downtown core that houses a deli, a nail salon, and a ski shop—to show what would happen in a redevelopment scenario:

> [The owner is] not going to redevelop that herself. But she may eventually sell it. And the developer is going to underwrite those [newly mandated] fees. Where that is going to be made up, that $2.5 million, is [in being passed on] to the woman who currently owns that property. She's not going to get as much when she sells that business, because the developer is going

to take it out of the selling price. So that's who's ultimately going to pay the price, the locals who own these [older] properties, because these [new] fees impact how much we're willing to pay for a property, now that the property has these liabilities in it.

Adam Frisch and others worried that an increase in fees may have a chilling impact on development, while a "break [in fees] will end up in the landlord's pocket."

Despite warnings from Karim Souki and Mark Hunt that the proposed regulations would either freeze or fundamentally alter development patterns in Aspen, not everyone gave their claims much credence. Former mayor Mick Ireland (2007–2013), in particular, cautioned council members not to heed too seriously the developers' concerns. In providing feedback during a public comment period, he told them, "I have to take issue with the unsupported assertion that imposing mitigations could result . . . in a complete shutdown in project development. Every time we propose a [land use] regulation, we're threatened with the complete demise of the real estate industry in town. And it never happens. There's no empirical foundation to support that statement." Instead, demand for Aspen has only grown, resulting in upscaling and supergentrification. With an eye on macro-level forces, Ireland offered a powerful reminder to the council that their regulations may accomplish little in light of broader economic trends. A spry sixty-something who, like many council members, rode his bike around town and appeared in chambers dressed in casual outdoor gear and fleece jackets, voiced his concerns:

> We have a combination of circumstances that's likely to bring a commercial flood. It's a combination of [federal] tax cuts for businesses and wealthy people, and a desire and ability to revoke restrictions on financial investments, like banks, and venture capitalists in general. My point is, this [real estate speculation] has happened here before. The consequences are fairly predictable. We had that happen in 1987 and we saw the effect of tax cuts and deregulation, which resulted in the transformation of your community's housing stock. We had another boom in the late 1990s. Money was loose and it triggered a transformation of your town.

Without making any explicit recommendations, Ireland cautioned the council *not* to step back from their regulatory impulses: "We have the opportunity to see through this process in advance and say, 'Do we really need to not obstruct redevelopment, when you're about to be hit with this tsunami from around the country and around the world, looking for a place to invest?'" In light of these global economic trends, which seemed to make investment capital ever more plentiful, Ireland warned that developers may simply be bluffing with their warnings of de-investment.

MONEY, POLITICS, AND POWER IN ASPEN

Throughout my research in Aspen, the role of developers and landlords intrigued and confounded me. Any basic understanding of economic activity, and any understanding of urban political economy, would lead to the assumption that developers in Aspen would work in concert with one another, and with local politicians and other place entrepreneurs, to pursue growth and to maximize profit. Yet, at least on the surface—as evidenced in council meetings, one-on-one interviews with developers, council members, property appraisers, and other key place-makers—this seemed not to be the case. There appeared to be no collective action on the part of developers to form a coalition with city officials to pursue growth strategies, nor did they appear to act collectively to oppose city land use regulations—even when regulations would cost them millions. Prospective homeowners did not lobby against the Real Estate Transfer Tax (RETT) when it periodically came up for renewal by the voters, nor did real estate professionals lobby against the city's extensive building fees—even when permitting fees alone could easily amount to $250,000–$350,000 for a new residential project. At times, individual wealthy homeowners did mount successful lawsuits against the City—protesting, for example, the development of a mixed-use business incubator and brew pub on the fringe of a residential area—yet their actions were not collective, nor were they directed at land use or fiscal policies. These dynamics raised questions about the city council's ability to impose a highly restrictive land use environment, and how this reflects Aspen's unique economic environment and place-based class culture.

It would be incorrect to suggest that developers, landlords, and others with interests in the business community exerted no influence on local politics. Since the strong growth-control regimes of the 1970s, different councils have varied in their approach to development, with pro-development forces, typically setting the pendulum in motion after national recessionary periods. About Mayor Helen Klanderud, who presided during the much-maligned infill years of 2001–2007, I heard it said: "She never met a development deal she didn't like." In recent years, Adam Frisch had the reputation of being more business friendly than other officials, a perception fueled by the fact that he and his wife both were business owners (one recreational, the other manufacturing) and by his friendly social relationships with developers, including Mark Hunt. Real estate professional Dennis Diamond, with forty years of local experience, took issue with the suggestion that developers do not attempt to push back against the council's anti-growth measures, describing a subtle form of regulatory capture, which happens when a political player or entity is co-opted to serve commercial or ideological interests.[9] "If Adam hears from twenty of his friends, 'Adam, what are you guys thinking? You can't raise the affordable housing mitigation fee,'" that plays a role in his decision-making, "and may have him say, 'Hey, you know, we really can't raise it quite this much. I think we should raise it less.'" More broadly, Diamond noted that many local planners in private practice formerly worked for the city, and now use their inside knowledge of land use processes, whether acting as consultants during the mortarium period or guiding their clients' development applications. "They're always at public meetings, and they're always trying to give their perspective about what this [regulation or policy] will do." Developers and architects also sit on city boards, including the Planning and Zoning Commission and the Historic Preservation Commission, where they have the opportunity to formally guide land use policy and its interpretation and implementation. Yet in these hearings, too, little opposition emerged to the city's plans to increase affordable housing mitigations, add second-tier space, and expand pedestrian amenity requirements. It is true, however, that in recent years a handful of developers were successful in lobbying for reductions in their housing mitigations in exchange for projects deemed "architecturally significant" or that otherwise made an important contribution to the community. They had not, however, lobbied to systematically eliminate or reduce housing mitigations. Despite Dennis Diamond's insistence that pushback and opposition from developers does exist, he concluded that "ultimately council ends up doing what it wants to do" and "that stuff kind of falls on deaf ears, if I'm being honest."

Perhaps little formal opposition emerged from developers to Aspen's "mitigation industrial complex" because many of them realized, in the words of real estate professional Dennis Diamond, that Aspen "is a great long-term play." Although mitigation and permitting fees may take an immediate toll on development projects, the place-making efforts of local officials virtually ensure that the eventual return on investment is high. Speaking at an Aspen Entrepreneurs event aimed at sharing insights about developing a successful business in Aspen, Tony Mazza—one of Aspen's largest commercial property owners, in partnership with Frank Woods in M&W Properties—spoke of its unique value. Having begun his career in the late 1970s, he reflected on the decision of progressive county commissioners to "downzone" the county in the mid-1970s, which limited the amount of land available for development: "Everyone was freaking out [about the downzoning], and I'm saying to my clients, 'Listen, if what they're doing is right, and if this place is so special, it's gonna make your property more valuable because people can't [build more].' And you can just take that forward to, to what has basically happened in Aspen and, therefore, the price-points we now have. . . . That's how the people who were here in the beginning did so bloody well—because they restricted supply." Jim DeFrancia, another developer with roots in the 1970s, echoed this position. "Any regulatory constraint has an impact on the community," he told me in a lunchtime interview, in that "constraining development reduces supply, therefore increasing values for demand." He continued: "If you can't go out [with a building's mass and scale], then you want to go up. If you can't go up [in height], then you can't go anywhere. . . . In the meantime, you're faced with increasing demand and you've constrained supply, which drives values up. If you're already in and you're an owner, that's fine. If you're not, that's a huge barrier to entry and ultimately it also impacts the broader community in the sense of affordability." When asked what advice he would give to someone deciding to develop in Aspen versus another resort with lighter regulations and lower barriers to entry, Mazza provided a perspective that shed light on why many developers seem to put forth some opposition, but ultimately go along with the program and choose to invest in Aspen: "I would probably go in Aspen. . . . Everywhere kind of wants to be an Aspen, or they think there will be another Aspen. But I haven't found one, and I've owned stuff in a lot of places. So, the reason why, besides all the caché and everything else, and all the beauty, and the music, and all the [cultural] stuff, you know, why—it's 'cause you can't build anymore." Yet Mazza understood one fundamental limitation of those who would seek to invest in Aspen. "I don't know how the hell you'd do it," he told the group of young, professionals gathered at the forum, "unless you're really rich." Given the free flow of capital for speculation and globally deep pockets, there are still "lots of people who will pay the premium," according to DeFrancia, to have their buildings and businesses associated with Aspen, yet access among people without ultra-high net worth or access to investment capital remained elusive.

Over time, the fundamental economics of the local real estate market, along with Aspen's undeniable beauty and sense of place, seemed to shape the ethos of local developers. John Sarpa, a developer with numerous hotel projects in his local portfolio—including the W Hotel with its open-to-the-public rooftop pool area—described the difference between his work in Aspen and elsewhere. "You really do have to listen" in order to work in this small, tightknit community, he told journalist Carolyn Sackariason, in a 2019 *Aspen Times* news story about the opening of the W Hotel. "You can't be here for very long without caring about the place."[10] For him, this means wanting it "to be better and more interesting and environmentally healthier and all of the things you need for a sustainable community." Other developers and architects, who have to deal with these regulatory constraints, similarly told me that there is no place they would rather do their work, given the aesthetic challenges and rewards, and the return on investment.

Although developers are often the ones who shoulder the upfront costs of building in Aspen, homeowners and vacationers—whose shopping and dining fuels the local economy—also pay a premium to be in Aspen. Yet they too mounted little opposition to the extractive policies that increased the price of being in Aspen, and subsidize housing and other programs for locals. Homebuyers pay a one-time Real Estate Transfer Tax, at the rate of 1.5 percent. For someone purchasing an $8 million home, this equates to $120,000 in funds for local programs, principally affordable housing; a person purchasing a home for $25 million makes a $375,000 contribution. Sales taxes in Aspen are 9.3 percent—the maximum allowed under Colorado law—so, purchasing a $3,500 Gucci handbag costs more there than it would virtually anywhere else in the United States. With very few stores catering to the needs of middle-class consumers, Aspen stores primarily carry goods with a luxury price-point, one made even higher through local taxation. And yet the visitors and second-home owners keep on coming.

Among the people I spoke to—from elected representatives to developers to people whose jobs are vital to the day-to-day functioning of the town—the consensus was that political power rested with local citizens and elected officials, and that those with economic power and influence tend to stay in their lane. Developer Jim DeFrancia explained why economic elites remain uninvolved in local politics, even as they pay the costs of extractive local policies:

> They don't vote here. In the vast majority of cases, this is not where they vote. And so, they look at our politics and roll their eyes. I think that if any one of them were inspired enough to take over the political scene, they all have the funds to literally crush what's going on in this town. If they wanted to dig up dirt on a couple of candidates, put their own candidates in place, they could do it. . . . It would not be hard for them. But they just don't care. I mean, you're working with people who have a net worth that is equivalent to the GDPs of small nations. They could own this town [politically] and they're smart enough to do it, but this just isn't worth it to them.

For a lot of wealthy people—the developers who pay $5 million in mitigation for a new project and the buyer who pays $375,000 on top of the $25 million price tag for a new home—these extractions amount to a rounding error. Instead, they invest their political efforts in broader national policies that impact their business and personal finances and pay these seemingly minor costs of access in Aspen—costs that may even pay off over time. Fourth-generation Aspenite Donald Ranstead gave substance to this idea, highlighting the discrepancy in how an economic elite may behave at home and how they may behave in Aspen: "I think there are plenty of people who are just like, 'You know, I might be a Republican, conservative, political person at home, but when I come to Aspen and I see those liberal, democratic, socialistic people doing their thing, it's hard to argue that it hasn't worked out to my benefit.'" Lo and behold, Aspen has a $120 municipal budget, which various sources estimate derives about 15 percent from taxes paid by local residents and 85 percent from visitors and part-year residents. These revenues fund schools, recreation, housing, and more, "and it's all paid for," DeFrancia said, "by all these people who don't vote here and who take little or no interest in the local politics, 'cause to them it's just the cost of living and they really don't care—which leaves us locals to benefit." Because of this, DeFrancia said, money "doesn't particularly talk in the political sector, because your largest voting block is not the economically upward end of the spectrum." Consequently, "there's a greater tendency for elected officials to be responsive to a working class, middle class, and their agenda, and not in need of tens or hundreds of thousands of dollars to run political campaigns, which would make them beholden to the traditional economic influences." Given these dynamics, the city council found itself tentatively measuring the threats of those developers who claimed that the new regulations would have a chilling effect on their business; weighing the ways they could preserve Aspen's charm and sense of place; and prioritize the needs of locals, given the fact that many of their policy proposals seemed to have conflicting outcomes.

CONCLUSION

In the closing days of the moratorium, after a full month of deliberations over the possible impacts of the proposed set of code amendments, the Aspen City Council passed an ordinance that increased mitigation rates, mandating that new developments (and significant remodels) mitigate for 65 percent of the new employees generated by their projects. They also reached a compromise that when redeveloped, buildings that had been built prior to the introduction of affordable housing mitigation would not be required to mitigate at the full rate; instead, there would be a phase-in process whereby the mitigation rate would start at 15 percent and gradually increase each year thereafter. Both of these decisions defied the advice of the city's planning staff, who recommended that the mitigation rate stay at 60 percent and that older buildings not be required to mitigate at

Figure 12. Public amenity spaces like this one outside Paradise Bakery allow public gathering, but reduce leasable space. Photo by Skippy Mesirow.

all. In passing these ordinances, the council was mindful that their decisions could shock the system and chill new development, but they also felt pressed to implement policies that honor statements in the Aspen Area Community Plan that prioritize the needs of working locals. Amid threats from some members of the development community, they attempted to steer a middle course and find the sweet spot that would ideally deliver second-tier retail spaces, a pedestrian experience that fosters enjoyment of nature and social interaction (see figure 12), and enough affordable housing to allow working locals to live the Aspen Dream.

Perhaps what these deliberations reveal most is that there are two pro-found contradictions at the heart of Aspen's sense of place and its class culture. First, the creation of growth and the production of affordable housing are two sides of the same coin. If Aspen wants to provide afford-able housing for working locals, who are vaunted as contributing to the area's authentic sense of place, it has to endure growth. It is, after all, growth—whether in the form of mitigations or real estate transfer taxes, the bigger the better—that fund affordable housing. And yet growth is inimical to this sense of authenticity. Additionally, local government's efforts to provide affordable lifestyles for locals—access to both housing and commercial spaces that provide everyday needs—simultaneously con-tribute to its problem of affordability. They do so by driving up the costs of development and the rents that landlords need to charge. The events that came to a head in this set of council meetings highlight these deep contra-dictions, and also reveal a hesitancy among some council members to use innovative, progressive tools to reproduce its sense of place.

Place-based class cultures are both an input and an output in the process of place-making. These analyses take a deep dive from examining place-making dynamics at thirty-five thousand feet to look at how they play out at the ground level, in this case through the careful deliberations of elected officials, place entrepreneurs, technical experts, and locals. These delibera-tions over how to deliver the ambitious objectives of the AACP—in light of the reality that their policy proposals may not "pencil out" for developers—are punctuated by distinctive moments that have the capacity to alter Aspen's place-based class culture. While these analyses show clearly *how* place-based class cultures influence the place-making process, it is less clear *what* their consequences will be. Despite the city council's commitment to protecting the housing and consumer needs of locals—thereby reproduc-ing the narrative that Aspen is a place where people from diverse social classes mix—their efforts are challenged by supergentrification and real estate speculation, fueled by global economic forces that make investment capital abundant. They are, moreover, threatened by internal contradictions in how to implement their own community values, and the unintended con-sequences that might result from their decisions.

Only time will tell how Aspen will be altered by this latest round of place-making vis-à-vis the land use code. With three thousand units in its existing affordable housing inventory and nearly three hundred more to be added in the near future, community support and funding for affordable housing remain strong. That said, supply will not be able to meet demand, given the community's preference for limiting growth and density and for preserving open space. Still, it appears that the capacity to house working residents within Aspen will remain, even if locals struggle to start their own businesses, enjoy a dinner on the town, or make spontaneous purchases to satisfy daily needs (online shopping has been a boon to working locals). While working locals can live and recreate in Aspen, they may not be able to shop or dine there. This portends a strange form of class segregation, where working locals are both ever present and curiously absent, within a community that lovingly embraces its egalitarian roots.

Other evidence suggests that some of the more dire warnings and prognostications of the new land use code may be coming true. Since the passage of these code amendments in 2017, new applications to build or remodel have slowed (even before the crisis surrounding the corona virus), and some of the more high-profile applications have been for one-story buildings—buildings that have the capacity to generate high rents from prime retail space and have limited mitigation responsibilities due to their modest size. To the extent that this becomes the new normal, Aspen will reap fewer benefits that accrue to working locals and will be less able to foster mixing between locals and visitors. Finally, since the moratorium, two of Aspen's most treasured businesses have closed or are threatened to close. Few businesses garnered as much praise during moratorium deliberations than Peach's Corner (a coffee and lunch spot) and Paradise Bakery (offering ice cream and baked goods). Packed from open until close, with visitors and locals alike, these businesses offered unique opportunities for social mixing, with low price points and seating arrangements that welcome families and their dogs, and pop-up performances by students at the summer music school. Although Peach's has been replaced by Aspen Brewing Company's restaurant and tap room, offering moderate prices and a community-friendly business model, Paradise Bakery and its legendary cookie-topped ice cream is set to be replaced by an expanded location for Italian cashmere retailer, Loro Piana. Say goodbye to $4 ice cream and hello to sweaters whose prices *begin* at $1,000.

6 A Mall at the Base of a Mountain?

Galena Street has been called "Aspen's Rodeo Drive." Upon first glance, the comparison to Beverly Hills' foremost luxury shopping street seems odd. Walking south on Galena Street, what most captures one's attention are the many historically designated red stone buildings that line the street and the epic mountain stretching out ahead—bright green and verdant in the summer, and brilliant white and dotted with skiers in the winter. Former mayor Bill Stirling (1983–1991) was among those who barely seemed to notice these stores, despite the fact that his former office in City Hall sits directly across from some of Aspen's foremost luxury retailers. What continued to capture his attention in Aspen were the mountains themselves, the independent bookstore, and the many community events, like the annual July Fourth Parade, where he and his silver coif are easily spotted.

Upon second glance, Galena Street's comparison to Rodeo Drive comes into focus. Housed in these beautifully restored relics from Aspen's mining era are international luxury retailers, including Prada, Valentino, Dolce and Gabbana, Gucci, and Christian Dior. In contrast to the glittering, ostentatious façades that typify high-end retail establishments in other global cities, in Aspen these retailers do not boldly announce themselves. Rather, they feature modest signage and otherwise blend into the historic

Figure 13. Luxury in an authentically Aspen Victorian-era package. Photo by Jenny Stuber.

streetscape, sharing the same historic architecture and vibrant floral window boxes that dot much of Aspen's downtown commercial core (see figure 13). But in spite of their relatively unobtrusive storefronts, some locals were keenly aware of their presence. Ben Wright, a longtime gallery owner, proclaimed that he refuses to go into "the Aspen Core" anymore—the twelve square blocks making up the town's commercial zone district—alienated and disgusted by the proliferation of high-end chains and splashy new developments. Galena Street and "Restaurant Row" sit just one block from his gallery, and yet he has erected a symbolic barrier between *his* Aspen and the *other* Aspen: the funkier version that drew him to town in the early 1990s and the one promoted in the town's glossy lifestyle magazines.

In the fall of 2016, the Ben Wrights of Aspen had had enough. Under the unlikely leadership of Jerry Murdock, a local billionaire and venture capitalist, a citizen's group joined forces to take on luxury retail. In assembling his team of advocates, Murdock recruited local business people who had felt the squeeze of Aspen's harsh retail environment, millennials who were hoping to realize their entrepreneurial dreams, and longtime civic stewards, like former mayors John Bennett and Bill Stirling, who up until that point had not fully identified luxury chains as a threat to Aspen's identity. In November of 2016, midway through the moratorium, this citizen's group introduced an ordinance to the Aspen City Council, aiming to regulate formula retail in town. Yet, unlike other municipalities that have pushed back against big-box retailers and chain stores (like Walmart), the Aspen initiative targeted high-end luxury retailers. Supporters of the proposed ordinance accused these retailers of altering the funky small-town character of Aspen and driving up commercial rents, thereby shutting out locally owned and locally serving retailers. Others lamented the loss of restaurant and commercial spaces where middle-class locals and affluent visitors rub shoulders—expressing that sense of *Aspen egalitarianism* that many see as making their community unique. And while the citizen's group was convened and backed by a billionaire, it gained leverage from the inclusion of middle- and upper-middle-class locals who used social class discourses that claimed their right to the city and expressed opposition to the global economic forces that seemed to be transforming the town they know and love.

On March 6, 2017, after nearly five months of consideration, the Aspen City Council passed Ordinance 6, which requires a conditional-use review process for any new chain stores wishing to locate in the downtown core. This chapter traces this process, from the identification and definition of a problem, through deliberations, and finally to the ordinance's passage. As a case study in place-making, I show how local residents with ample social, political, and economic capital pushed back against perceived threats to authenticity and economic well-being, as they engaged with various stakeholders to "keep Aspen, Aspen." In addition, I show how other community stakeholders, namely those representing commerce, staked out a different position, claiming that luxury retail has a rightful place in Aspen, both with respect to landlords' property rights and in promoting the Aspen brand. Finally, I illustrate the reaction of the Aspen City Council and their efforts to mediate the interests of different stakeholders. Ultimately, the watered-down piece of legislation passed by the city council gave each constituent group something to celebrate; yet, in the attempt to balance the interests of stakeholders with diverse class interests, the council kicked the can down the road hoping to find a solution that would more aggressively serve the economic needs of its year-round middle- and upper-middle-class locals.

SUPERGENTRIFICATION AND UPSCALING IN THE RETAIL SECTOR

Obvious or intentional efforts at place-making kick into high gear when stakeholders feel a sense of anxiety, anxiety that may stem from feelings of alienation or dislocation. In Aspen, upscaling within the retail sector has inspired such anxieties. As shown in Sharon Zukin's work on New York City, retail gentrification—also called boutiquing—occurs when retail spaces become increasingly filled with products and services that cater to tourists and the most affluent segments of the community.[1] In more mundane instances, retailers like the Gap, Zara, and Footlocker, replace the independent sneaker dealer on the corner or the store selling women's housecoats and "foundations." In more extreme versions, retail gentrification brings retailers whose products carefully blend a taste for the "authentic" and the upscale. Rough-hewn wooden serving pieces, industrial lighting and kitchen items, and artisan woolen goods fill stores adjacent to those whose shelves are stocked with local and organic food items, like small-batch jams and farm-raised eggs.

In Aspen, retail gentrification is so extreme that only a handful of retailers sell clothing with price points lower than $300, and the few that do, deal mostly in outdoor clothing and fitness gear—not the ideal look if you unexpectedly land a job interview or get invited to a fundraiser. Moderately priced stores like The Gap and Banana Republic are mere memories of a more affordable time in Aspen's retail landscape. For parents with growing children, socks, underwear, and other basics are an hour away in Glenwood Springs—unless children's clothing from upscale brands like Kenzo and Stella McCartney (yes, Paul's daughter), with price points in excess of $100 are in the budget. Retail gentrification in Aspen has brought not just high-end luxury retailers like Gucci and Prada but also storefronts filled by art galleries, jewelry stores, and real estate offices.

Although lower-priced options exist for lunch, going out for dinner almost universally means spending more than $20 for a burger or a lowly bowl of pasta and upwards of $35 for a proper entree. A careful observer may spot the Domino's Pizza on the edge of downtown, but otherwise, fast food or chain restaurants are nowhere to be found.

In Aspen, as in New York, San Francisco, and London, the direct impact of retail gentrification involves the proliferation of higher-priced goods and increased commercial rents—which makes it difficult for locals to access basic services or open small businesses of their own. While affluent residents and visitors may enjoy the unique and innovative retail environment that boutiquing brings, and may even be drawn to the town for these shopping options, upscaling disrupts economic opportunities for locals— even those who are relatively affluent.[2] Where can a man go to get a $15 haircut when the barber shop has been replaced by a store selling $15,000 vintage watches? Need to replace a set of bed sheets, and Target's $40 king set is in your budget, but Frette's $700 set is not? Good luck. Threats to basic goods and services are so deeply felt by local Aspenites that during the moratorium, council member Bert Myrin frequently invoked the importance of using zoning tools to ensure that the parking lots outside of the town's two grocery stores be protected, rather than opening them up to development for their "highest and best use." Indeed, mere grocery stores are so sacred to Aspen's fabric, and so representative of Aspen egalitarianism that locals routinely give the award for the town's best gathering place to "City Market," a Kroger grocery store subsidiary.

The displacement brought about by retail gentrification can also impact social networks, in some cases enhancing them. Consumption spaces, like the bars and cafes that Ray Oldenberg called "third places," allow neighborhood residents to congregate for work or recreation and meet neighbors with similar interests.[3] Yet depictions of newly upscaled areas of Harlem, Brooklyn, and Chicago show that for longtime locals, retail gentrification may mean the destruction of social networks. The new bars and cafes to which middle-class folks flock simultaneously shut out older residents, whether because of price or taste. In his ethnographic work on retail gentrification in Venice, California, Andrew Deener quotes a longtime resident as saying: "I used to know every single person on my block. Now I hardly know anyone. I've never even had a conversation with my next-door neighbor and he's been in there for three years."[4] When upscaling attracts not just more affluent locals, but also tourists and, ostensibly, affluent part-year residents, "the city centre belongs to affluent visitors rather than to residents, resulting in the exclusion of working-class residents from the core."[5] Where, in Aspen, do the local journalists and first responders go for a drink after work, and spontaneously rub shoulders with other community members? Where do local retirees gather over coffee to talk about the weather, their health problems, or politics? During 2016 and 2017, Aspen's two local newspapers were filled with reporting, editorials, and anxious letters to the editor lamenting the loss of much beloved local eateries, like Boogie's Diner, Main Street Bakery, Little Annie's, and the Weinerstube. When retail gentrification comes to town, the lack of viable "third places" inhibits the ability to build social capital and, consequently, weakens social control, reciprocity, and other mechanisms that create well-functioning communities.

While it may not threaten access to housing or jobs, the hegemonic global urbanism that often accompanies retail gentrification may bring about an increasingly sanitized landscape; one in which architecture, tastes, cultural preferences, and ideologies converge into a homogenized worldview and a way of life that submerges local character. Even for the relatively affluent, upscaling can have deleterious social and psychological effects. Urban sociologist Sharon Zukin notes that such processes may inspire a "crisis of authenticity," wherein the shifting tides of gentrification spark "a broader and more metaphysical set of problems" that involve "our common inability to grasp the shifting meanings of space and time, as well as the search for sources of our own 'real' identity."[6] This crisis of authenticity, feelings of connectedness, and questions about the nature of one's community clearly fueled the battle over formula retail in Aspen.

In many gentrified and gentrifying spaces, locals lack the social, political, and cultural capital to push back against these forces. Yet Aspen is not such a place, and neither are the thirty-some municipalities across the United States that have passed some form of restrictions on chain stores, including quota systems, conditional review processes, or even outright bans. These explicit efforts at place-making have played out in wealthy communities, especially those that are historic or possess a unique resort atmosphere, including Nantucket, Massachusetts, Sanibel Island, Florida, and California's Carmel-by-the-Sea. In these communities, citizens have channeled their anxieties over local place-character through efforts to regulate chain retail. Elsewhere, these battles against homogenization have been directed at chains like McDonald's, Subway, Dunkin' Donuts, and Starbucks—businesses that locals see as compromising the sense of authenticity, history, and enchantment that independent retailers bring. During the lead-up to her town's eventual restrictions on formula retail, one resident of York, Maine, expressed her opposition thusly: "I think Dunkin' Donuts would ruin our town's historical value. This town has hundreds of years built into it and putting the first fast food place [in York] would start something that would wreck our town. . . . All those things we learned in fifth grade about this town's history could be destroyed by a donut shop."[7] Her letter to the city council suggests that the small, quaint, historically designated structures—likely made of wood, natural quarried stone, or other organic materials—must be defended against the brightly colored, plastic, back-lit signs of retailers like Dunkin' Donuts, with their highly identifiable pink and orange service-mark. Golden Arches? Heaven's, no.

While efforts to regulate formula retail are not new, none of the existing efforts have targeted high-end, luxury retail. But then again, as affluent and special as these other communities may be, they are not Aspen. Where other communities have experienced gentrification and homogenization through the influx of chains like Starbucks, H&M, and Whole Foods, Aspen has experienced supergentrification—locally described as the process by which the billionaires have pushed out the millionaires. In Aspen, luxury chain stores represent a triple threat, threatening the local character and treasured notions of cross-class fraternizing, the ability of locals to become independent retailers and entrepreneurs, and locals' access to daily goods and services. Yet, these high-end stores also serve an important function in this upscale mountain town, drawing visitors during the winter and summer seasons and filling the town's coffers with sales tax revenues—revenues that trickle down and serve the public good. Thus, the battle over formula retail in this upscale mountain town raises the question of "Aspen for whom?" and shows how stakeholders and the city council work together to balance diverse class interests and preserve the place character of their beloved town.

THE PROBLEM OF FORMULA RETAIL:
FRAMING THE ISSUE

When venture capitalist Jerry Murdock and his citizens' coalition presented to Aspen's city council a *conditional use* ordinance for formula retail in November of 2016, the council had been engaged in the land use moratorium for more than six months. With respect to commercial development, the AACP establishes these goals:[8]

> Encourage a commercial mix that is balanced, diverse and vital and meets the needs of year-round residents and visitors.

> Facilitate the sustainability of essential businesses that provide basic community needs.

> Ensure that the City Land Use Code results in development that . . . [protects] our small town community character and historical heritage.

As noted in chapters 4 and 5, the city council was focused on finding a set of tools that would bring to life these promises. Yet the council lacked an appetite to approach this problem through regulatory measures and thus sought out a set of design-based solutions that would create "nook-and-cranny" or second-tier commercial spaces. Despite efforts to achieve these goals through these design requirements, some members of the community felt that city officials were not doing enough to provide a balanced set of retail options and essential businesses that serve basic community needs. In a town where citizens play an active role in shaping and sometimes even implementing local politics, a group advocating for a particular issue was nothing new. What was fairly unprecedented was the fact that Jerry Murdock's citizen group, after hiring a local land use attorney, presented to the city council a fully drafted ordinance, with the formatting and technical wording that mirrors legislation produced by the council itself. This draft ordinance proposed a conditional-use review process for "formula retail," which was defined as any business operating more than eleven locations in the United States, where those locations have standard merchandise or services, as well as uniform branding and signage ("service-mark"). Applicants would be granted a business license if, for example, the conditional review process determined that the business would either meet the daily needs of locals or offer one-of-a-kind experiences—dining, retail, or recreation—not currently available in town.

And so, November 28, 2016, began five months of public deliberations over the place of formula retail in Aspen, and the invocation of discourses reflecting deeply held notions concerning the town's place character and how class should be done. Throughout this five-month period, competing discourses were offered by members of Jerry Murdock's citizens' group, aspiring and current business owners, and town residents, as well as council members, business groups, developers and their lawyers. Conversations and contestations took place in formal proceedings within City Hall, letter-writing campaigns and efforts to elicit public feedback, and behind closed doors. In some cases, discourses about social class were made explicit, as in claims suggesting that a unique aspect of Aspen's place character is that it offers the opportunity for cross-class fraternizing. In other cases, references to class interests were implied, as stakeholders worked to assert their unique interests via-à-vis formula retail. Amid these discourses, the city council worked to adjudicate these concerns as the formal arbiter in Aspen's struggle to define itself.

As in other towns that have enacted regulations for formula retail, the most frequently invoked reason for opposing chain stores was the threat to community character. In a place where a sense of exceptionalism characterizes local place narratives, Aspen residents opined that the loss of locally owned businesses and the rise of upscale chains meant the "erosion of character." This "homogenization" of the retail landscape threatened Aspen's uniqueness, its brand, and its sense of community. At the November city council meeting in which Murdock's group introduced the proposal to regulate formula retail, former mayor John Bennett spoke on behalf of the group, lamenting Aspen's increased homogeneity: "For the last half century, Aspen has been one of the most unique, special, small towns in the universe, certainly on this planet. We also know that year by year . . . it starts to feel a little less special all the time. A big part of that is you walk around town and see more these familiar [retail] names, and it's same-o-same-o. We could become a mountain with a mall at the bottom. Our uniqueness is not automatic." Due to its high rents and affluent clientele, "same-o same-o" meant not Starbucks, Gap, H&M, or Sephora— but high-end luxury chains, chains that threatened Aspen in various ways.

From an economic standpoint, Aspen residents accused these global brands of having the unfair advantage of vertical integration in their production chains and of being able to operate stores in Aspen even if they did not generate a profit. Indeed, due to the seasonal nature of the economy, many of Aspen's stores generate profits for only six months out of the year. The ability of chain stores to subsidize their losses through corporate backing, locals argued, shut out lower-priced locally owned or locally serving entities, which do not have deep pockets to sustain seasonal lulls and cannot pay the rents that luxury competitors can. Luxury chains were also perceived as a social and symbolic threat. Mayor Bennett and others raised the specter of Denver's upscale Cherry Creek Mall: while its upscale nature may resonate with Aspen's clientele, its easily recognized brands and their lack of local charm do not, making them anathema to Aspen's small-town character and celebrated "messy vitality."

Indeed, since the 1970s, notions of "funkiness" and "messy vitality" have been formally inscribed into Aspen's community-planning documents. As noted in previous chapters, the 1993 Aspen Area Community Plan states that, "Aspen as a community should avoid an environment that is too structured, too perfect, and that eliminates the funkiness that once characterized this town."[9] "Too structured" and "too perfect" aptly describe "formula retail," whose business plans typically require large and fully renovated spaces with uniform design features. The treasured and historically imagined "funkiness" that is both embedded in the AACP and routinely invoked by community members honors Aspen's days of yore, where the buildings that remained after the silver mining crash stood side by side with the Alpine-style buildings that began to proliferate after the founding of the ski industry in the 1950s. These different sizes and styles are what make Aspen "exceptional," providing the "messy vitality" that makes it different from the high-end malls dotting suburban America and—again—from Vail, a planned and uniform resort community that figures prominently as the antithetical touchstone in Aspen's modern planning history.

At the same November council meeting in which Murdock and his team introduced their ordinance, lodge manager Bob Morris attested to the demand for uniqueness in Aspen's retail environment. "I hear a lot of comments from guests," he said, "and one of the comments I hear is that with Gucci and all of the other stores, 'I feel like I'm walking down Michigan

Avenue in Chicago. . . . It's the things that make Aspen different that I come to Aspen for, not to see the same stores with the same fur coats and $20,000 purses.'" For Bob Morris's guests, the problem is not that chain stores stock expensive furs and purses; it's that shoppers want to encounter expensive furs and purses that are *different* from the ones they see in their hometowns or other travel destinations. As Bob Morris's comment suggests, the perceived problem with formula retail was not always agreed upon: amid the plentiful objection to Prada and their ilk, some objected to their exclusive price points, while others objected to their ubiquity in other locales.

In their efforts to frame the problem posed by formula retail, some locals claimed that the standardized business practices of formula retail undermine the social relationships that emerge from independent retail—social relationships that ultimately sustain long-term economic benefits. Speaking at a community roundtable at the Aspen Institute, Giselle Leal, owner of a small accessory store in the commercial core, said that what fundamentally differentiates her business from the international chains is "the storytelling element"—which she described as the opportunity to curate her merchandise, establish relationships with producers and artisans, and then share their stories with her customers—who each year keep coming back for more:

> [This] is why people shop at Magasin; they're recreational shoppers. . . . I shop for the same customer, year after year, season after season. I see their families grow; it's so warm and fuzzy. The products are from local designers or they are handmade. I'm not even sure that people are buying it because they love the product, but they love the story. I am a source of entertainment for them. That's what's different from going to a Prada or a Burberry. From me, they're buying twenty minutes of their day to have a conversation with a local.

Throughout these discussions, locals characterized the shopping environment of upscale chains as cold and rigid, suggesting that locally owned stores allow for greater vitality by inviting friends and customers in to chat and linger. At the same community roundtable, a woman named Patty noted: "It used to be that everyone was out, everyone was talking and congregating in one place or another." Now, she and others noted, those locals

have moved down valley—thirty minutes away in Basalt and Carbondale
—where housing and commercial rents are lower. A feeling of energy,
spontaneity, and street-level vitality have been eroded, some locals feel,
by the introduction of chain stores that they see as boring, beyond their
financial means, and even hostile to allowing them to visit friends at work.
This change to the retail environment speaks to the loss of community and
social capital that other theorists have described as the collateral costs of
upscaling.[10]

In describing her store, Magasin, Giselle invoked one of the most common tropes about the Aspen "brand": that it is a place that provides repeat
visitors and part-year residents the opportunity to interact with "local characters." Katrina DeVore, a third-generation Aspenite and a millennial-aged
member of Murdock's citizens' group, echoed this sentiment in describing
her work as a ski instructor: "I have a lot of really high-end people flying
into Aspen from all over the world, and they tell me that they can shop
in those [upscale] stores in New York and L.A. But they come to Aspen
because it's different, and they want to get involved with the locals and they
want to know what the locals are into." Speaking at the Aspen Institute
roundtable, a resident named Chris expanded on this theme; drawing on
Aspen's unique history, he explained his opposition to chain stores: "We're
not a purpose-build resort. We're not Vail, we're not Whistler; we're not
what Squaw Valley's becoming. We're funky, unique. That's why Hunter S.
Thompson called this place home. I love the local bars and the fact that you
can go out and meet locals and meet tourists at the same time." In addition
to drawing a symbolic boundary between Aspen and less-authentic resorts,
Chris referenced the storied notion of Aspen egalitarianism: the idea that
there was a time when anyone, of any social class, could pull up a bar stool
and find themselves having a beer or whisky next to celebrity renegades
like the gonzo journalist Hunter S. Thompson or the actor Jack Nicholson.
Luxury chain stores and high-end restaurants, with their homogeneity and
exclusive price points, were seen as a threat to those types of interactions
and, by extension, to the class dynamics that make Aspen unique.

While references to class dynamics were merely implied in some locals'
opposition to chain stores, other community members offered explicitly
classed narratives when framing the problem of upscale chains in Aspen.
Like Chris's nostalgic lamentation of the days of sharing bar stools with

celebrities at the storied Hotel Jerome, several respondents questioned the proliferation of high-end retail in Aspen, given the town's history as a place where social classes mix. At the Aspen Institute roundtable, the town's biggest developer, Chicago-based Mark Hunt, recounted: "One of the things I hear about what people miss about Aspen is everyone coming together in one space. . . . It's the haves and have-nots, the young and the old, everyone rubbing shoulders. I've heard that story over and over, about why Aspen is different." The mixing of the "haves and have-nots"—an explicit reference to class differences—heralds the time when lowly ski-lift operators or ski instructors would chat together while riding the chair lift (or the more upscale gondola, in recent times) or share a slice and a beer at New York Pizza with venture capitalists or Hollywood types.

Although Mark Hunt's properties house upscale chains like Dolce and Gabbana, he supported the idea of *incentivizing* locally owned businesses, rather than *restricting* chain stores. Many local residents saw him as the "architect" of Galena Street and poster-child of upscale retail in Aspen, yet he framed himself as a supporter of local retail, especially in terms of the social ties it fosters: "I really believe there are businesses that are important to Aspen, some of which are now gone, that may never make money. They bring us all together in one way or another, which is important to the community." Hunt was among several locals who waxed nostalgic about now-shuttered places like Main Street Bakery, the Weinerstube, and Boogie's Diner, where, in the words of former owner Boogie Weinberg himself, "locals went there, tourists went there, wealthy people came there, poor people came there." When replaced, the buildings are likely to house upscale formula retail or high-end restaurants that serve not the $10 grilled cheeses and $6 milk shakes featured at Boogie's Diner, but $40 branzino entrees and $18 glasses of wine. Such a shift would surely inhibit Aspen's much-valued mixing of social classes.

Clearly, local stakeholders differed in how they defined the "problem" posed by high-end retail. While some emphasized the threats to community character brought by retail homogeneity, others suggested that the problem, more broadly, was and is the increasingly high cost of living and doing business in Aspen. This point was made cleverly and succinctly by Charles Cunniffe, a local architect: "We don't have the [year-round] population density to support locally serving businesses. Especially with people being pushed down valley. There's no incentive to come up to do shopping. In order to have a local-town character, you have to have local characters living in the town." From this perspective, the problem is much larger than whether a $5,000 hand bag should be sold in a Prada store or in an independently owned boutique—it's a question of how housing prices and the physical location of the workforce impact community character. To protect the Aspen brand and resist supergentrification, residents advocated a variety of strategies to limit the residential displacement of locals and foster the mixing of social classes. These suggestions included local tax subsidies for affordable retail, funds for incubator spaces, and the expansion of affordable housing within city limits. Yet with the immediacy of the ordinance proposed by Murdock and his group, these suggestions were largely bracketed from the moratorium discussion of how to make Aspen more accessible to working locals.

In articulating how the issue of formula retail made its way to the city council, Mayor Steve Skadron addressed head-on the existential anxieties felt by many of Aspen's locals, anxieties brought about by growing class disparities and the spatial separation caused by supergentrification. During the lengthy November city council meeting in which Jerry Murdock introduced his ordinance, Mayor Skadron pushed the ordinance's sponsors and other community members to articulate why they believed formula retail to be a threat to the community. Late in the meeting, he summarized his own sentiments:

> So what is the core issue [motivating opposition to formula retail]? I'll tell you my answer. It's the angst that I am being rejected by my own town. I think there's a sense that the town has been co-opted by the wealthy, and that the soul of community is missing. And that affects the brand perception of Aspen, which speaks to local character, and I equate local character with our shared experience in the [downtown] core. That shared experience, which now seems to be lacking, cuts through the economic stratification that, in effect, is causing some of this angst. We want to celebrate Aspen's beautiful dichotomy [of affluent visitors and less-affluent locals], and I think some of that's been taken away.

Indeed, whether or not the influx of formula retail itself is the cause of the problem, Mayor Skadron concluded that its consequences are bad for locals' sense of belonging in their own community and for the mixing of social classes that is central to Aspen's identity. Even if its locals are more affluent and have more resources than those being displaced in places like New York, San Francisco, and London, they face the same existential threat and a similarly compromised sense of belonging within their own city.

In shifting the frame from concerns about local character to concerns about local economic opportunities, some residents identified high-end formula retail as the reason why locally serving businesses struggled and why aspiring local entrepreneurs had a hard time obtaining a foothold in the economy. High-end luxury retail and locally owned businesses were seen as unequal competitors in a zero-sum game—especially in a town with stringent land use codes and growth limitations. In describing why he initiated this ordinance, billionaire venture capitalist Jerry Murdock —who could surely afford to shop anywhere in town—spoke of the loss of a beloved local bike shop, Fletcher's. This loss, he said, prompted him to ask the question: What can we do to level the playing field so that locally owned businesses can continue to exist? "I was motivated," Murdock said at the March, 2017, city council meeting where the ordinance ultimately passed, "by talking to kids at the local high school here and CMC [Colorado Mountain College, a local community college]. Nobody who grows up in Aspen thinks they have a chance to have a business in the core." The perception that the playing field was not level was pervasive, with locals pointing to the deep pockets and complex business operations that sustain upscale chain retailers. In an email to city officials, a local named Cat wrote: "The greedy landlords are to blame as small locally owned stores cannot afford the high rents. Thus only the Gucci, Prada, Louis Vuitton, etc. chains can afford these rents. They probably lose funds regularly, but they can say they are in 'Aspen' on their shopping bags." From Murdock's perspective, changing the rules of the game would prevent high-end retail from "spreading like cancer through the whole town." Using less dramatic language, former mayor John Bennett lent his support to the initiative, speaking in favor of the economic opportunities for locals, stating that regulating chain stores "might help level the playing field, a little bit, for the young entrepreneur starting off, if he or she doesn't have to compete with Prada or Gucci." Throughout these deliberations, proponents of the measure invoked the need to "level the playing field," suggesting that something needed to be done to protect the economic interests of working locals from the unfair advantages posed by global economic forces.

As the bike shop owner whose store closing prompted Jerry Murdock to sponsor this ordinance, Fletcher Yaw rallied around the cause and provided support for the initiative. Speaking at a city council meeting, Fletcher echoed the notion that this regulation would level the playing field and provide protection for aspiring entrepreneurs:

> Being born and raised here, and having two children who go to school here, I want people who are local to have the ability to have entrepreneur dreams and to be able to move forward with them. I'm seeing that it's slowly getting harder and harder for people like myself to get into the game, because we're almost priced out from the beginning. So I think what this conversation can do is maybe limit some entities' ability to drive up prices and keep the locals [out]. . . . It seems like everything is getting more weighted towards the high end, and that it's weeding out . . . the funky old stores.

Throughout these deliberations, millennial-aged locals provided similar testimony, articulating a desire for themselves or their children to be able to open bike stores, ski shops, restaurants, and more.

Shifting the emphasis from the impact of high-end retail on locally *owned* businesses to the impact on locally *serving* businesses, a commentator named Anne posted on a community forum: "I cannot buy shoes, underwear, jeans or a top in Aspen these days unless it is used." She did not, however, support increased regulations on chain stores. Like others, she wished the city council would make greater efforts to incentivize locally serving businesses. Indeed, a number of residents commented that some chains that once provided affordable goods have now been replaced by independently owned retailers that sell luxury goods. While these independently owned retailers may contribute to local character, they do not make it any easier for local characters to shop in town. Phyllis Bronson, a political gad-about and local character in her own right, commented during a November 2016 city council meeting: "A lot of us who actually work miss the Banana Republic." While it's unclear who her reference to people who *actually* work was directed at, she suggested that opposition to chains may be the privilege of wealthy individuals who have the money to shop at the remaining independently owned boutiques.

Developer Jim DeFrancia characterized the retail landscape accordingly: "In Aspen we have groceries and we have Gucci and we have nothing in between. I can't get my watch repaired here, I can't buy work boots here, I can't get my car serviced here. If I need those basic services, it's a ninety-mile trip to Glenwood and back." Although the city council had been trying to address some of those needs during the moratorium through its effort to mandate "nook and cranny spaces," Murdock, his associates, and other community supporters called for a more aggressive approach. Accordingly, the group moved forward with their proposal to regulate formula retail, seeking the buy-in of the city council and the Community Development staff, the government body charged with implementing the AACP and its call to meet the "the [commercial] needs of year-round residents and visitors."

A SOLUTION IN SEARCH OF A PROBLEM: ASPEN'S LANDLORDS PUSH BACK

In a town as small and interconnected as Aspen, it did not take long for landlords and other commercial interests to catch wind of the percolating efforts to regulate formula retail. Indeed, awareness of Murdock's efforts was surely known among key economic players prior to the unveiling of the draft ordinance on November 29, because just two days later, on December 1, 2016, one local land use attorney submitted an open records request to the City on behalf of his clients, influential landlords Andy and Nikos Hecht (who developed the Aspen Core building, a.k.a., the Tangerine Monster). Their goal was to gain insight into who the key players involved in the issue were and the degree to which the council was involved. This would allow them to gauge the legal issues at hand and develop a response on behalf of local commercial interests. Over the next month, their concerns with the proposed ordinance grew, as evident in their own behind-the-scenes meetings and mounting legal threats. Jerry Murdock and his team agreed to host a stakeholders' roundtable at the Aspen Institute in January 2017, where the city council, local business owners, and landlords would have the opportunity to dialogue with Murdock and his supporters.

Building ownership in Aspen's commercial core is concentrated among a small group, with an estimated 90 percent of commercial real estate owned by five key players. While the age and quality of their buildings varied, placing regulations on the use of their properties could compromise the owners' material interests and, potentially, violate their property rights. For some local developers, especially Mark Hunt, their core business model relies on placing luxury chain stores in ground-floor spaces, where they pay premium rents and effectively subsidize the rents paid by tenants in the building's non-prime spaces. Throughout their public and private deliberations with the city, these building owners asserted that regulating formula retail would infringe on their property rights, constituting a mid-game rule change that was contrary to the business model that guided their purchase of these buildings. Moreover, they claimed that luxury retailers do, in fact, play a valuable role shaping Aspen's sense of place.

In an environment where prime retail spaces may rent for as much as $200 a square foot, local landlords pushed back against the proposed regulations, noting that even for them—the top marquee players—doing business in Aspen was already hard enough. Aspen's largest commercial landlord, Mark Hunt, said during the Aspen Institute roundtable that it was a myth that there is "a long list of chains that want to come to Aspen." Given the high rents and seasonal nature of the economy, even without the proposed regulations, he did not envision that more and more luxury retail would come to populate Aspen's commercial core. Indeed, several new buildings stood largely vacant, finding it difficult to fill retail space located just two blocks beyond the highly trafficked commercial core. At the same roundtable, landlord Charif Souki warned that more such vacancies would be likely if these regulations passed. Like other observers, he noted that restricting formula retail would do nothing to lower the price of commercial rents, whose prices are dictated by a combination of market forces and the steep mitigations and fees required for commercial development. Accordingly, he and others doubted the claim that regulating formula retail would do anything to level the playing field for aspiring local entrepreneurs. Moreover, he questioned the claim made by Jerry Murdock and his group of millennial supporters that there is a backlog of locals who are genuinely willing and able to get into commercial spaces, asserting that these aspiring business owners would rather "ski 100 days a year" than put the necessary energy into sustaining a business.

Although the value of the Aspen brand is surely sustained by the town's extensive land use regulations, and this value translates into some owners being able to rent some of their spaces for $200 a square foot, some landlords had had enough. Charif Souki, the principal player in Ajax Holdings, asserted that having a committee review applications submitted by chain stores constituted inappropriate government overreach and infringed on the authority of landlords to make decisions about their properties. "You're regulating something that you don't know how to regulate," he stated at the Aspen Institute roundtable; he found the notion of "substituting your [city government's] permission to someone else's" to be illogical, undermining the expertise of long-time business operators. At the same event, landlord Tony Mazza made a plea directly to the city council members in attendance: "Please Adam and Bert, don't add more regulation. The only thing that I can still do in my buildings that isn't regulated is breathe."

Frustrations with Aspen's perpetual move toward social engineering were also evident in the response of conservative blogger Elizabeth Milias, who likely had no material interests at stake in this issue but whose ideological sensibilities were deeply offended by Jerry Murdock and his group of "whiny millennials."[11] As Aspen's most vocal proponent of the free market, Milias spoke in a regular city council meeting, characterizing this effort as "a solution in search of a problem" and likening the review process for chain stores to a "retail death panel." Local government has no place, she asserted, in picking winners and losers within the retail landscape. Moreover, she characterized the millennial supporters of this cause as "straw men posing as the dispossessed," installed, she intimated, by Mayor Skadron and the city planning office in their relentless effort to wage class warfare in Aspen.

While supporters of the chain regulations pointed to the lack of opportunities for locals to shop and start a business as evidence of a problem, opposition to the proposed regulations stood firmly on the argument that Aspen's retail environment is not broken. "How is it broken," landlord Tony Mazza asked, "when sales taxes and real estate taxes are up, occupancy is up, the farmers market is packed every weekend, and everyone wants to come here? Some are saying this model [based on high-end formula retail] doesn't work; maybe it doesn't work philosophically for some of the people here, but factually it is clearly working." Setting aside questions of small-town character and economic opportunities for locals, Mazza offered local tax receipts as the key metric of interest, suggesting that the Aspen brand is as valuable as ever and that high-end retail plays a role in drawing people to town.

The sense that formula retail *is* working for some—including landlords and deep-pocketed visitors—inspired some stakeholders to threaten lawsuits against the City of Aspen. Discussions of possible lawsuits took place primarily outside of the public's eye, where according to Bill Stirling, former mayor and member of Murdock's coalition, attorneys for some local landlords were on Mr. Murdock's group "like a wet blanket." The most visible threat was issued by Brooke Peterson, partner with Charif Souki in Ajax Holdings, who characterized the effort to regulate formula retail as "discriminatory" and "inappropriate." In a letter to the city council dated February 13, 2017, Mr. Peterson wrote: "There is no basis to conclude that these stores fail to support our community," pointing toward their trickle-down benefits for employment, taxes, and charitable contributions. In closing his letter, he wrote: "If the City proceeds to enact this legislation, we will initiate legal action to prevent its enforcement." Some weeks earlier, at the Aspen Institute roundtable, Charif Souki stated that if this ordinance passed, he would make no further improvements to his buildings, essentially reducing their value and the kinds of tenants they might bring to Aspen. With incredibly deep pockets and the ability to subsidize his Aspen businesses through his other global investments, this threat was not idle.

DON'T KILL THE GOLDEN GOOSE: CITY COUNCIL DELIBERATES

So how did the City respond, both to the meticulously drafted ordinance submitted by Jerry Murdock and his millennial supporters and to the pushback against the proposal by local landlords? As the local legislative body, Aspen's city council stood as the arbiter in these deliberations. To promote community well-being, council members had to consider how

formula retail shapes both community character and the economic opportunities for locals and visitors, as articulated by the Aspen Area Community Plan. Questions about the legalities of the proposal also guided their
process. In adjudicating these concerns, council members brought forth
implicit and explicit considerations of social class, as they considered
the divergent economic interests of community stakeholders. They also
focused on the value of the Aspen brand, seen by many as an authentic
community with a funky small-town feel and luxury amenities, situated
next to a world-class mountain. This quality was repeatedly referred to as
Aspen's "golden goose"—the thing that lays the golden egg and provides
considerable benefit to the community. To keep the golden goose laying
the golden eggs, Mayor Skadron and his colleagues were forced to consider how Aspen's diverse constituencies are locked together in a complex,
interdependent relationship.

Perhaps more than any other voice within city government, council
member Adam Frisch continually drew attention back to the value that
chain stores and their shoppers provide to the community. Speaking in a
February, 2017, city council work session, he addressed the delicate balance of social class interests that he and his colleagues are tasked with
striking:

> One of the golden gooses this town has is that there are relatively few people
> here who spend a tremendous amount of money, and pay for what I call the
> community's bar bill of about $100 million a year.[12] Regardless of the locals'
> wealth, whether we're [local residents] 10 or 15 percent of that $100 million
> generation, we have to understand that the people who come here put a
> tremendous amount of money into this town, and they're happy to. But
> those same people who come here also want a community-based resort, and
> then want the funkiness and they want to go into the shops and restaurants.
> That's a golden goose we don't want to kill.

Explicit in this statement is the acknowledgment that luxury retail has
become a part of the local character, not something that is inimical to it,
and that visitors and part-year residents are drawn to this character—
especially when housed in mining-era buildings that hug the landscape
and provide exceptional views of the mountain. This twin combination of
luxury and authenticity draws the spending of these visitors, which then
trickles down and funds the city's budget. Whether from retail taxes, real

estate taxes, the one-time Real Estate Transfer Tax (RETT), or the mitigations paid by developers, it was conventional wisdom within the city council that non-locals and developers contribute disproportionately to the city budget and the programs that locals rely on to make Aspen their home.

In his role as mayor, Steve Skadron challenged supporters of the chain store regulations to consider the broader impacts of their proposal. While supporters generally viewed these regulations as something that would benefit less-affluent locals by creating opportunities for locally owned and locally -serving businesses, Skadron prompted them to consider the positive impacts of luxury chains. In a tense exchange with Gina Murdock, wife of Jerry Murdock, the mayor asked if she valued how Aspen's subsidized housing program, public transit system, childcare, and Open Space and Trails Program contribute to the town's character. Acknowledging that she did, Mayor Skadron tersely replied: "All of those things flow from sales taxes. Those sales taxes are generated by those very stores you're wanting to replace with other kinds of stores." Providing a thumbnail sketch of this contribution, during the Aspen Institute roundtable, property owner Mark Hunt estimated that luxury retail contributes taxes from $100 to $120 million in sales to the community, and that his portfolio of buildings alone "will probably contribute $12 to $15 million for affordable housing; [and] millions and millions for other things in permitting fees that go to things like busses and trails and hospitals and schools."

Mediating the concerns of building owners like Mark Hunt and aspiring business owners like those on Murdock's team, Mayor Skadron and other council members raised questions about how to measure the positive impacts of locally owned and locally serving stores versus those of luxury chains. Clearly, both have positive impacts on the community and on locals, including the higher wages and benefits paid by luxury chains, as compared to locally owned businesses. In balancing these interests, Mayor Skadron said: "We're kind of dealing with the beauty and terror of capitalism right before us," hinting at the economic returns that free market competition can bring, along with the damage it can do to local communities. In trying to adjudicate these competing interests, Mayor Skadron expressed a desire to work from facts about the economic impact of various types of retail on the community, rather than the "feel-good spirit" of the proposal.

The fact that Aspen has engaged in tremendous "social engineering" over the years was evident throughout these proceedings, as both the current and former mayors commented on the ways that progressive politics and heavy regulations have been institutionalized in Aspen, and how they have simultaneously drawn affluent people to the community and permitted middle-class locals to call it home. Perhaps no one expressed this tension as vividly as council member Adam Frisch, who asked versions of this question, throughout the year-long moratorium: "Aspen has been top-notch, community-focused resort town for sixty-plus years. I truly believe that. I also believe that Aspen has tinkered over the years with how to enter the economic spectrum that runs from Ayn Rand Free-Market Land to what happens in Kim Jong-Un's North Korea. And the question is whether Aspen has thrived *in spite of* or *because of* us doing more tinkering than most communities anywhere in the world. I would argue that it's a little bit of both, but mostly we are great because of it." This kind of social engineering, Frisch noted, is what creates Aspen's golden goose— the Aspen brand that brings in visitors and part-year residents, who lay the "golden egg" that pays for Aspen's extensive array of housing and amenities that are utilized by the local, voting, "subsidy class." In understanding their role in preserving Aspen's brand, while also sustaining the way of life experienced by the middle-class locals who elect them, city council members found themselves in a precarious position as they weighed the proposed regulations on chain stores.

PASSING AN "IMPERFECT ORDINANCE": HOW THE COUNCIL KEPT THE PEACE AND PRESERVED ITS OWN POLITICAL LEGITIMACY

On March 6, 2017, after nearly five months of consideration, the Aspen City Council unanimously passed Ordinance 6, which established a conditional-use review process for formula retailers who wish to locate in town.[13] That night, Mayor Steve Skadron called it an "imperfect ordinance"—perhaps because no solution could adequately satisfy the complex and interconnected needs of Aspen's diverse class constituencies. From the standpoint of Aspen's struggle over class interests, the passage of Ordinance 6 provided benefits to each stakeholder, but no clear-cut victory for any single party. Although it may take years to see how it plays out, it represents yet another method of institutionalizing the interests of different constituencies through the land use codes. It also revealed threats to the council's political legitimacy and how they manage threats from politically active residents, especially those who are motivated to defend locals' economic interests.

For landlords representing elite interests—including investors and visitors who enjoy Aspen's upscale shopping environment—the passage of Ordinance 6 was a material victory. For both legal and technical reasons, the final ordinance contained significant exemptions: formula retail continues to be permitted *by right* in all existing buildings and in the twenty-one development projects in the approvals' pipeline at the time of passage. Only stores wishing to locate in developments yet to be built (or those that undergo significant renovations) would be subject to the conditional review; as such, it may be ten to fifteen years before this legislation has a tangible effect. In the meantime, Aspen's premier landlords retain the right to lease to whomever they want and command the $200-per-square-foot rents found in Aspen's top-tier retail spaces.

The threat of a lawsuit certainly figured into this victory for elite interests. While Brooke Peterson was the only player to publicly threaten to sue, other local lawyers indicated to me that their clients had contacted them to explore their legal options if a chain store "ban" were passed. The legal basis of these threats emerged from the "dormant commerce clause," a clause in the U.S. Constitution that prohibits laws that provide economic protections for some business interests and limits the rights of others. The goal of protecting locals seemed to be part of this initiative, as evident in the public discourse that regulations on formula retail would "level the playing field" and create opportunities for aspiring local entrepreneurs. In an interview with Brian Cottrell (pseudonym), a local land use attorney, he described these claims as a "tell" of the sponsors' motivations and contextualized how these claims problematized supporters' push for the ordinance:

> They were trying to say, "Hey, let's create some protective spaces using governmental power to help our home-grown kids get a leg up in business versus someone who moves here from . . . Illinois [where Mark Hunt came from]." I think that was revelatory of what they were really trying to do, to

be protectionist. . . . It's when the government starts saying who you can and cannot rent to that judges and lawyers start getting uncomfortable. I mean, it wasn't more than sixty years ago that we overcame restrictive covenants in this country, where you can't rent your house to a Black person or you can't sell you a house to a Black person in that subdivision. We are all very nervous when the government's saying I can't rent my property, which I own outright, to a certain class of person.

In a one-on-one post mortem conversation, council member Frisch noted that these legal concerns led to the addition of significant exemptions in the final version of the ordinance, in part because the city wanted to reduce the threat of legal action and, in part, because Jerry Murdock himself remained sympathetic to the free-market interests of landlords.

A symbolic victory was won by Jerry Murdock's citizens' group and community stakeholders representing the economic and business interests of locals. Aspen's city council affirmed that their claims to uniqueness and character, and the ability to defend their town against global economic forces, are important and deserving of protection. While Mayor Skadron cautioned against voting based on the "feel-good" sentiments inspired by the proposed legislation, council member Frisch repeatedly affirmed the value of Aspen's "sense of place," and the hope that this legislation would preserve the community's character and hedge against the homogenizing forces of retail gentrification. In a city council meeting, citizens' group co-leader and former mayor John Bennett characterized this legislation as an "insurance policy," one that protects local interests and sends "a salvo across the bow," warning developers who may seek to locate high-end formula retail in Aspen in the future.

Even though considerable exemptions were built into the final version of the ordinance, Mr. Murdock and his team expressed a sense of victory. After the legislation unanimously passed via a roll-call vote, cheers erupted in the council chambers, and the ordinance's sponsors approached the bench with hugs and handshakes. Conversing with me four months later, Mr. Murdock said that he was "very happy" with the result, and that he expected that in a decade's time, supporters would be able to say, "Look at what [buildings] didn't get torn down [and turned into formula retail]; look at the diversity of businesses; look at the participation of locals in the local economy, with their own businesses." Still, many of those involved in this process questioned the ability of this ordinance to significantly reduce the cost of doing business in Aspen and create opportunities for locals, given the high rents, permitting fees, and mitigation rates. Therefore, it is highly debatable whether this ordinance will effectively institutionalize the economic interests of middle- and upper-middle-class locals, or provide legitimate fodder for those discourses that attest to Aspen's sense of egalitarianism.

Arguably, the Aspen City Council won a political victory. From the standpoint of the town's middle-class voters, passage of the ordinance showed political leadership within the context of a community that has felt the anxieties of supergentrification and the attendant feelings of lost authenticity. While efforts to regulate formula retail had been made by previous administrations, this was the first initiative that built sufficient community support, got the legal details right, and made good on the pledge to "pursue more aggressive measures to ensure the needs of the community are met, and to preserve our unique community character," as enumerated in the AACP.[14]

Yet, not all local stakeholders were satisfied by the scope of the ordinance. Outside of council chambers there were rumblings that a separate citizens' group would place a similar ordinance on the May, 2017, ballot, to be voted on by locals—the same locals who vote for council members and constitute "the subsidy class." At one city council meeting, Katrinho Devore, longtime local and mother of two Aspen millennials and aspiring entrepreneurs, warned the council: "There are people out there who want something much, much more extreme. If it ends up going to petition, to the people, you might get something more difficult to work with." Gina Murdock agreed: "If you table it [the ordinance]," she warned, "a citizens' group will put a stronger version on the table, which I think would pass." These were not idle threats. Indeed, Aspen had developed a reputation as a place where middle-class locals engage in citizen-sponsored initiatives to protect their town, as in 2015's Referendum 1 case, when they used their power to vote down a proposal by Mark Hunt to build what he packaged as an affordable lodge, but which many locals worried was granted too many variances (modifications to code) in the building plans, thereby compromising the trickle-down benefits to locals.

Due to the threat of a ballot initiative, and perhaps to preserve their own political legitimacy, the council passed this ordinance. Throughout, the council voiced a preference to shepherd this ordinance through the formal political process rather than a citizen-initiated ballot initiative, given that doing so allows a more careful, rigorous approach, requiring the presentation of facts, debate, and formal community input (none of which is required by a ballot initiative). On the night that the ordinance passed, prior to calling the matter to a vote, Mayor Skadron showed his hand: "My preference is to try to get something done at this council table. I think any form [of this ordinance] would pass, come the May election. I think a more stringent version would pass, as well. Just 'cause it can, doesn't mean it should. If council has the ability to pass something, I think using the referendum should be saved for when the majority of the community doesn't like something we do at this table." Fellow council members agreed, thereby preserving their political power within a town where middle- and upper-middle-class voters have considerable political leverage. That evening, the Aspen City Council unanimously passed the ordinance regulating formula retail, with significant exemptions for local property owners, which essentially kept the peace and kicked the can down the road for future struggles over community character and class interests in Aspen.

CONCLUSION

While many Aspen conversations about authenticity and character explicitly invoke notions of funkiness and messy vitality, they are often implicitly about economic opportunity and feelings of belonging. Long a community known for attracting bohemians and celebrities wishing to maintain a low-key lifestyle, in recent decades, Aspen has attracted flashier, more visible celebrities, global elites, and year-round and part-year residents, whose fortunes have been made possible through technological innovations and financialization in the economy. Yet the value of the Aspen brand hinges in part on maintaining its feel as a funky mountain town—a trait made possible by the presence of local ski bums, bohemians, and members of the creative class. Incidentally, these locals also elect a city council to defend their interests and pass legislation that preserves this sense of community; this legislation makes their lives possible, through initiatives like the affordable housing program. Aspen's class dynamics mean that the council must balance the interests of less-affluent locals and the interests of more-affluent parties, in this case developers and the formula retailers that are housed in their buildings, as well as visitors and residents who seek out these upscale experiences. In their formal deliberations over policy and place-making, council members are keenly aware that it is the taxes and mitigations paid by the more affluent that make possible the things that keep less-affluent locals in town and help generate the funky mountain lifestyle.

The struggle over formula retail in Aspen sheds light on local antipathy toward global economic forces and the anxieties that have emerged in response to upscaling and supergentrification. While the social class lines in this struggle are not always clear, they suggest tensions that pit less-affluent locals, who feel that their unique local culture and economic opportunities have been eroded, against more-affluent locals, developers, and visitors, who come to Aspen to partake in the funky mountain character but then change it by bringing upscale expectations and amenities with them. Situated as the official arbiters in this struggle are Aspen's city council and their associated committees and staff members. Attentive to legal, economic, and political concerns, they balance the interests of various community stakeholders, often arriving at imperfect solutions.

With respect to the concept of place-based class cultures, these deliberations illustrate an effort to preserve older, more valued ways of doing social class, and resistance to the threat of supergentrification. The discourses used show support for Aspen exceptionalism and Aspen egalitarianism, while also highlighting counternarratives about the ways that affluence—and even ostentation—constitutes a legitimate way of doing class in Aspen; this more consumerist way of doing class, is critical to the town's existence, contributing to its symbolic identity as well as its material existence. The resulting ordinance shows how discourse can motivate social action, but butts up against material realities as it gets institutionalized in local policy.

These findings highlight the limits and possibilities of local governments to mediate class tensions. Local political leaders have many tools at their disposal for shaping the communities they serve. In this instance, they can use land use codes to define what a community looks like aesthetically, what uses can take place where, and the mass and scale of these structures.

They can also regulate the costs of doing business, which in Aspen are intentionally high, given the community sentiment that development must "pay its own way." Yet local politicians are not all-powerful. The market operates according to its own logic, stimulated by broader economic forces. Local politicians can aspire to exploit, harness, or blunt larger market forces, knowing that economic growth is often essential to a community's long-term viability.[15] In this case, Aspen's city council balanced the competing needs and claims of a number of local stakeholders, ultimately passing an imperfect ordinance that promises to preserve local character but may have little impact on blunting the forces of global capital and making Aspen a more affordable place to do business.

7 Buscando el Sueño Americano

LATINOS IN THE VALLEY

Every morning at 4 a.m., the cycle begins. At a dark and barren parking lot adjacent to the Colorado River, a Roaring Fork Valley Transit Authority bus begins the journey up valley, picking up the largely Latino laborers who keep Aspen running. Two hours later, with the sun peeking out over Independence Pass, riders from Rifle, Silt, Newcastle, Glenwood Springs, Carbondale, and Basalt disembark and scatter to begin their days working at Aspen's hotels, restaurants, and construction sites. As the town comes to life, with local journalists and city employees picking up their morning coffee at Spring Street Café and tourists beginning their stroll on the pedestrian mall, there are few Latinos in sight. This changes around 3 p.m., as tired clusters of workers gather at the town's bus stops. With backpacks on their laps and grocery bags at their feet, they begin the journey home, quietly chatting with friends, scrolling on their phones, or staring off at the mountains in the distance as the sun begins to set over Glenwood Canyon.

Latinos are both essential to the functioning of Aspen, Colorado, and conspicuously absent from many of its settings. They comprise less than 10 percent of the town's residents, but more than 30 percent of its workforce. Down valley, in Carbondale, they represent 48 percent of all residents, and 63 percent of the district's students.[1] Latinos fuel the valley's workforce, populate local schools, and maintain an important presence through small business ownership, but because many of these residents are undocumented or foreign born, they have limited impact on electoral politics.[2] Through both their presence and their absence, Latinos play a powerful role in shaping life in Aspen and the Roaring Fork Valley, as well as in the place-making endeavors that are the focus of these analyses. According to political scientist Cynthia Horan, race—or in this case ethnicity—is always already an independent factor shaping urban regimes.[3] In addition to the intersecting dynamics of those who influence politics and those who influence the economy, a logic of race— both in terms of who is there and who is not—also shapes the conditions of possibility for what gets done and whose interests are served. In Aspen, Whiteness serves as an invisible resource in shaping the town's character and its redistributive policies. Yet Latinos are an integral part of the community, and their experiences must be examined to develop a fuller picture of local place-making efforts.

While Latinos make up about 18 percent of the U.S. population, they are not distributed evenly across the nation. They are concentrated in Texas, California, and New Mexico, and in larger cities like Miami and smaller cities such as Hartford, Connecticut. Yet they can also be found in the small meat-packing towns of the Midwest. Their experiences are diverse— contingent upon their history in the area, the specific nationalities or even regional groups represented (e.g., Puerto Rican versus Mexican, or even Zacateco versus Sonoran), and the local economy. Some are multigenerational residents of the United States and others are newcomers. For many Latinos, the journey to and life within the United States requires the continual crossing of borders. The first border, as described by Mike Davis and Alessandra Moctezuma, involves making it to the United States and crossing the official boundary of the state—whether by land, water, or air.[4] For both newcomers and long-term residents, daily life may also require them to contend with the second border—the formal immigration enforcement apparatus that patrols roadways and workplaces, most visibly represented by Immigration Customs Enforcement (ICE) and other law enforcement agencies. Having legal documentation does not automatically liberate one from having to cross this border, though documentation does help if someone gets caught in its grasp. The third border is the most invisible, and it too is one that both migrants and native-born Latinos must navigate. It is comprised of the legal, spatial, and cultural norms that structure daily interactions between migrants and residents. It involves local policies, such as seemingly race-neutral restrictions on how many people can occupy a housing unit, as well as norms that govern social interactions, such as attitudes toward speaking Spanish in school and in public. Together, these three interrelated but separate systems structure immigrants' experiences and exert control over their bodies and liveli-hoods. And just like the physical boundary that spans the United States' southern border, the second and third borders vary in terms of their height and permeability. Local laws and customs shape the formal and informal modalities by which newcomers navigate this third boundary, and the extent to which they are able to breach the wall. They shape, for example, the degree to which migrant workers can expect an ICE raid at their place of employment and the manner in which Latino worshippers are greeted at a local church. These analyses show that place-based class cultures, and the ways that social class and race intersect, also structure the permeability of this third border.

This chapter speaks to the experiences of Latinos living and working amid affluence, especially within the relatively well-educated and progres-sive climate of the "New West."[5] It explores the experiences of Latino resi-dents of the Roaring Fork Valley. Drawing on interviews with local Latino service workers, they address the same questions that animate my explo-ration of White, middle- and upper-middle-class residents: How do they navigate life in the Roaring Fork Valley, and how they do they make sense of class differences, given the area's stark economic inequalities? I show that while they experience some barriers and boundaries, their lives and livelihoods are positively influenced by the local place-based class culture.

LATINOS AMID AFFLUENCE

The scholarly work on Latinos living and working amid affluence does not present one singular picture of their experiences. Indeed, as told by scholars across fields, the experiences of Latino residents cannot be disentangled from the broader context in which they reside—its spatial qualities, its histories, its hierarchies, and its contradictions. The research shows a variety of experiences, ranging from overt efforts to exclude migrant populations to a nostalgic, if Pollyannaish, embrace. Even in Aspen, different vantage points and historical moments reveal different attitudes toward and experiences among Latino residents. Lisa S. Park and David N. Pellow's *The Slums of Aspen*, for example, portrays overt hostilities toward Latinos.[6] Centered on a 1999 local government resolution to restrict immigration to the United States, Park and Pellow examine a case of nativist environmentalism, where racist themes animate local efforts to protect the environment. Highlighting the work of Aspen city council member Terry Paulson and local letter writer and rabble-rouser Mike McGarry, they show how allegations that immigrants' large family sizes exact a toll on natural resources constitute a thinly veiled form of racism; they point out the irony that local efforts to protect the environment lack a critique of the excessive carbon footprint of elites, who fly to Aspen in their private jets and build mountain estates that contribute to environmental degradation. Justin Farrell finds this same hypocrisy within the environmental activism of uber elites of Wyoming's Teton County.[7]

Since publication of Park and Pellow's book, Aspenites have been sympathetic to allegations of environmental privilege and critiques that they have not tackled the outsized impacts of elites on the environment, but they have contested the portrayal of locals as racist or nativist. Long-time elected official Rachel Richards argued that passing this resolution was fundamentally about growth—a persistent theme of local politics—and that critics glossed over wording in the ordinance that called for "equitable wages and benefits for workers."[8] There is no doubt, however, that the ability of elites in Aspen and other New West destinations like Jackson Hole, Wyoming, to recreate in a rural paradise is built on the backs of the Latino workers. To that end, Park and Pellow also describe the exploitation faced by the area's largely Mexican and El Salvadoran service workers, who spend their days in jobs that do not pay a living wage or provide other employment benefits, and spend their nights in cramped and poorly maintained housing—the *slums of Aspen* referring to the dilapidated trailer parks that dot the flood plains of local rivers—where they perpetually face the threat of eviction. The specter of ICE (the federal Immigration, Customs, and Enforcement agency) raids haunts documented and undocumented workers alike, constraining their autonomy and desire to push for more workplace rights, even as they are aware that ICE agents rarely make incursions into Aspen— where a hands-off approach reflects an understanding that Latino workers' labor is essential for maintaining elites' enjoyment of the good life.

Where some affluent communities may call for explicit, legal limitations on Latino residents, others may engage in more subtle exclusionary tactics. As discussed in the introduction, affluent residents in Mount Kisco, New York, called for tighter regulations on the Latino day laborers who gather in the town square each morning to solicit work. While affluent residents marshalled race-neutral discourses, claiming that day laborers pose a general safety risk, geographers James S. and Nancy G. Duncan argued that racialized fears motivated locals' objections. They argued that in passing an ordinance that moved the day laborers' meetup spot to a less visible location, residents of this affluent community acted upon concerns that the "presence of racially marked outsiders offends the aesthetic homogeneity necessary to maintenance" of their exclusive community.[9] Such racial anxieties also typify Corey Dolgon's portrayal of how affluent residents of the Hamptons responded to the growth of the Latino service class. There, some local residents and business owners objected to the influx of cars and public gatherings that accompanied Latino's Sunday soccer games. Paraphrasing a Colombian soccer player, Dolgon writes that "the merchants in Montauk [were] happy to have Latinos working for them washing dishes in their kitchens and cleaning rooms in their hotels," but did not "like to see these same workers have fun in town."[10]

Subtle exclusionary tactics can also emerge through land use planning. Once again, Duncan and Duncan argue that "the invisible walls of zoning" may not be built with racialized intentions, but they certainly have racialized consequences.[11] Through downzoning—which often increases lot sizes and mandates single-family housing—and the creation of conservation easements, affluent residents of Bedford, New York, create scarcity in the built environment; this scarcity becomes a financial and a symbolic resource for affluent residents, and a barrier to lower-income residents. By offering justifications that center the importance of nature and history, affluent residents are able to depoliticize class and racial struggles, reducing them to "mere" aesthetic preferences rather than overt acts of exclusion and domination. Although Duncan and Duncan characterize these as class struggles, such struggles have become more pitched as the Latino population has grown. It is impossible, then, to separate the role of race and ethnicity from these struggles. As scholars Laura Pulido and Adolf Reed note, not seeing these struggles as racialized perpetuates normalization of Whiteness in studies of place and overlooks the tendency among scholars of urban regimes and community politics to approach their subjects as raceless.[12]

Whereas the exclusion of lower-income and Latino people has be realized through the tools of the land use code, additional forms of spatial exclusion also shape feelings of belonging. In communities experiencing a growth of Latino residents, "parallel worlds" can exist where Anglos and Latinos have limited interaction with one another.[13] As a critical mass of Latino residents lays down roots, stores, churches, restaurants, and childcare facilities emerge to take care of their needs. A fragmented geography—where Latinos and Anglos live in separate areas of town—can contribute to both the invisibility of Latinos and their feelings of marginality. Pulled into town by people they already know, newcomers make their homes in the largely Latino mobile home parks on the edge of town. As Lise Nelson and Nancy Hiemstra show, Latino residents of Lake County, Colorado, lacking cars but having access to a bus that ferries them from the trailer parks to the resorts in which they work, spend more time in Vail—an hour away—than in Leadville, the town on whose outskirts they live.[14] Moreover, temporal distinctions in the lives of Latinos and Anglo residents mean that Latino residents return to town later in the evenings, where they frequent grocery stores, pharmacies, and restaurants after most of the Anglo residents—who are considerably less likely to work in the adjacent county's resort economy—have gone home. These fragmented geographies, the authors write, "inhibit immigrants from developing a sense of belonging in the community and work against the breakdown of prejudicial assumptions held by some nonimmigrant residents, particularly those who continue to be the community's most economically and politically powerful actors."[15] Nelson and Hiemstra's work shows that space, itself, can sometimes be an actor shaping intergroup relations; that exclusion can be affected and maintained by seemingly race-neutral geographic patterns, whereby Whiteness becomes an invisible actor creating a sense of place and access to resources like affordable housing.

Finally, in contrast to those who actively or semi-actively exclude Latino newcomers some affluent residents seem to welcome them as friends and intimates. Drawing from fieldwork in Teton County, Wyoming—a community that closely resembles Aspen and the Roaring Fork Valley—Justin Farrell found members of the nation's elite wax nostalgic about their friendships with locals, including Latino service workers. Uber-wealthy individuals, he argues, use these relationships to reconcile discomforts they have with their wealth, and an attraction to cowboy boots, Wrangler jeans, and the authentic locals who wear them functions as way to reclaim a sense of normality in their lives.[16] Latino residents, however, were more circumspect about these relationships. Whereas many migrants describe the positive impact that wealthy folks have on the local community, and express a sense of gratitude for being able to work in a safe community with a strong economy, they did not see these relationships as friendships. Latino activists, specifically, asserted that wealthy residents were more concerned with protecting the wolves than with providing a fair wage to workers, and saw relationships with elites hierarchical and exploitative— more akin to patron and servant than reciprocal friendships.[17]

BUSCANDO EL SUEÑO AMERICANO (SEEKING THE AMERICAN DREAM)

Typical of Latinos living in the United States, those living in the Roaring Fork Valley comprise both multigenerational residents and new arrivals. Like many generations of immigrants, these recent arrivals come seeking safety and economic opportunity. In Colorado, an estimated 39 percent of the foreign-born population are naturalized, while 37 percent are undocumented.[18] Like their Anglo counterparts profiled in chapter 2, Latino migrants to the Roaring Fork Valley are seeking "the good life"; the difference, though, is that "the good life" for Latinos involves more fundamental needs. Stable jobs and the ability to earn a good income motivated many of their moves. Lorena, who migrated to the United States from El Salvador in her late twenties, described a deeply entrenched system of immobility in her home country. She came to the United States with a dream of improving herself: "My country doesn't have that possibility. You can study, but you don't have the possibility—it wasn't until recently that you have the opportunity to study and get a good job. Because those who would get the jobs are those whose family members already have those jobs. So, there is really no use in studying." With a father and a sister living in the area, Lorena set out for a place that promised to pay more than "five or seven dollars a day." Having lived in the United States for seventeen years, Lorena says that she loves living in Colorado, where she and her husband have been able to purchase a trailer home of their own. Alejandro, another El Salvadoran respondent, echoed this point: "There [in El Salvador], they earn $5 a day, while here you're making $20 per hour. That's a huge difference." Though he was sad to abandon his university studies, Alejandro recognized that earning a college degree in El Salvador may not pay off: "Even those who study, who are licensed and have a PhD, they make $10 a day, too." Carlos, who was brought to Colorado from El Salvador at age thirteen, made similar economic comparisons. Having graduated from high school in Basalt, and now working full-time at a café, he reflected: "Put it this way, here you're making $127 or $140 a day; there you're earning $7 a day. It's a big difference." These numbers may be a slight exaggeration, but about one-third of all Salvadorans live in poverty and median per capita incomes are less than $4,000 annually, or $333 per month.[19]

In addition to seeking economic opportunity, migrants to the Roaring Fork Valley described more basic, existential reasons for their moves. Having been in the United States for two months, Alejandro described the conditions that motivated him to leave his native El Salvador: "In my country, I was a student studying for a language degree, but it's just not safe. If you go out, the gangs can murder you, kidnap you, or whatever, so I decided to come here so that I wouldn't have to take that risk. . . . I made the decision to come because of, let's say, more than anything else, the circumstances of my country." With the highest murder rate in the world, El Salvador is a notoriously difficult place for young men, who face extraordinary gang violence. With a primary job as a housekeeper in a hotel and a secondary job in construction, Alejandro acknowledged that coming to the United States, and especially crossing the border, posed some risks. In El Salvador, however, there is a "fifty-fifty chance you'll get out of your house and return alive," he said. Understanding this threat, he set out to join his uncle in Colorado, knowing that "crossing the border was twenty-two days of risk," whereas "in El Salvador you're at risk practically your whole life."

Maria, a forty-seven-year-old El Salvadoreña, who works in a hotel in Snowmass and lives in Glenwood, was forced to confront the risks to her son. Her journey to the United States began thirteen years prior, when she left her six-year-old son to be raised by his grandmother, hoping to move back home eventually. Yet as her son approached the age when "gangs would try to lure him in," Maria's mother convinced her that he would be safer in Colorado. Resistance to the gang's efforts, she knew, could result in bribes, abductions, and even murder. Although some fellow migrants find the transition to rural Colorado difficult—coming primarily from cities, including San Salvador—she now sees her life in Colorado as permanent. "It's so peaceful here," she says; now that her son has lived with her in the United States for four years, "it never crosses my mind that he could be in danger. Not here, thank God."

Compared to the lifestyle migrants who came to Aspen and found that they had to downgrade their career aspirations, these migrants (along with a few 1.5- and 2nd-generation Latinos) experienced a more conventional version of the American Dream—at least with respect to their occupational opportunities. Carlos used vivid language when he was asked to describe local economic conditions. "Vivimos en una mina de oro," this twenty-year-old Salvadoran said, meaning "We live in a gold mine." Though he acknowledged the high cost of living, he said it all balances out. Even as he dreamed of attending culinary school, and came close to attending but lost out in the final round of scholarship qualifications due to his legal status, he remained positive. "There's always work, good work, pays well." Maria, who worked at a large, full-service hotel in Snowmass also heaped praise on the area's economic opportunities. Twice in her interview, she referred to Aspen as "our fountain of jobs."[20] "When I first moved here," she said, "I worked two jobs. Day and night. Day and night." She did not, however, say this with a sense of drudgery. Instead, she saw the ample access to service jobs—virtually all of which pay at least $14 per hour—as allowing her to "keep moving ahead," whereas in El Salvador, "even if you're going to clean, you have to have a degree." Sofia, a Brazilian who worked as a nanny for a few years in New York prior to moving to Colorado, also spoke positively about the economic opportunities. When she first came to the valley, she placed an ad in the local papers to provide house cleaning services. "That was the best job ever," she said, "I've never made so much money." She left that line of work and became an aesthetician, however, because so many migrants came to the valley offering similar services, which drove down the price she was able to command.

A more recent arrival to the United States, Alejandro was not so unequivocally positive about the valley's job opportunities. "Sometimes they tell you it's easy," he said, characterizing the messages he received prior to migrating. "But it's nothing like that; I mean, you have to work every day, get up early and earn enough to survive." Still adjusting to the local culture of work, he stated that "having to work all the time is no way to live. In my country," he continued, "you can get by and things are a little easier. But [considering the violence] in my country, no one would consider moving back." Achieving the American Dream, then, requires constant comparisons and evaluations. Whereas many Anglo lifestyle migrants felt that their economic fortunes in Aspen sometimes fell short of what they might achieve living in a larger city like Denver or Chicago, for these Latino economic and political migrants, the work opportunities in the Roaring Fork Valley looked pretty good when compared to a constant threat of violence or thwarted job prospects in their home country.

Even if the economic benefits of working in Aspen were the primary draw for these Latino residents, some of them, like the Anglo lifestyle migrants, appreciated some of the other unique benefits of working in this area. With a lighthearted vibe, Javier, a twenty-three-year old El Salvadoran, described his treacherous journey to the valley. Describing crossing the border from Mexico into the United States, he said, "We walked for almost five hours. Immigration almost caught me. Luckily, they didn't see me crawling through everything. The coyote [the person who is paid to guide migrants through the journey] told us to go to the ground and shut up, and I threw myself into a cactus. It hurt a lot. Then, after you cross the river, you have to run to where they are waiting to pick you up." Five years after arriving in Colorado, this hotel housekeeper and landscaper, still sends some of his earnings back home; still, he is able to enjoy other job perks for himself: "They [employers] give you a monthly bus ticket and a ski pass. Sometimes, they give you a ticket to—what, what do you call it, go down the river [take a rafting trip]. My benefits are also, less expenses. Here [at this hotel], they give you food [a daily meal]. When I worked in Aspen, they fed us lunch on Fridays." One of the few lifestyle migrants among the Latino residents, José moved to Colorado from Puerto Rico specifically for the opportunity to snowboard. "Getting a job here is the easiest thing ever," he said. "There are lots of jobs. I also feel like if I am not tied to a job, if I don't like it, I'll just leave and find another job. It's not like Puerto Rico or Miami where you have to be looking on the internet or on Indeed." Admittedly, José's experiences are shaped by the fact that having been born in Puerto Rico, he has legal documentation to work in the United States. Yet beyond just simply access to work, José pointed to the unique benefits of many jobs in this area. His jobs at a hotel and at the airport provided benefits that suit his lifestyle: "I came here because I wanted to move to a ski resort, and I found out that if you work for Ski Co., you get a ski pass. The benefits are excellent here, really. At the hotel, they provide me with a ski pass and food. I work at the airport, and I get flight benefits." The benefit of a ski pass can be considerable, since a season pass can sell for upwards of $2,000, and a daily lift ticket retails for $179. Many locals jockeyed to work as a gate agent as the airport, where working just a few shifts a month yields some level of flight benefits. Sounding just like his Anglo counterparts, José also praised local employers for allowing employees to take an hour to ski on their lunch breaks.

Although many Latino workers received similar employment benefits, they did not tout them as the reason for moving to this ski resort, nor did they describe making extensive use of benefits like ski passes and tickets for river rafting trips. To a large extent, their busy work schedules and long commutes did not allow for lunchtime ski runs, and as adults who had grown up in warm climates, skiing was not an activity with which they were familiar. For the second generation, however, or those who came to the United States in their youth—sometimes called the 1.5 generation—this was changing. Graduates of Basalt High School, like Javier, Ernesto, and Carlos, were all avid snowboarders, and maintained service jobs in the resort in part to gain access to ski passes. With higher levels of education, an economic cushion provided by their parents' hard work, and in some cases having legal documentation, these Latino residents were gravitating toward the Aspen Dream, and away from the immigrant dream of relentless hard work and betterment of one's family.

Exploitation of immigrant labor is endemic to the American Dream, and legal status and limited English-language skills can limit advancement at work and create the conditions for exploitation. These Latino residents provided a mixed portrait of the degree to which they experienced exploitation or other limitations at work. Alejandro, for example, expressed deep faith in the power of one's work ethic, stating: "You have the opportunity to stand out; you just have to take advantage of them." Hard work and being a good person, he believed, would trump any efforts to limit his advancement. Like many respondents, Blanca stated that opportunities at work grew in relation to one's ability to speak English. Born in the United States, but raised speaking Spanish at home, she said that her employers "take good care" of her, and that after working at the hotel for five years, she ascended to a supervisory position. Native-Spanish speakers whose "English is not perfect," she said, had also been promoted to managers of housekeeping and chief of engineering.

Enrique, a fifty-five-year old employee at a fast-paced lunch restaurant, was one of the few respondents to argue that Hispanics face barriers at work—simply because they are Hispanic. "Even though I've lived here for so long," he said, "I've had experiences, experiences in my area of expertise, where people stereotype me. They act like because, I'm Hispanic, I'm from Mexico, I can't progress. In whatever position I'm at, I won't be able to do better." Having completed a college degree in Mexico, he maintained an easy banter with the Anglos with whom he worked. Yet, despite this social ease, he held a deeper pain, "I've felt invisible," he said, having to "keep greetings in [his] mouth," after numerous experiences where Anglos gave him the cold shoulder. His critique of workplace opportunities in Aspen, however, gained nuance by drawing on broader national and phenotypic distinctions: "Generally, if you look Hispanic, they will not give you a job waitressing or bartending. They will offer you a job cleaning tables. Even if you speak English, they want to know, 'Do you know anything about wines?' If your skin is darker, if you're a person of color [de ese grupo étnico] and have black hair, it [getting a customer-facing job as a tipped employee] will be difficult." He and other respondents saw a hierarchy operating in the valley—not just between Anglos and Latinos, but among Latinos: "Latinos are most vulnerable, starting from Mexico and Central America. Colombians, Venezuelans, Peruvians, Argentinians, Brazilians, they are placed on a higher level [un nivel más alto]. An Argentinian can be better treated for his skin color and light eyes than a Mexican or Central American." An Argentinian with a J1 visa (a short-term visa for cultural and educational exchange) and lighter phenotype may, he said, get a job as a waiter, even if they do not speak perfect English, ahead of a Mexican immigrant who has worked in the same restaurant as a busser.

For some Latino workers in the valley, professional limitations and experiences at work are more subtly influenced by race and ethnicity. Cecelia, who worked as a preschool teacher in Aspen, described local parents as warm and welcoming. "They appreciate me," she said, "because I teach their kids Spanish and they see that I am also a mother who fights for their kids [the kids she teaches] and wants to better myself." She has, however, had experiences with Anglo coworkers, whom she described as having "a sense of professional jealousy" stemming from her desire to learn more and improve herself. In fact, she was working toward a master's degree and had a certification in early-childhood learning—which other preschool teachers lacked. Despite her strong qualifications, she described a "sad" experience at work where she was denied the opportunity to participate in a breakfast hosted by the parent-teacher association. She wrote an email to her principal and superintendent, expressing a sense of hurt and exclusion, and found support from her principal. She said that her coworkers, however, were "bothered" by the fact that she stood up for herself, demanding that "we [preschool teachers] deserve respect." This type of interaction constitutes the third border that migrants may confront on a daily basis, where they navigate social norms that shape assumptions about who they are and where they belong.

For some respondents, the opportunity to work, to advance at work, and to receive other work-place benefits was shaped by legal status; it constituted a second border to be navigated. In some cases, individuals without legal documentation were paid under the table or found work through employment agencies. With their labor being contracted out, these workers likely did not have access to perks like ski passes, let alone health insurance; nor did they receive the full value of their hourly wage, but gave up a portion to the employment agency. Though she had been born in the United States, Perla continually worried about her mother's ability to maintain stable employment. Even though "ella no tiene sus papeles" (she does not have papers), Perla's mother was able to find cleaning jobs "through the grace of God." Perla's mother had been arrested, but had never been deported; Perla feared for her, even when she went to county offices simply to pay for her car tags. Her friends, too, increasingly found themselves in precarious positions under the Trump administration, unsure of whether their ability to work would be extended under the DACA program (Deferred Access to Childhood Arrivals, a program that provides some benefits to undocumented immigrants who were brought to the United States as children). Access to Medicaid, too, had become more precarious, as new software programs began requiring a higher level of documentation. She canceled her mother's Medicaid and advised her sister not to apply. "Now," she said, they "want to know your legal status, if you're a citizen and whatnot. The application says it's confidential, but one never knows." At her job, where she helps new hotel employees navigate the Medicaid application process, she has found that "many families don't want to apply because of fear, and that's affecting us big time." Because she was born in the United States, Perla has not had to navigate this second border herself. Instead, she "love[s] [her] employer because she's given me so many raises in just three years . . . and she doesn't want me to leave." That said, fear for others was part of her day-to-day experience. Together, these narratives depict diverse work experiences in the Roaring Fork Valley. Phenotype, national origin, duration in the United States, one's own legal status, and proximity to others without legal status, all shape the degree to which Latino residents have been able tap into the "gold mine" of jobs in Aspen.

FINDING HOUSING: THE RACIALIZATION
OF THE ASPEN DREAM

In the minds of many, achieving the American Dream is one part social mobility through employment and one part independence and autonomy through housing, often via home ownership. As noted throughout, due to the prohibitively expensive housing market, achieving the latter is often elusive for middle-class residents of the Roaring Fork Valley. After first moving to town and living with family or friends, and then moving onto a shared apartment, residents of the area seem to spend the greater part of their thirties hoping to win a unit in the affordable housing "lottery" program, which would put them in close proximity to their jobs, recreation, and the cultural amenities that make Aspen such a draw. This "typical pattern" is, however, racialized. Similar to White lifestyle migrants, Latino migrants arrived in the valley though family connections and immediately moved in with them; subsequently, their paths diverged. Due the complex interplay of push and pull factors, the end result is a dramatically segregated landscape—certainly not unusual in the United States—which renders Aspen a markedly White space and creates Latino enclaves farther down valley.

Housing choices are always shaped by cultural norms and preferences, and this is no less so among residents of the Roaring Fork Valley. These cultural norms and preferences include notions of who comprises an ideal household, what kind of structure is desirable or acceptable, and how housing fits into life course goals. These, and other factors, exert a "pull" on housing choices, resulting in Latinos living down valley from their jobs in Aspen. Trailers were the modal home type for Latino residents. Whereas Anglo lifestyle migrants generally saw trailers as a transitional housing option, Latinos found them to be both an initial landing place and a desirable permanent option. Trailer homes allowed multigenerational families to remain together and provided a comfortable place to unite or reunite— especially after an arduous border crossing. Contrary to the image of trailer homes packed with single, unattached male migrants portrayed in Park and Pellow's work *The Slums of Aspen*, these respondents described trailer parks as clean and friendly places where they were able to own their own home.[21]

While Blanca had recently obtained affordable housing through her hotel job in Snowmass, her narrative makes clear why the town of Basalt, where she grew up and attended high school, maintains a pull on many Latinos. "In Basalt," she said, "you feel like you're at home. Everyone knows each other, whereas here [in Snowmass], it's more tourism. Here, you meet a ton of different people, but once the peak season is over, it's so quiet. Barely anyone stays in town, and the stores close down. But in Basalt, we all know each other; it's like family." Indeed, both Basalt and Carbondale are home to Catholic churches that offer Spanish programming throughout the week. There are more stores—bakeries, butcher shops, and food markets—that cater to Hispanic customers. Sixty percent of the students at the Basalt and Carbondale schools are Hispanic, so bilingual education programs are well established. Moreover, unlike Aspen and Snowmass, fewer local residents leave during the off-season, making the year-round population more stable. With higher concentrations of Latinos, Maria provided a very simple explanation for the valley's segregation: "I prefer to live where I know my neighbors." Finally, another factor that pulled Latinos farther down valley is the climate. Towns like Carbondale, Glenwood, and New Castle are at lower elevations, so they are more temperate throughout the year and accumulate fewer inches of snow. With wide-open vistas, these communities may feel more familiar than the rugged mountains of Aspen, depending on where in Mexico the migrants grew up. Together, these factors mean that towns like Carbondale and Glenwood Springs simply feel more like home.

Differences in life course patterns also play a role in residential segregation. For many Anglo lifestyle migrants, the move to Aspen did not start out as permanent. In many cases, Aspen was a post-college gig that turned into a more durable career, or a stop on the way farther west, that gradually became home. For these reasons, many White residents did not feel the pressure to find stable housing. Still dating into their thirties or on an extended journey to "find themselves," they often ended up sharing rooms and occupying suboptimal housing for years on end. Although Latino migrants sometimes yearned to return home, hoping that the violence would subside and they could reunite with their families, the safety and economic opportunity they experienced in the Roaring Fork Valley quickly solidified their moves. In addition, many of them married earlier and became parents earlier, altering their housing needs. Latino residents did not have the luxury of waiting to win the affordable housing lottery, nor were they willing to make sacrifices simply to live in close proximity to social amenities—like Kathryn Henderson, who was willing to pay more to live in Aspen because she could stay out late, do karaoke, and not worry about having to catch the bus. To live there, Cecelia said, "there are wait lists for the government housing. You spend years waiting, and I am no position to be waiting in line for years." Instead, Latinos relied on *otros moditos*—other methods, like the newspaper and internet—to find immediate housing, which often landed them down valley. About her decision, this teacher from Mexico said, "I love Basalt. It's beautiful, very similar to Aspen . . . but cheaper." With two rivers flowing through it and high canyon cliffs rimming the community, she was not wrong.

Push factors also structured Latinos' housing choices and produced a racialized geography. Rather than being pulled toward a friendly community of co-ethnics, Javier described feeling pushed out of Aspen. One of the few respondents to describe a sense of discomfort while occupying public spaces in Aspen, this young Salvadoran migrant said: "I lived in Aspen for two weeks when I first came here. It was very different. You're surrounded by Americans and I didn't speak English, and I let that bring me down. . . . Sometimes I would go to the park and guys would try to talk to me, but because I couldn't speak the language, they would look down on me. It made me feel like an outcast." Because of these feelings, Javier "took the initiative to move to El Jebel, where there are a lot more Hispanics." He now feels pulled toward his down valley community. "This is my thing," he said, "I've made friends here, among Latinos, and now I feel comfortable."

Perhaps the biggest push out of Aspen was the sense that housing there was simply too expensive. Most of these migrants never looked for housing there, and did not consider doing so, given the fact that a two-bedroom apartment in Aspen might rent for $3,600, whereas down valley in Basalt or Glenwood Springs, a similar unit may rent for $2,600 or $2,100, respectively. Using a class discourse more than a race discourse, respondents said, quite simply, that Aspen "is for the rich." Paola, a thirty-something café employee said that it had never even occurred to her to look for housing in Aspen because she knew that the prices were beyond her means ("porque siempre supe que era caro"). Adding texture to this economic explanation, Sofia, a Brazilian woman who married an Anglo Aspen native, noted that even if she and her husband could find housing in Aspen, childcare for their son would be prohibitively expensive.

While it is true that very few affordable apartments exist within Aspen's free market, these migrants also did not seek housing through the affordable housing program. Some respondents were placed in employee housing because they held jobs in hotels or the school system, but virtually none of them sought out the Aspen Pitkin County Housing Authority—which maintained nearly fifteen hundred units for rent and another fifteen hundred for purchase. Indeed, many respondents seemed unfamiliar with the program. When asked what they knew about APCHA (¿Que sabes sobre APCHA, el programa de viviendas asequibles?), many respondents, like Carlos, replied: "I don't know anything." In some cases, respondents did not know the program by its formal name. In other cases, they believed that the program was composed only of units for purchase, placing it beyond their reach. Respondents also disliked the fact that units do not appreciate in value, so that owners can only sell their unit back at a price consistent with cost of living increases. For individuals who hoped to work hard and purchase property that would allow them to generate wealth, APCHA did not provide access to the version of the American Dream they sought.

Yet perhaps the biggest push factor that structured migrants' housing choices was the fact that living in Aspen would require them to continually navigate the second and third borders of life in the United States. Qualifying for a unit within the affordable housing program requires extensive documentation—documentation that many Latinos might not have. In addition to requiring copies of state and federal tax returns, the process also requires a state or federal identification card, and a signature attesting to lawful residency in the United States. For those wanting to enter the lottery to purchase a home, the mortgage process posed similar barriers. With an estimated 37 percent of Colorado migrants not having legal status, applying for APCHA housing would be virtually impossible; even for those who have a social security number, if they work under the table or off the books—which some employers prefer—they would not be able to produce a W2. When asked if she had ever applied for the affordable housing program, Maria, a hotel employee from El Salvador, dismissed the question, stating: "Sometimes one doesn't search for these programs because you have to have a social security number, or something else you just don't have." She and her husband have created their own version of the American Dream, buying a trailer home in Glenwood Springs, where they pay a private party without incurring interest, and look forward to the day when the home will eventually be theirs. Yet even in situations like these, Latino residents remained vulnerable, with several high-profile cases where residents were evicted from trailer parks that were threatened by flood waters or when the land was claimed for other uses through immanent domain.[22]

These housing dynamics highlight the complex intersection of race and social class in Aspen and the Roaring Fork Valley. While cultural preferences and differences in life course trajectories partially explain the area's segregated housing patterns, the second and third borders play additional roles in erecting boundaries. With respect to the second border, legal regulations foreclose the possibility of many migrants applying for affordable housing. The third border—made up of cultural norms and expectations—also segregates, as migrants like Javier and Guadalupe feel alternately pushed out of and pulled toward communities that feel more like home. Many Latino employees are either unable to qualify or afraid of the process. Even if they have proper documentation, another member of their household may not, and many would prefer not to expose themselves to deportation or other legal sanctions. With respect to *place-based class cultures*, these findings show that the same mechanism that was designed to institutionalize the class interests of working people within Aspen and Pitkin County simultaneously produces a racialized landscape. Alas, though many members of the community benefit from the labor of Latinos, Latinos "don't benefit from" these programs, Cecelia said, because "they don't have that legal status."

ASPEN EXCEPTIONALISM AND EGALITARIANISM, REVISITED

If places do indeed have class cultures, these cultures should be widely recognized among those who live, work, and visit these locales. While members of the community may differ on the degree to which claims about social class are more myth than reality, part of what makes a culture a culture is that it is widely shared, forming a common touchstone. These beliefs constitute what Pierre Bourdieu called the *doxa*—roughly meaning common sense—which then informs social action.[23] In his portrayal of Teton County, Wyoming, Justin Farrell found that on a relatively superficial level, uber-wealthy residents and working folks—Anglos and

Latinos, alike—agree on the nature of cross-class relations, but that Latino activists, who had spent time struggling on behalf of their community, were more cynical of elites' claims to friendship. It is somewhat surprising, then, that Latino residents of the Roaring Fork Valley provided class narratives that were remarkably similar to those offered by middle- and upper-middle-class Anglos.

First, Latino residents shared the belief that uber-wealthy people provide economic opportunity to the area. Like Clint Jones, the White private chef who said, "I like the 1percent; the 1 percent allows me the life that I like to live," these Latino residents of different classes see themselves as having economic fates that are intertwined with the wealthy. When asked how he saw wealthy people influencing life in the valley, Carlos, a twenty-year-old married barista, replied: "They pay more taxes, which means that they help us more—like with safety and all of that. The money they lose is money that goes to us." Javier extended this belief, offering a more specific observation. Like Clint Jones and even my own father, whose art careers were supported by clients who became friends after doing manual labor in their homes, Javier described an example where employment relations had indeed taken on complexity. "Once you gain their trust," he said, "they may ask you to watch their house, because they trust you to take care of it as they want. My uncle and his wife know a wealthy man who owns a house here but lives in Texas. They take care of the home when they [wealthy homeowners] come here on vacation. If you build a relationship with the wealthy, you know how to communicate with them, and they like you, you may end up with a decent job." While this relationship is more purely transactional than the experiences of my father and Clint Jones, it is worth noting that the word "trust" appears several times in Javier's response, suggesting a degree of familiarity that is authentically felt *and* becomes a resource.

For other respondents, the benefits provided by the wealthy were both individual and communal. In his analysis of environmental issues in Teton County, Wyoming, Justin Farrell critiqued the role of wealthy Anglos for their philanthropic support of environmental issues. He viewed it as an expression of their economic guilt, and some Latino activists he spoke to pointed out that the generosity of wealthy community members did not extend to the workers in their midst. Although Aspen and Teton County have similar economic profiles and wealthy residents who are similarly committed to the environment, these respondents described the support they had received from philanthropic organizations. "The rich naturally help us and are the ones who contribute the most," Lorena noted; they "are the ones who provide scholarships, the ones who give to the schools. I can't say they are rich and smug." Cecelia provided a more personal example. "I've never seen a community this small create so many nonprofits, which help Latinos most." She described speaking at a museum-like home on Red Mountain at an event to raise money for Ingles en Accion, an organization she has been involved in for more than a decade. This program, she said, had "created some nice friendships" between Hispanics and the largely White, middle-class Aspenites who help teach English. More generally, she said, "programs like these help our community—enroll with a doctor, find cheaper clinics, support them, and report employment issues. But more than anything, they know the laws of this country." She and her church had developed an outreach program with the local police, and brought officers into the church to build a sense of community. Cecelia described church members as applauding when the officer told them, "We are not immigration. We fight for your well-being and the safety of people." While it would be easy to view this outreach event as a veiled surveillance effort, these respondents instead described law enforcement as "friendly and helpful" (Monica). They did so, moreover, in interviews conducted in Spanish, with native-Spanish interviewers.[24]

In some cases, respondents recognized that positive police-community relations were a product of class dynamics. Even if Latinos are not necessarily welcome in the community, Paola said, they are "needed." "Without immigrants," she said, "Aspen is nothing." Whether in the hotel industry or the service industry, "Aspen without Latinos does not function." This fundamental understanding led to a relatively hands-off approach by local law enforcement and by federal agencies, as well. Sebastian discovered this relatively early on in his work at a hotel. One day, his sister-in-law called him from Glenwood Springs, telling him of a rumor that ICE was in the valley. His coworkers in Aspen shrugged this off. "I asked some other cooks," he said, "and they said they've never seen immigration in Aspen in the twenty to twenty-five years they had worked there." Carolina, a forty-something housekeeper, asked a rhetorical question and provided

220   BUSCANDO EL SUEÑO AMERICANO

her own answer: "Why don't they [ICE] come here when it's high season and all the people are working illegally? It's tactical, they need people." Even if ICE raids almost never happened in the area, employment audits had resulted in undocumented workers being let go; for this reason, many Latino residents still carried a bit of fear with them on a daily basis.

Aspen exceptionalism also infused Latinos' views on more affluent community members. Aspen exceptionalism is partially captured by the notion of *mind, body, and spirit*, where intellectualism and curiosity are integral to the local culture. Numerous respondents commented that Anglos are especially interested in learning and practicing Spanish, and becoming more familiar with Latin culture. Monica, a twenty-eight-year old Salvadoran said, "I've had the opportunity to work in the houses of millionaires and when Latinos talk about things, they are interested." Asked to give an example, she recounted sharing stories of holiday traditions with one of the families for whom she worked. She found it amusing that families are dressed in pajamas Christmas and New Year's Eve (sometimes getting a match set for their dog), in contrast to Latinos, who dress up. From these experiences, she said, she learned that millionaires are . . . "super humildes y les encanta nuestra cultura)" (super humble and love our culture). For Paola, this appreciation of Latin culture was evident in the community more broadly. She said that there is a lot of promotion of Latino events and efforts to include Latinos in community events. She pointed specifically to the monthly outreach event for Latinos at the Aspen Art Museum, as well as a recent event where a mariachi band played and tacos were served. Each year, the Independence Day parade features a traditional Mexican folkloric dance troupe, which often wins the audience choice award (see figure 14). Interethnic relations can be a tricky thing to balance, and it is possible that these events were simply ways for Anglos to consume Latin culture; yet it is also possible that when Anglos describe a local culture that is worldly and embraces classical music, the arts, and lectures on physics and global security threats, that their cultural curiosities apply to Latin culture as well.

Even notions of *Aspen egalitarianism* permeated Latino's class narratives. Like the Anglos who said that it was sometimes difficult to discern someone's social class background because of the common embrace of an outdoorsy aesthetic, José a Puerto Rican who came to Aspen in part to

Figure 14. An award-winning dance ensemble participates in the Independence Day Parade. Photo by Jenny Stuber.

snowboard, said: "You'll see a person in flip-flops and shorts, and perhaps they're the wealthiest person you can possibly imagine." Repeating Monica's characterization, he described wealthy people in Aspen as "very humble," so humble that "sometimes they look like poor people." Having lived in Miami, he was especially attuned to how class cultures differ across locales. "In Miami," he said, "they have the urge to be flashy. They drive expensive cars; they wear expensive watches. Even the people who don't have a lot feel the need to show off. They might have a small studio apartment, but they drive a BMW." Like many Anglos who had lived in Aspen for years, he described the local class culture as unpretentious: "that vibe just doesn't exist; you don't feel left out if you don't have an expensive car." Other respondents agreed: class distinctions are more muted in Aspen. Only when a person begins to talk and to display their education and cultural views, Maria told our team, "can you really tell if they are wealthy."

"But not here . . ." was a surprising refrain among Latino residents in the Roaring Fork Valley. Police were unfriendly in North Carolina where her sister lived, Maria claimed, but not in Aspen. It is mainly "other states" that are dangerous, Javier asserted, where if you are walking home after work at 2 a.m., "you get robbed, or worse." Reflecting on her life in the United States, Lorena remarked that "a veces hay racismo; aquí en Colorado, no, pero en California, si lo experimenté." That is, there is racism at times in the United States, and she has experienced it in California, but not in Colorado. Paola offered nuance to this claim. When asked to provide an example of racism, she described an incident at the Walmart Supercenter in Glenwood Springs, where residents "with fewer resources look at you when you speak Spanish." She described another incident in which a man wearing a "Make American Great Again" hat and shirt seemed to be following Latino customers around the store. Like other respondents, when asked about racism in the community, Paola was quick to add, "Aquí in Aspen, no" (Not here in Aspen). The education level in Aspen, several respondents claimed, made people there more curious and accepting of Latinos and, in turn, made their own lives more comfortable. This attention to spatial distinctions—to spatialized differences in attitudes toward Spanish speakers and the likelihood of having troubles with law enforcement—illustrates the dangers of making generalizations about "Aspen" or "Teton County" writ large, and the need to attend to variations within these regions.

Extending the idea that Colorado and the Aspen area are *different*, when asked about class relations in the valley, Alejandro said that "classes aren't divided here like they are elsewhere." With just a few short months in the United States, Alejandro had already absorbed some of the class narratives that pervaded the area. Although policies used by the affordable housing program clearly limited participation by undocumented workers, Sofia praised it as a policy that has promoted working-class inclusion in town. Seated at her station in the salon where she worked, Sofia reflected on the housing program: "One very good thing about Aspen is that they made that so it's not just for the millionaires and billionaires. So the working class can actually live in town, as well, so there is not that [class] discrimination." Finally, a sense of class egalitarianism was also reflected in the words of Lorena, a forty-something manager at a lunch restaurant.

Like Jose, who pointed to the casual, flip-flop-wearing millionaire (or billionaire) as indicative of Aspen's unpretentious class culture, Lorena noted: "The rich are the ones who wear the simplest shirt, and we are the ones trying to look like a different person." Ultimately, "There is no difference, here, like there is in many other countries. Here, the rich sit at the same table as everyone else." Indeed, even for Latino immigrants to the area—some with long tenure and other recent arrivals; some from Brazil and others from El Salvador and Mexico; some working behind the scenes and others with intimate contact—Aspen is different.

CONCLUSION

"Aspen is my sweet home" (*dulce hogar*), said Maria, a hotel worker from El Salvador. She, like many Latino migrants, spoke about her life in the Roaring Fork Valley with a sense of affection and gratitude. They described the area as safe and marveled at the fact that they were able to leave their houses and cars unlocked, and could walk around at night without fear. Indeed, these respondents seemed more afraid of local wildlife than they were of local law enforcement. Admittedly, possible encounters with ICE—which are more common down valley in Glenwood than in Aspen—struck legitimate fear into these respondents. It is a place, José said, that is "super pacifica, de temple de paz" (filled with peace-minded people); Perla described them as "muy buena onda aquí" (very chill). The fact that there is "no crime here, compared to Puerto Rico where they are killing people in the daytime and everything . . . it gives you mental and psychological peace." And when it doesn't, some of these migrants use the same strategies used by Anglo lifestyle migrants: they turn to nature. "If I feel stressed," Lorena recounted, "I go hiking. There, I cry, I talk to myself, I put my headphones on and I sing. These mountains hold a lot of secrets." She would not consider moving elsewhere, she said, because in the Roaring Fork Valley, "me siento libre" (I feel free).

These accounts sound almost too good to be true, and don't match the accounts of Lisa Sun-Hee Park and David Pellow, who interviewed migrants from the same area, or those of Justin Farrell, who interviewed Latinos in the very similar community of Teton County, Wyoming. The reasons for these different findings are complex, and no single answer can suffice. One reason for these differences is that respondents adhered to the cultural norm of politeness; one where speaking too critically about the United States to a stranger might be considered poor taste. In addition, Latino residents may have been careful not to disclose details or experiences that would risk their residency in the United States or livelihood with current employers. Although several respondents did spontaneously disclose that they had, themselves, crossed the border or that relatives were living in the United States without documentation, interviewers were explicitly instructed not to probe too deeply into respondents' documentation status—not wanting to compromise themselves, the project, or respondents—should they uncover illegal activity. Unfortunately, our research team was not able to have the detailed, personal conversations about deportations and other such fears that Leah Schmalzbauer presents in her eloquent study, *The Last Best Place: Gender, Family and Migration in the New West*.[25] Perhaps, then, the scope of these residents' fears or the trials they have dealt with were not revealed. Further, the fact that these interviews were conducted in Spanish, with native speakers, allowed for the creation of rapport; yet the fact that the interviewers were young college students, may have led some respondents—especially older respondents—to provide more sanitized accounts of their experiences, wanting to protect them from the reality of their experiences.

It is also possible that some of these respondents are either unaware or nonreflexive with regard to the ways in which they experience exploitation or oppression. They may have uncritically absorbed the ideology of the American Dream and the virtues of hard work, or notions of Aspen egalitarianism, inhibiting their ability to see more fully the conditions of their existence. In *Billionaire's Wilderness*, Justin Farrell characterizes Latino migrants as relying on "talking scripts"—suggesting that they are inclined to offer pre-reflexive accounts of their experiences, rather than deep, thoughtful narratives. Although humans do differ from one to the next in terms of how introspective or reflexive they are, I work from the assumption that qualitative research yields meaningful accounts and that interviewees are expert narrators of their lives. Sometimes these narratives can contain self-delusion, but a complete reading of an account—the entirety of an interview, especially alongside other such interviews—typically provides texture and nuance to the human experience, rather than "true" insights or delusions. In that regard, these interviews collectively contain a mix of positive and negative. While respondents described the area as providing incredible economic opportunity, they also commented that the cost of living is quite expensive; they also lamented that English is often needed to move up at work, but that work schedules do not allow time for learning English. They discussed concerns about deportation, alongside claims that local police are nice and cooperative. They argued that there was not much racism in Aspen, yet also described moments when they had been given dirty looks for speaking Spanish. A pattern emerged in which these respondents legitimately described their lives in the Roaring Fork Valley in positive terms. While the data presented by different scholars may differ, given differences in their research questions, it is likely that considerable overlap exists in the data themselves.

The positive narratives offered by these respondents must also be put into context: these interviews focused on understanding why these individuals chose to live in the Roaring Fork Valley and how it compares to the places from which they came or other places to which they might move. From this vantage point, Aspen, Basalt, and the local environment have many advantages over the very dangerous communities from which many of these migrants came. For the mothers and young men interviewed, not having to worry about death or abduction at the hands of a gang, simply being able to go to work and to return home each night, was a blessing. Within this context, dirty looks from Anglos were occasionally experienced as alienating and unfriendly, but may have been considered tolerable in relation to threats posed in their home countries. While working day and night may not have been ideal, being able to earn incomes that kept pace with the cost of living and allowed them to send money to family members was considered preferable to earning a college degree back home, only to earn a fraction of what they earned in Colorado.

Finally, the experiences of Latino residents in navigating the second and third borders of life in the United States should be situated within the local *place-based class culture*. As a culture, its components are widely held *and* institutionalized within norms and policies. For these reasons, the culture impacts Latinos and Anglos, alike. Even if the institutionalization of class interests excluded undocumented residents from the affordable housing program, the same class ethos provided transportation and ski passes to local workers. Additionally, the institutionalization of class interests advanced the needs of affluent residents for cheap labor, which simultaneously provided protection to local laborers from ICE incursions and led local law enforcement offers to maintain a hands-off approach. Aspen exceptionalism similarly seemed to shape these residents' experiences. They described locals as kind and welcoming and affluent visitors as curious and interested in their culture. Some respondents noted that they often felt more exclusion and disdain from lower income Anglos living down valley in Glenwood than they did in rarefied Aspen. After all, class competition was scant in Aspen, resulting in few class-based anxieties and little need to scapegoat migrant workers. Aspen egalitarianism similarly seems to have made it into these residents' consciousness, reflected in beliefs that fewer class distinctions or conflicts exist in Aspen. Although these analyses cannot show how such beliefs are absorbed, these interviews suggest that even Latino residents have a sense that class is done *differently* in Aspen, and that pretensions and social exclusion are not a part of how class differences are manifest.

Although our experiences of race and class reflect relatively enduring aspects of a culture, they also change over time. When the Aspen City Council and Pitkin County Commission passed anti-immigrant ordinances in 1999 and 2000, the country was in a recessionary period, reacting to the burst of the dot-com bubble. In Aspen, residents used immigration policy as a scapegoating tool. This anti-immigration mood was not unique to Aspen; indeed, it was widely shared across the western United States. Today, local officials and citizens of Aspen barely remember these ordinances, and to the extent they do, they remember them as an expression of a deeply held anti-growth ethos, rather than rooted in racism. When Donald Trump pledged to build a wall, this platform gained little traction in Pitkin County, where 70 percent of the voters cast a ballot for Hillary Clinton. The day after Trump was elected in 2016, local officials pledged to protect Latino residents and school children, assuring them that law enforcement would not be allowed to intrude on their lives. Respondents in this study called Trump a "sick man" and an "ugly man," and felt threatened by changes in data collection procedures with programs like Medicaid. Interestingly, they did not comment on the increased use of deportations and E-verify under the Obama administration. Generally speaking, they described feeling safe within Aspen and Pitkin County.

There is no doubt, however, that the community has a long way to go in promoting equity and inclusion in the affordable housing program. Aspen's Whiteness has worked as an asset, protecting this program from scrutiny. The fact that the program largely serves "people like us"—Anglos who work in the community, send their children to school, and reproduce the authentic, outdoor-loving culture that makes Aspen Aspen—provides incredible financial and philosophical support to the program. If and when its housing programs reexamine and revise the way that immigration status impacts access to housing, we will have a better understanding of the degree to which Aspen's exceptionalism and egalitarianism genuinely extends across racial and ethnic lines.

Conclusion

THE LIMITS AND POSSIBILITIES OF PLACE-MAKING IN THE ERA OF SUPERGENTRIFICATION

> What we did for the last year is try to write a code that delivers the built environment we want, and allows for appropriate development, which delivers the things we need. I can't stand up right now and say, "Yes, it's absolutely going to deliver," because we're working against market forces like nobody's ever seen. We're trying to work alongside those market forces; in perhaps the world's most unique economic environment. But we tried.
>
> —Aspen Mayor Steve Skadron, in the final stages of the land use moratorium

When the Aspen City Council declared a land use moratorium in March of 2016, they did so to stop the pendulum swing that had created an environment that was seen as overly friendly to developers and to reinscribe the authentic, small-town character that has made the upscale resort famous. Simultaneously, the council sought to implement more fully into the land use code the wording of the Aspen Area Community Plan, especially wording that foregrounds working locals' access to affordable housing and businesses that serve their daily needs. In the end, the revised land use code aimed at restoring small-town character by reducing the size of buildings, creating more spaces that foster interactions between locals and visitors and that allow for the enjoyment of mountain scenery, and specifying the aesthetic codes that capture Aspen's sense of design innovation and its authentic mountain-town feel. Other ordinances focused on the needs of locals, including increased mitigation rates paid by developers for affordable housing and requirements that developers incorporate "nook-and-cranny" spaces into their projects. In addition, local activists pushed to reinforce Aspen's sense of distinctiveness and its identity as a place that attends to the needs of working locals by imposing regulations on chain retailers; this was motivated by the concern that high-end retailers were a threat to both. The primary goal throughout this process was to use the tools of urban planning to preserve the "golden goose"—Aspen's identity as an exclusive, yet authentic enclave—so that it, in turn, would continue drawing the visitors and investors whose economic contributions fund the programs that make middle-class life possible.

This book makes an important contribution to urban sociology and studies of place-making. It does so by centering an analysis of social class within understandings of how places get made, what makes them distinctive, and how conflicts over place emerge and get resolved. To date, studies of urban scholars have framed monied elites as almost exclusively motivated by economic interests. The growth coalitions that pursue growth and profit have only gained strength with the rise of neoliberalism, as shown in Jason Hackworth's work on the *neoliberal city* and in Miriam Greenberg and Alessandro Busá's case studies of New York City, which portray the branding of New York in pursuit of profit and the destruction of the city's unique working-class communities on account of this pursuit, respectively.[1] Although scholars may attend to the cultural meaning or branding of these places as central to their ability to generate profit, the cultural aspects of social class have remained under-theorized. Only recently have urban scholars begun to consider how the intersecting dimensions of social class—its economic and cultural aspects—shape place-making. Zachary Hyde, for example, sees developers as neither focused exclusively on profits nor driven by altruism when they seek to incorporate affordable housing or public spaces into their projects.[2] Instead, he sees them as *giving back to get ahead*, which frames their development efforts as the ineluctably joint pursuit of economic capital and symbolic capital, of profits *and* reputational prestige. My work contributes to this tradition and complicates understandings of what place-makers seek to maximize and how class interests shape these processes.

This work also seeks to complicate understandings of how residents "do" social class in place. To date, many urban scholars have produced interesting, but fairly homogeneous portraits of how affluent people do social class. Their studies have largely framed affluent people as motivated by exclusion. Whether seeking to protect the economic or the symbolic value of their land, affluent people within affluent communities are portrayed as supporting place-making policies that exclude less affluent people.[3] Even in communities undergoing change, as the forces of gentrification set in, researchers have provided relatively predictable insights into how class interests and class actions play out. Gentrifiers have been painted with a broad brush, bringing deep pockets and upscale tastes to their new communities, which force the displacement of locals. Long-term residents, by contrast, are portrayed as powerless and disenfranchised, though they may occasionally marshal social capital or locally resonant discourses to resist the tide. Voices are emerging, however, which complicate understandings of how social class works in specific locales. Japonica Brown-Saracino, for example, was among the first to show that among gentrifiers, social-class location and cultural interests and motivations do not neatly map onto one another.[4] Her portrait of social preservationists shows how some gentrifiers actively support the long-term locals who have shaped the neighborhoods into which gentrifiers have moved. Her work on sexual identity communities is also instructive. While not about social class, she shows that sexual identities emerge differently in different places, so that it is reasonable that social class cultures will also be variable.[5] British geographers, too, have recently drawn attention to the place-specific understandings of class and the locally contingent nature in which class struggles play out. My work adds to this tradition as well, showing that precisely which class boundaries and identities are relevant and how actors seek to mobilize those identities and institutionalize their interests, depend on a complex combination of local factors.[6]

The model of *place-based class cultures* adds nuance and complexity to understandings of how social class is done in place. Within the context of Aspen and the Roaring Fork Valley, we see that place narratives frame Aspen as an exceptional place; one that is authentic, with a history emerging from its origins as a real mining town. Over time, this sense of exceptionalism gathered strength, as Aspen transformed into a landing place for people pursuing a lifestyle that combines mind, body, and spirit. Local understandings of social class intertwine with these narratives, foregrounding Aspen as a place of storied egalitarianism. What makes Aspen exceptional, many locals believe, is that it is a place where social classes mix and mutually enrich one another. It is a place of undeniable affluence and luxury, but also one with an expectation that this luxury manifest in unpretentious ways, intersecting with and respecting local expressions of authenticity. These narratives do not capture mere understandings or ideas. Indeed, they lead to the institutionalization of class interests, which in turn form a recursive loop that shapes these narratives. Both ideas of how social class should be done, and how these ideas are implemented in laws and policies, are made possible by the material conditions that enable or constrain place-making endeavors.

These analyses use the model of *place-based class cultures* to explain how one municipality sought to meet the needs of its diverse class communities, molding it into a place that strives simultaneously to meet the needs of working locals and affluent visitors and investors. The contribution, however, is not simply in illustrating how one community sought to meet the seemingly disparate interests of its diverse class constituencies. The model of place-based class cultures is as a tool that can be used to understand how class is "done" in place, more broadly. While Aspen may be unique in the coherence and consensus of its narratives and while it may present conditions not widely found elsewhere, each of the model's constituent elements—place narratives, narratives of social class, institutionalization of class interests, and material conditions—exist in all communities. Therefore, this conceptual tool can be used on a broader level to understand how social class shapes and is shaped by place-making processes. It can be used in discrete cases, for instance, to understand locally specific approaches to affordable housing and economic development, and why supergentrification may play out much differently in London and San Francisco than it does in Aspen. It may be even more applicable in helping to explain, for example, variations among affluent resort communities. While many affluent resort communities have expensive housing markets, they differ in how they strive to meet the housing needs of working locals. The model can help explain why, for example, Aspen has more affordable housing than Teton County, Wyoming, or why it may more aggressively tamp down the spread of luxury retailers compared to Park City, Utah. Their unique social class narratives and the local laws and policies can help illuminate how different communities "do" social class and, especially, class inequality.

A second contribution of this work is identifying an approach to growth and development that is not explicitly no-, low-, or pro-growth, but something more complex. Low-growth agendas, which seek to preserve quality of life, can generally be thought of as prioritizing use value over exchange value. Beginning in the 1970s, Aspen City Council members and Pitkin County commissioners pursued an explicitly low-growth agenda. Most significantly, they downzoned the county, which limited density by regulating how many residences the community would allow. Additionally, they used a growth management quota system to establish annual limits for new square footage for residences, hotels, and commercial structures. These are some of the initial tools that guaranteed scarcity in Aspen's built environment. A strong low-growth constituency still exists in Aspen, evident in the positions taken by some elected officials, planning experts, and citizen activists and letter writers. At the extreme, they advocate for policies that would limit the number of vehicles allowed into town, a move that would emulate the quaint, car-free Alpine town of Zermatt, Switzerland. Some interpret their desires to raise mitigations on affordable housing not as a way to provide much-needed housing, but as a way to freeze growth by imposing burdensome fees on developers. As in other locales experiencing a changing sense of place, some Aspenites accuse the low-growth faction of wanting to "dip the town in amber" or "pull up the drawbridge," so that the quaint Aspen they know and love can endure.

Today, rather than a low- or no-growth agenda, municipal officials seem to pursue a modified growth strategy; one that seeks to maximize both use value and exchange value. I refer to this as a *hybrid growth* strategy, where local stakeholders' actions seem designed to meet the needs of both locals and investors. The enduring emphasis on use value, or quality of life, is evident in the 2017 code amendments that protect views of the mountain and provide increased pedestrian amenity spaces for everyone's enjoyment, and in those that specifically address the needs of locals—namely, by increasing affordable housing mitigations and mandating "second-tier" commercial spaces. Aspen's pursuit of exchange value is more hidden. Rather than overtly court development by offering tax abatements or other economic incentives, it uses the land use code and its accompanying design standards (aesthetic guidelines) to create scarcity and quality in the built environment. This appeals to developers who recognize that Aspen is a long-term play, a location where the initial costs of development—which include significant land costs, building fees, and mitigations—ultimately pencil out, in part, due to municipal government and other stakeholders' persistent efforts to preserve the town's unique sense of place. As a result, Aspen can afford to limit development because doing so results in high-end projects. It is only hotels like the St. Regis and the W, and retailers like Gucci and Prada, that can afford Aspen's rent, and by drawing these brands to town, Aspen can afford to limit development thanks to the tax revenues generated by these projects. To date, the hybridization of use value and exchange value has served Aspen and the surrounding communities well, and has resulted in significant benefits for both working locals and more affluent visitors and investors. As Leonard Nevarez notes, integration of both use and exchange value is possible in unique cases, where local defenders of quality of life—who have the right mix of social and cultural capital—are able to guide capital investments in ways that yield profit, but may not result in growth, per se.[7] Later, I consider the limitations of this approach, exploring whether this model can persist within Aspen and whether it can be exported beyond.

But taking a moment to look at the possibilities implied in these analyses, it is clear that Aspen and Pitkin County have achieved remarkable things through the land use code. Drawing on the regulatory tools of urban planning, local officials have used the land use code, alongside a host of other local policies, to engineer a version of the American Dream. First and foremost, it has established a housing market where a significant portion of working locals are able to find a home, despite the free-market forces that almost entirely preclude their existence. The implementation of an extensive affordable housing program solves Aspen's "impossible math equation," making it possible for residents with median household incomes around $73,000 to live in a place where the median home price in the free market hovers around $4 million, and where modest two-bedroom apartments rent for $4,000 per month. The Aspen Pitkin County Housing Association maintains a stock of three thousand units with prices that do not "rent burden" the majority of its residents. Second, it has been able to pass supplementary taxes that subsidize programs that enhance access to outdoor amenities and cultural opportunities, and provide supplementary funding to the public schools. During his tenure on city council, Adam Frisch often asked, "Is Aspen great in spite of or because of" the extensive social engineering it has orchestrated over the years. He has repeatedly concluded that "Aspen is mostly great because of it."

These insights have value above and beyond recognizing Aspen's history of progressive politics and its unique ways of managing class differences. This book shows that even within affluent communities, the land use code can be used as a tool to include, not merely exclude. Affluent communities have a history of using exclusionary zoning to accomplish exactly what the name denotes: exclusion. This has been done by mandating large lot sizes and expressing a preference for single-family over multifamily dwellings. At both the municipal and home association level, exclusion is further orchestrated through aesthetic codes that, on the surface, seem like neutral expressions of taste but, upon closer inspection, reveal themselves as tools that enhance the financial and symbolic value of Aspen's home owners and erect boundaries against outsiders or aspiring residents. Low- and mixed-income housing projects have famously fallen victim to NIMBY-ism, as affluent residents organize to oppose housing developments that they find problematic or distasteful. Aspen, by contrast, employs a unique version of YIMBY-ism—where voters say "Yes, in my backyard" to affordable housing developments, as long as they are not too dense and do not compromise views of the mountain. The land use code, similarly, has been engineered to *include* locals; in the current iteration it does so by providing solutions aimed at increasing locals' opportunities to start their own businesses and limiting high-end chain stores that would price them out of the market and undermine the "messy vitality" that contributes to the town's sense of place. While other studies have examined the efforts of municipalities to use zoning and the land use code to craft a sense of place and even to maximize use value, few have considered the possibility that the tools of urban planning can successfully be used to include those less-affluent members of a community. In both discourse and institutionalization, Aspen's locals are seen as a valuable asset in the town's place-making efforts. This book provides an empirical case that establishes that possibility and provides a conceptual model that outlines the conditions under which such dynamics are possible. My hope is that other researchers will adopt this conceptual model and use it to enhance our understandings of how class works, especially in terms of urban planning and the institutionalization of class interests.

ASPEN AND THE LIMITS OF THE LAND USE CODE

Despite these considerable accomplishments, there are clear limits to what Aspen has achieved with the land use code and to what it might be able to achieve as time goes on. The key question is whether the town will be able to maintain its unique place character, its embrace of messy vitality, and its desire to foster social class mixing, for the foreseeable future. In many ways, Aspen may be a victim of its own success; whereby the combination of its conscientious attention to place-making and global market forces push its value ever higher, ultimately squeezing out the working locals who have been credited with shaping the town's unique sense of place. It is a basic economic fact, then, that the vast majority of working locals cannot live, eat, or shop there without extensive social engineering.

By 2027, the Greater Roaring Fork Valley Region—an area spanning Pitkin, Garfield, and Eagle counties, and home to one hundred and three thousand individuals—is expected to face a shortfall of fifty-seven hundred affordable housing units; the upper-valley area, comprised of Aspen and Snowmass, is expected to have a deficit of thirty-four hundred units.[8] In the municipalities outside of Pitkin County, one of the main barriers to building affordable housing is a lack of funding, eventuating the need for innovative public-private partnerships to step into the marketplace. In Aspen and Snowmass, however, the problem is less about money and more about the lack of buildable parcels of land and opposition to housing structures that violate aesthetic considerations. Pitkin County's low-density policies and open-spaces programs place real limits on where affordable housing can be built; and while smaller spaces could be suitable for higher densities, erecting structures higher than three stories is usually not an option, given the privileged place of mountain views. In late 2017, for example, the city council considered the application for an affordable housing project that would have been four stories high. Instead, they approved a smaller three-story development comprised of twenty-four units, reducing the size of the development by four units. In their 3-2 vote, the council demonstrated sympathy for neighboring residents' concerns, in the words of their legal representative, that the project was "not sensitive to the scale and character of the neighborhood."[9] Opposition was strong enough that the council feared that existing residents might sue the city if they approved the four-story version.

With his eyes keenly focused on Aspen's sense of place, council member Adam Frisch consistently questioned whether Aspen could or should try to build its way out of its affordability crisis. Although the community strongly supports its affordable housing program, addressing housing needs is just one facet of the problem. Regulating commercial spaces and providing access to locally owned and locally serving businesses was another. Yet, the city council displayed little interest in providing affordable commercial spaces. Regulating the market for housing, where winners are chosen by lottery, was one thing; Frisch worried, however, that tipping the scales on local businesses and picking the winners and losers who would benefit from rent subsidies would take Aspen too far into "Kim Jong-un's North Korea." Moreover, as Frisch noted during the mortarium: "The idea of making Aspen cheaper is just not going to happen. We would have to build so much commercial space, that it would be a whole different town and you [locals who are attracted to its character] wouldn't want to be here, and the seller wouldn't want to sell here." Instead, the city council and other stakeholders remained fixated on the "golden goose"—the small built environment that funds the programs that make middle-class life possible. With supergentrification having its way with Aspen's commercial scene, it appears that at least within the near term, the town is headed toward a unique form of segregation, where working locals live and recreate in town, but are increasingly shut out of its restaurants and retail spaces. With these dynamics, more middle- and upper-middle-class residents are moving down valley to Willits and Carbondale, where it is still possible to buy a home for $600,000. As they do, they bring new energy to those communities, contributing to their vitality—a vitality also stimulated by Latino grocery stores and other immigrant-owned businesses. As middle- and upper-middle-class workers from Aspen gentrify these communities, working-class Latinos get pushed farther and farther down valley.

At the end of the moratorium process, Mayor Steve Skadron spoke of his desire to end the pendulum swing of development—from periods of bust to boom and back again—and asked his colleagues and staff of urban planners about the latest batch of land use regulations: "Are we sufficiently protected against the next speculative development boom?" Unfortunately, the answer is most certainly "No." While the land use code and broader economic forces intertwine to shape how a community looks, feels, and functions, they are also autonomous forces. The land use code is an element of local political economy; it surely influences local economic conditions and can be altered to respond to changing economic conditions. Yet with the globalization of production, intensive use of technology in virtually all employment sectors, and worldwide deregulation of financial markets, individual municipalities may be overwhelmed by forces originating beyond their borders. Former mayor Mick Ireland described this as a "tsunami" of money from around the world, "looking for a place to invest." In light of these forces, council member Adam Frisch wondered whether their efforts to revise the land use code were tantamount to bringing "a knife to a bazooka fight."

While council members and other stakeholders recognized the immense challenge that they were up against, they sometimes seemed caught flat-footed, trapped in a state of mild paralysis, as they contemplated using land use tools that have served the town so well in the past versus implementing newer, more innovative tools. The history of progressive politics in Aspen has achieved considerable benefits for locals through downzoning and growth controls, which have included high mitigations on developers. Yet in terms of advancing opportunities for locals to own businesses or access businesses that serve their daily needs (car repair, dry cleaners, barber shops, grocery stores), the council seemed either reticent to adopt new tools to address this widely recognized problem or unable to envision alternative models of economic development. Indeed, and perhaps somewhat remarkably, neither Aspen nor Pitkin County governments maintained an economic development office. This likely reflects the fact that they have historically pursued a low-growth path and because investment has found its way to Aspen without it. Speaking as a representative the Aspen Chamber and Resort Association, the group that represents local business owners, attorney Maria Marrow asked, "Can we think of nothing other than mitigation to find the sweet spots?" Whether designed to punish developers, ward against growth, or provide assets to working locals, mitigations proved to be a wonderfully effective and flexible tool over the years. Marrow, however, encouraged the council to "look beyond the land use code and extractions to deliver the goal" of creating a vital climate for local businesses. Beyond the land use code, she and many other small business owners were concerned that building and permitting fees—beyond mitigations on affordable housing—were too high to promote flexibility in the marketplace, especially among local business owners who are not subsidized by larger corporate parent companies. Karim Souki, the son of one of Aspen's largest landlords, chastised the council for persistently using an approach to development that is "always stick, never any carrot." He and others were frustrated that in Aspen, "it's all restrictions and hurdles the developers have to overcome," whereas in "other markets, there's tax incentives and waivers of fee to allow more affordable options." During the moratorium period, when questions emerged about other ways of creating a business climate that would meet the needs of locals and visitors alike, council rebuffed those concerns, arguing that broader issues of fees, permitting, and economic development were beyond the scope of the land use code revisions. Reacting to their somewhat muted response, some local citizens accused the council of being out of touch with the progressive, innovative roots that created the town's treasured "messy vitality," and with taking a more reactionary stance. In the words of millennial-aged small-business owner Tucker Chase, they are "just reacting to the squeaky wheel [and the] fire [they] have to put out," rather than looking for the new wave of solutions to meet locals' needs and keep Aspen fun and funky. If the council and other place-makers continue to compartmentalize the challenges to affordability and rely on old tools to deal with new and mounting challenges, Aspen will find it increasingly difficult to live up to its claims of being an authentic place that promotes the mixing and well-being of visitors and locals.

Finally, one limit to Aspen's ability to use the land use code to achieve its complex community values is that land use planning is almost always followed by the emergence of unintended consequences. In some cases, unintended consequences result from the fact that users of spaces respond to land use challenges in ways that are creative and unanticipated. In Aspen and London, for example, the land use code limits residential lot sizes and the amount of square footage that can be built on a lot. In response, affluent homeowners have circumvented these requirements by building "mega-basements," that double or even triple the dwelling's total square footage. In 2014, after one developer in Aspen broke ground on a project with a forty-foot basement, council passed new regulations limiting basement depths to fifteen feet.[10] In other cases, unintended consequences can emerge from well-intentioned efforts that, when combined with global market forces, take on a life of their own. During the moratorium, former mayor Mick Ireland (2007–2013) addressed this possibility, asking about the council's efforts to restore small-town character: "Are we setting the stage for redevelopment of something like the Butcher's Block [deli, housed in an older building] into a high-end space? That will be beautiful, and pedestrian friendly, and will have canopies and arcades, but will be just another high-end use?" His question foregrounded the council's efforts to create a sense of place through the land use code, but wondered whether the costs associated with these well-intentioned efforts will ultimately get passed on in the form of higher rents, once these older properties renovate. As noted in chapter 5, when this question was directed at the city council, they recognized that their efforts would surely result in a more expensive built environment, and that this required them to make some careful decisions. They gave shockingly little attention, however, to the question of whether their decisions would eventually yield conditions that stand in direct contradiction to the community values they sought to fulfill. If this turns out to be the case, we may be left to wonder whether these consequences were, in fact, unintended, of if they were the predictable outcome of a council that had either strayed from the town's earlier progressive orientation or hesitated to use new tools to solve old problems.

LESSONS FROM ASPEN AND THEIR LIMITS FOR OTHER LOCALES

Disruption and displacement brought about by gentrification and super-gentrification are not unique to Aspen. While manifesting in different ways, the influx of global capital and the crisis of affordable housing—one of the causes and one of the effects of these processes—are affecting many communities in the United States and beyond. The ways that other communities experience and address these challenges are shaped by their own place-based class cultures. To date, few communities have been as successful as Aspen in protecting the needs of working locals, in the context of extreme inequality. There are numerous reasons for this, as well as numerous reasons why Aspen's "formula" may be difficult to replicate elsewhere. Aspen is remarkable, for example, in terms of the cohesiveness of narratives surrounding place and social class. This is made possible by the fact that the community is rather small to begin with, but also because so many people who live there have something in common: the desire to recreate and live their lives in close proximity to nature. The fact that 90 percent of the community is White no doubt contributes to its homogenous views. It shares some characteristics with the White cities that Louise Seamster has described and what cultural critic Rich Benjamin calls a *whitopia*, a place where "whites are not drawn to a place explicitly because it teems with other white people. Rather, the place's very whiteness implies other perceived qualities."[11] Having these demographic and cultural traits in common surely cements a sense of cohesiveness in the community and strengthens residents' commitment to the affordable housing program, framing it as a program for "people like us" rather than an incursion by some less-advantaged other. Larger municipalities and those with more diverse populations are likely to lack this profound sense of "we-ness" and, as a result, may be less likely to act with a sense of class solidarity.

Other place-bound factors similarly limit the degree to which Aspen's commitment to affordable housing and attention to the needs of working locals can be emulated elsewhere. In some ways, Aspen and the Bay Area share important qualities. Both areas celebrate their bohemian histories and currently have higher-than-average median household incomes. In fact, San Francisco has the highest median household income for a large city within the United States at $96,000, compared to Aspen's $73,000. Both, similarly, have made forays into protecting local businesses. In the era of supergentrification, in 2015 San Francisco passed Proposition J, a measure that uses local taxes to subsidize "legacy businesses" that have made a contribution to local character and are in danger of being priced out of the marketplace. Yet San Francisco has struggled to pass new taxes that would help create affordable housing and address the city's staggering problem with homelessness. In 2016, a "tech tax" that would have imposed a 1.5 percent payroll tax on tech companies failed to make it out of committee of the city's board of supervisors. Mayor Ed Lee called it a "job killing" initiative. Various schemes to tax highly paid CEOs have also failed to make it to the ballot, suggesting that local officials lack the appetite to support measures that have the feel-good effect of taking a swipe at local tech giants but may incur economic costs.[12] Moreover, voters in San Francisco would have to marshal considerable support—two-thirds of all voters—for the measure to pass. In 1978, California passed Proposition 13, which limits the passage of new property taxes; only a few other states have successfully passed similar "tax revolt" measures. Colorado, ironically, has the most aggressive such legislation, with its 1992 TABOR laws (Tax Payer Bill of Rights). Today, voters must approve all new tax levies, and taxes like the real estate transfer tax (RETT) that substantially funds Aspen's affordable housing program are banned entirely. Fortunately for Aspen locals, its supplemental tax on real estate transactions was adopted in 1979, well before the passage of TABOR. Now, even similar Colorado communities—one's like Telluride and Crested Butte, that pride themselves on authenticity and are facing an affordable housing crisis—are hamstrung in their efforts to levy taxes that could be used to subsidize local residents. Teton County, Wyoming, in particular, would be reticent to adopt additional tax levies, bolstered as it is by high-net-wealth individuals who seek it out as a resort community within the nation's most "tax-friendly" state.[13] Accordingly, aside from place-specific discourses of social class and community character, municipalities lack not just the will to pass legislation that would fund affordable housing, but the political mechanisms that would allow them to do so.

RESEARCH LIMITATIONS AND LINGERING QUESTIONS

As with virtually any research project, this one has its limitations. Although the data is composed of a wide array of sources, including observation at

242   CONCLUSION

council meetings and interviews with individual council members, planners, developers, and citizens, they contain limited insight into "back room dealings" and conversations. Because of this, it is unclear whether and how developers exert their influence on the planning process, both in terms of gaining approvals on individual projects and shaping land use code revisions. Such data would provide context to or confirmation for the claim that developers are not aggressively involved in trying to influence the regulatory environment. Similarly, although the data include interviews with individual developers, these conversations focused on their professional involvement in Aspen in a general sense, eliciting insight into why they have chosen Aspen as a setting for their work and the challenges and rewards they experience working in the community. These conversations did not drill down into developers' work on individual projects, exploring how they understand and attempt to manage the demands of the land use code in specific instances. Therefore, while there is evidence that Aspen developers enact the "give back to get ahead" strategy described by Zachary Hyde, whereby they are motivated by both economic incentives and the reputational prestige they garner by making contributions to affordable housing and other community objectives, it is unclear how they weigh the economic costs of doing business in Aspen with possible gains of symbolic capital as they try to "pencil out" their projects. Such data would provide more fine-grained insight into how developers calculate the costs and benefits associated with working in Aspen and their own roles in place-making.

Perhaps the most persistent and important lingering question has to do with how race and ethnicity influence Aspen's ability to offer a modified version of the American Dream. Aspen, Colorado, is profoundly White; those who work there are not, nor are the residents of the broader Roaring Fork Valley. Although Lisa Sun-Hee Park and David Pellow, in *The Slums of Aspen*, portray a community that is overtly hostile to immigrants, seeking to exclude them through legislative efforts and marginalize them within substandard housing, these data are much more oblique on the question of how race and ethnicity work in Aspen. The affordable housing program, like Aspen and Pitkin County itself, serves a largely White demographic. The fact that relatively few Latinos live in Aspen's affordable housing reflects feelings of exclusion, a lack of outreach or awareness of the program, and lack of legal status, along with their choice to live else-where given cultural preferences and life course needs (e.g., residences for families, not just singles). Latino residents may feel pulled toward Carbon-dale and points beyond. There, they have more opportunities for afford-able housing and space, fewer regulations on what they can do with their properties, and access to churches and businesses that serve their needs. Interviews with Latino workers depict a community in which they feel safe and welcomed, even if they do not have the financial means to dine in local restaurants or shop in local boutiques. The tensions they describe are not between themselves and the community's Anglo residents, but among Latinos, between Mexicans and Salvadorans, for example. Today, Aspen does not feel like the *whitopias* described by Rich Benjamin, where hostil-ity to immigrants and people of color may be a defining feature. Instead, my data and experiences reveal a recognition that Latinos play a critical role in making the community function. The concern that immigrants pose a disproportionate environmental impact, as suggested by Park and Pel-low, currently seems both incorrect and quite quaint. Now, it is the carbon footprints of those who fly into Aspen on private planes and who use their mega-mansions for just two months out of the year that are viewed as pos-ing an existential threat to the community. Ultimately, it seems that rather than overt racial exclusion, Whiteness in Aspen functions as a resource that allows consensus and drives political mobilization. I call upon future scholars to direct their attention to this issue more directly and to consider how racial and ethnic homogeneity intersects with socioeconomic charac-teristics to influence the institutionalization of class interests.

IN CLOSING

In considering the "impossible math of Aspen, Colorado," and the ability to use the land use code to serve disparate class interests, it is clear that the model that works in this upscale mountain town is unique and that can be replicated only under very specific circumstances. Not every com-munity is blessed with the natural beauty that makes Aspen so special. Further, not every community has an active and powerful middle-class base; a base that works incredibly hard to implement its economic and political interests. And perhaps most importantly, Aspen seems unique in that the global elite who make Aspen their part-time home or otherwise bring their business interests to the community are very rarely registered to vote locally. Accordingly, middle- and upper-middle-class locals constitute a significant voting bloc; to date, affluent interests have not engaged in concerted efforts to challenge the high rates of taxation or dismantle what council member Frisch dubbed "the mitigation-industrial complex." Given these reasons, it is unclear whether there are lessons here for other communities typified by great wealth and significant gaps between the super-rich and everyone else. Yet to the extent that such communities can develop narratives about their uniqueness while harnessing the power of local residents and political institutions, there may be hope for other locales to both preserve and market their character in ways that maintain citizens' right to the city.

Acknowledgments

I want to thank, first and foremost, my father, because without him this project would not exist. In fact, it is entirely conceivable that without him, I would never have become a sociologist at all. It is because of my dad that I was introduced to Aspen, and through my introduction to Aspen, I became acquainted with many of the contradictions surrounding social class. I brought these observations with me to campus as an undergraduate at Northwestern University, where they were a source of pain, confusion, and inspiration. There, as a lower-income, first-generation college student, I found that I typically had enough cultural capital to help me navigate elite higher education, but never enough financial capital to feel as if I fully belonged. These feelings of being betwixt and between, both insider and outsider, have made for one heck of a sociological imagination.

I am especially grateful for the time spent with my dad during the many months of fieldwork, and the ability to deepen our relationship in adulthood. I will always treasure our adventures in gallery hopping, runs to Clark's Market, trying new cocktails, and especially waiting to get picked up by "the rock." I want to thank Susan, as well, for sustaining us both physically and intellectually, with cups of coffee in the morning, delicious salads in the evening, and great conversation throughout.

Other Aspen people who deserve special kudos are those who generously shared their time with me, peeled back the layers, and helped me push my reflections into deeper territories. These folks include Skippy Mesirow, Adam Frisch, Curtis Wackerle, Michael Miracle, and Philip Supino.

I want to thank the University of North Florida for financially supporting this research. Money from the Dean's Research Grant, Presidential Leadership Award, and Faculty Affairs Summer Research Grant made this project possible, funding both travel and a cadre of talented research assistants. These research assistants contributed, of course, critical help with transcription, but they also helped bring the project to life through their questions about and explorations of Aspen. These assistants include Erin, Kayla, Shannon, Ashley, Sally Ann, Sara, Rosario, Monica, Lauren, Carolina, and Paula.

I also want to share my gratitude with my editor, Naomi Schneider, and her team, along with the anonymous reviewers of this manuscript. Thank you for making this a seamless process and for pushing me to more authentically inhabit the role of urban sociologist. I own an enduring debt of gratitude to Elizabeth A. Armstrong, who has always been an inspiration to me, and who has always helped me achieve my intellectual goals.

APPENDIX   Methodology

Aspen is a place filled with social class mysteries and contradictions. I have observed these contradictions firsthand for much of my life. Over time, they have shaped my sociological imagine and the projects I have chosen, including this one.

THE BACKSTORY

I was five years old the first time I rode in an airplane; it was the private plane of 1970s pop-folk music legend, John Denver. Depending on your age and musical interests, that name may not ring a bell, but in 1976, he was a pretty big deal. At the time I boarded his private plane, headed from Minnesota to Aspen, Colorado, I was also a five-year-old kid on welfare (AFCD) and Medicaid, one who knew the stigma of standing in a line marked "Free and Reduced Lunch" and the pain of hearing statements like, "We'll have to wait until my benefits check comes on the first of the month." When my parents divorced in the mid-1970s, my dad moved to Aspen to exorcise the demons that followed him home from the war in Vietnam and to pursue the "Rocky Mountain High" lifestyle that Aspen made famous during that decade. There, he hustled for work as a skilled carpenter, couch surfing from apartment to apartment, and rubbing shoulders with wealthy people, celebrities, and other movers and shakers. Given Aspen's sense of egalitarianism, the worlds of work and leisure would frequently intersect; at a party crowded with various bons vivants, for instance, my dad would leave with new friends *and* new clients, the line between them frequently blurred. This is how he came to know John Denver, for whom he built custom furniture, and how I came to ride on John Denver's sleek private plane. It was a super-cool experience, even though we were not allowed to touch the catered meat and cheese tray that was there, presumably, for more important passengers. During the summers and winters of my childhood and teen years, my sister and I would make annual trips to see our dad in Aspen. While we never knew where we would be staying, or what our duties would be if we were house sitting—one time we were tasked with misting indoor marijuana plants—we always knew that it would be interesting.

Over the years, Aspen has imparted to me many lessons about social class and culture. Some of these lessons I brought with me as a scholarship student at Northwestern University, where I deployed the cultural capital I acquired in Aspen as best I could. Several dorm mates, for example, were intrigued that my dad had a long-term romance with gonzo journalist Hunter S. Thompson's ex-wife. Meanwhile, I struggled both with basic living expenses and the deep desire to pass as any other privileged student on campus. The tensions between my adequate stock of cultural capital and inadequate stock of financial capital presented opportunities and insights that eventually led me to major in sociology, a discipline with a language and set of tools that would allow me to systematically explore the mysteries of class difference that surrounded me. Throughout graduate school and as an assistant professor, I blended my own life experiences and my sociological tool kit, pursuing research questions that helped me understand how students from different social classes experience and navigate elite higher education.

With a sabbatical on the way in the fall of 2016, there was no question about where I wanted to spend it. Over the years, my questions about how social class "works" in Aspen only intensified. The most persistent questions emerged directly from my father's life: Why do people choose to live in Aspen when doing so entails so many challenges, especially the challenge of finding affordable housing? During his four decades of living in the Roaring Fork Valley, my dad variously lived in his workshop, rented houses and apartments, put his artistic stamp on a trailer home adjacent to the Roaring Fork River, and purchased a beautiful townhome in a gated community in Carbondale. But when my little sister was born, the pull toward Aspen—the culture, the families, the schools—was so profound that my dad and his family relocated to a friend's carriage house apartment, where they exchanged a twelve-hundred-square-foot residence with a community pool and a club house plus steadily appreciating home values for a four-hundred-square-foot dwelling. The decision to trade housing security for access to and association with Aspen raised many questions for me about "the American Dream" and why people choose to live where they live.

Meanwhile, my dad continued working as a carpenter and rubbing shoulders with elites. By day, he supervised the building of $20 million homes; by night, he retreated to his own modest residence. What is it like, I wondered, to build the homes of America's elite, crafting beautiful finishes and clever design solutions, when the hopes of winning even a modest townhome through Aspen's affordable housing lottery were continually dashed? As he got to know the clients on his construction jobs, my dad occasionally formed friendships with them. Talking about their art collections—whose value well exceeded the value of the homes in which they were displayed—he shared with them his artistic knowledge and skills, which sometimes led to these clients becoming my dad's art patrons, purchasing from him sculptures and photographs. I observed this dynamic with some of my other friends in Aspen, where an initial business relationship transformed into a personal relationship, and where the line between friendship and employee seemed, at least from an outsider's perspective, blurred. What is it like, I wondered, to navigate these lines of friendship and economic interdependence, beset with stark differences of power and wealth yet filled with genuine appreciation for one another's personality, talents, and cultural knowledge? This localized version of class egalitarianism is something I wanted to know more about.

FINDING THE STORY

While I knew that Aspen was where I wanted to spend my sabbatical in the fall of 2016, when I arrived that September, I did not have a firm research plan. What I learned that fall is that good ethnography is sometimes found at the intersection of a keen sociological eye and serendipity. My initial goal was to explore *coming of age in paradise*, which would focus on understandings of class privilege and the transition to adulthood among youth who grow up in Aspen; I especially wanted to capture the insights and experiences of high school seniors, as they prepare to leave home (more than 90 percent of Aspen High graduates enter some form of postsecondary education; most of the remaining 10 percent train for competitive sports or take a structured gap year, embarking, for example, on a medical mission). Despite all of the admonitions and life lessons imparted by Annette Lareau in the methodological appendix to her book *Home Advantage*, I did not adequately communicate to gatekeepers at Aspen High School what I was doing and how I hoped they could help me, so by the time I arrived in Aspen, I had no formal access to high school students, and a ticking sabbatical clock. With a nascent interest in place-making and questions about the many mysteries of what Aspen *is*, I went to the place where place-making takes place, where no one could deny my access. I did, in other words, what any self-respecting yet panicked ethnographer would do in such a situation: I began attending city government meetings. After attending several meetings and feeling lost—having to play catch-up with the new language of city government and city-planner-ese—I discovered that I had landed in the middle of a major place-making event: the effort to rewrite Aspen's land use code so that it would better reflect the community's "comp plan,"

locally titled the Aspen Area Community Plan. Once I understood the sociological significance of where serendipity had landed me, I quickly crafted a research
design that would allow me to explore the intersecting dynamics of social class
and culture in Aspen's place-making process.

DATA COLLECTION

To understand how place is made in Aspen, and how class and culture inform
this process, I collected a diverse array of ethnographic data. These data included
observation at public meetings; in-depth interviews; primary documents like
studies, reports, and municipal ordinances; and secondary accounts drawn from
newspapers, magazines, and other such sources. Each form of data presented a
unique perspective on how Aspen works; together they provided both official and
unofficial accounts and insider and outsider perspectives on what Aspen is, how
it is understood, and how it gets made and, occasionally, remade.

Observations at Public Meetings

While place-making is, in fact, an ongoing process without a clear beginning or
end, the building moratorium that Aspen City Council declared in March 2016
constitutes a bookended period for observing this process. During this period, I
attended many official proceedings in person, including those of the Aspen City
Council, the Historic Preservation Commission (HPC), the Planning and Zoning Commission (P&Z), and community outreach meetings. The city council is
made up of five elected, modestly paid officials, one of whom is the mayor. Each
commission is made up of eight members; unpaid and appointed by the city
council, these commissioners typically have expert knowledge of the community,
whether as architects, developers, environmental advocates, lawyers, or former
or aspiring council members. Meetings that I was not able to attend, I observed
from afar, through video recordings posted on the City's website. The field notes
for this study include a comprehensive, verbatim transcript of proceedings at
all of the official city council meetings and work sessions in which the revision
of the land use code was discussed. These meetings document decision-making
processes, featuring dialogue and debate between and among the five elected
council members and the city's planning staff, presentations made by hired
consultants, who represent both national firms and planners in local private
practice, and feedback provided by members of the public. This set of field notes
also includes a subset of meetings of the Historic Preservation Commission
and the Planning and Zoning Commission, which provided insight into how
these commissions evaluated land use applications submitted for residences
and commercial projects in Aspen, as well as feedback given by members to the

proposed revisions of the land use codes. These meetings involved members of the respective commissions; the City's planning staff, which lent guidance and expertise; developers and their planning staffs; and community members. These meetings, then, provided perspectives on what Aspen is and what it should be from multiple stakeholders.

Analytically, these field notes provide insight into the process by which Aspen is made through the land use code. The final product is the set of newly passed land use codes and ordinances that will guide the future of development in Aspen; they constitute the institutionalization of class interests, along with the meaning of Aspen and the materiality of Aspen. The fieldnotes also reveal the insights and concerns of various stakeholders within the community, and reveal debates and critical decision points in this process; in this sense, they constitute the narratives that both reflect and constitute place-making. In total, I observed twenty-seven separate city council meetings for a total of sixty-nine hours. Additionally, I observed nine meetings of the Historic Preservation Commission for approximately twenty hours, and seven meetings of the Planning and Zoning Commission for approximately thirteen hours. Although not sponsored by Aspen municipal officials, notes also contain a five-hour roundtable discussion about the proposed regulations on chain stores. In total, these analyses are based on nearly 110 hours of meetings involving Aspen city officials. Because these data result in a final product—a revised land use code—they were analyzed in a linear fashion, with coding focused on how information and discourses were used to make an argument, the degree to which these arguments received traction, and how they influenced the final policies.

In-Depth Interviews

Although attending official meetings is a staple of community ethnography, such meetings can become too much of a good thing, Japonica Brown-Saracino and Meaghan Stiman warn, "potentially preventing the ethnographer from generating a holistic portrait of and understanding of a place."[1] The dangers of overreliance on official meetings include being limited to observing only an organized, public, and premeditated window into the community and failing to tap into the networks and voices of those not represented at such meetings. Attentive to these dangers, I gathered many additional sources of data, including in-depth interviews. I conducted eighty in-depth interviews with three separate populations: (a) elected officials and other professionals with insight into politics and urban planning; (b) middle- and upper-middle-class year-round residents of the Roaring Fork Valley; and (c) working-class Latino residents of the Roaring Fork Valley. While each population was selected based on their unique insights into life in Aspen and the surrounding area, collectively they provide a portrait of how and why they have chosen to make the Roaring Fork Valley their home, what benefits

Table A1   Respondents: Elected Officials and Land Use Experts

Name	Position of Authority	Profession
Steve Skadron	Mayor	Various
Adam Frisch	Council member	Business owner
Ann Mullins	Council member	Landscape architect
Bert Myrin	Council member	Attorney and real estate broker
Bill Stirling	Former mayor	Real estate broker
John Bennett	Former mayor	Environmental activism
Cindy Christensen	Affordable housing	NA
Mike Kosdrosky	Affordable housing	NA
Amy Simon	Municipal planning	NA
Maggie Carson*	Municipal planning	NA
Cindy Houben	Municipal planning	NA
Heidi Hartmann*	City board	Architect
Jim DeFrancia	City board	Developer
Clark Demming*	City board	Developer
Skippy Mesirow	City board	Real estate
Brent Osterman*	City board	Architect
Dave Marshall*	Land use lawyer	NA
Brian Cottrell*	Land use lawyer	NA
Natalie Lundin*	Land use lawyer	NA
Art Russell*	Former city planner	Architect
Jerry Murdock	Activist	Hedge fund manager
Dennis Diamond*	Real estate professional	NA

* = Pseudonym

and challenges they face there, and how they understand Aspen and especially the class culture and class interactions of those who live and visit there.

First, to complement my observations of official government meetings, I conducted twenty-two interviews with elected city officials, city employees, commission members, and other professionals with insight into development and land use in Aspen (lawyers, architects, property appraisers, and developers, see table A1). The goal of these interviews was to pull back the curtain on the public process and explore decisions made and interactions taking place behind the scenes. I also used these interviews to explore what daylight, if any, existed between each individual's perspective and the policies that eventually emerged through the process. In some cases, I used these meetings to gather factual information, for example, about the affordable housing program, or to receive clarification on the technical concepts about which I was learning (e.g., floor area ratios, or FAR). While the goal of each interview was to elicit each professional's take on place-making in Aspen, and a history of their own relationship to the place, the structure of each interview varied and was tailored to each respondent's professional expertise. The length of these interviews ranged from thirty minutes to an hour and a half. I interviewed some respondents more than once, including Adam Frisch, Ann Mullins, Maggie Carson, and Skippy Mesirow, which allowed me to gauge their insight and analyses at various points in the process. All of these respondents were provided with the option of remaining confidential. Half of them wished to participate in an official or professional capacity, and allowed me to use their names. The other half requested confidentiality, wanting to speak freely while also protecting their professional reputation or clients.

A second set of interviews was conducted with middle- and upper-middle-class residents of the Roaring Fork Valley (see table A2). These interviews fill an important niche: whereas existing research has examined the experiences of lower-income Hispanic service workers, seasonal hospitality workers, and uber-wealthy residents, no research has examined the experiences of the middle-and upper-middle class residents who are both the modal group making up this community and those who shape its political landscape. Their narratives are important for several reasons: first, these individuals have choice in where they live; they are not constrained by limited human capital or circumstances. While some of these interviewees were born and raised in this community, others are lifestyle migrants. The fact that they choose to live in an unequal community with a high cost of living when they could earn more money living elsewhere reveals some of the complicated contours surrounding social class and the politics of place. These interviews also provide insight into why year-round residents have chosen to make this area their home and how they navigate housing, careers, and family life in an environment characterized by a high cost of living and steep socioeconomic inequalities. Additionally, these interviews provided place narratives that reveal detailed descriptions of what Aspen is like and how they experience it as a working local. They generated insight into what Aspen is like from a socioeconomic perspective: which classes live in Aspen; where the respondent "stands" with respect to others; how members of different class strata interact with one another; and how their class interests intersect.

These thirty-nine interviewees represent every stage of adulthood, ranging from twenty-four years old to mid-seventies. A few respondents were born in Aspen and one arrived in his sixties, but the modal respondent arrived in Aspen around age twenty-two, soon after college graduation. Many of them came to Aspen because they had a family member living nearby, and were offered an

Table A2 Respondents: Middle- and Upper-Middle-Class Residents (Pseudonyms)

Name	Residence	Occupation	Age	Arrival	Interview Length
Woody Bateman	Basalt	Architect	62	1971	100
Kimberly Chase	Aspen	Mental health counseling	32	2005	68
Donald Ranstead	Snowmass	Accountant	55	Born	80
Clint Jones	Snowmass	Hospitality	51	1987	67
Glenn Sweeney	Old Snowmass	Journalism	76	Mid-50s	68
Sarah Peters	Aspen	Journalism; marketing	24	2012	54
Rosie Sorrentino	El Jebel	Education	53	1999	65
Eugenia Rappaport	Aspen	Graduate student	25	Born	50
Kara Mason	Aspen	Gallerist; hospitality	36	2001	72
Caroline Picard	Aspen	Nanny	25	2002	62
Payton Dillon	Aspen	Outdoor education	24	Born	60
Kathryn Henderson	Aspen	Marketing; retail	45	2004	52
Karl Paulsen	Basalt	Author	67	1984	81
Jesse Hanks	Carbondale	Author	71	1972	88
Julie Kane	Aspen	Retail; miscellaneous	66	1971	52
Willie Dayton	Aspen	Law enforcement	52	1989	52
Toni Wilson	Aspen	Real estate professional	62	1978	125
Andre Lewandowski	Aspen	Outdoor education; misc.	49	1990	54
Howie Schumacher	Aspen	IT	70	1976	82

Donna Orthey	Aspen	Real estate professional	68	1976	88
Greg Clendenning	Aspen	Beverage sales	66	1974	72
CiCi Catalano	Snowmass	Journalism; marketing	34	2006	65
Nadia Telpiz	Aspen	Retail	30	2014	45
Tanya Reyes	Aspen	Counseling; ministry	26	2011	80
Emma Schumacher	Aspen	Counseling	35	Born	85
Scott Bailey	Aspen	Beverage sales	36	2004	72
Mitch Nelson	Carbondale	Architect	35	2004	82
John Weston	Basalt	Real estate professional	62	Mid-60s	77
Zach Waugh	Aspen	Real estate professional	37	2008	71
Jess Adams	Aspen	Marketing	47	2016	53
Marcia Gold	Basalt	Artist	71	1977	62
Theo Parenti	Aspen	Gallerist; artist	72		67
Charlie Capper	Aspen	Hospitality	33	2005	32
Tucker Chase	Aspen	Entrepreneur (hospitality)	32	2006	72
Doug Donaldson	Aspen	Pastor	66	2014	85
Jim Brantley	Aspen	Real estate professional	57	Mid-80s	85
Okasana Baldwin	Missouri Heights	Interior decorator	32	2011	44
Mason Ward	Carbondale	Journalist	28	2015	58
Simone Davies	Aspen	Entrepreneur (retail)	38	2009	43
N= 39			47		68

opportunity to be a "ski bum" after college or otherwise take what they assumed would be a gap year. Another set moved to Aspen explicitly for a job, in some cases having been transferred there and in a few cases after applying to an advertised position. The respondents in this group represent an array of occupations, including retail, hospitality, law enforcement, counseling, journalism, marketing, real estate, and more. Because the sample contains respondents who arrived in every decade since the 1960s, their accounts provide insight into how Aspen has evolved over time, highlighting points of continuity and change in housing and job markets, place character, and the local culture as it applies to social class. All names are pseudonyms.

Respondents were recruited using a variety of methods. First, random sampling was used to cast a wide net and identify people occupying diverse positions. I obtained a sample of five hundred names and addresses from the marketing firm, InfoUSA, delimited by residence within ten miles of Aspen's center and incomes between $40,000 and $250,000. From this list, I selected a subset to whom I mailed a letter of introduction and invitation to participate in the study. Because Aspen has a transitory population—sometimes due to housing instability and in other cases due to chosen lifestyle mobilities—it is impossible to know how many of these individuals received the recruitment letter. Of the two hundred individuals contacted, only five consented to and completed interviews; thirty-five of the letters were returned to sender. I used other sampling strategies, then, to assemble my population. I used theoretical sampling to target people occupying positions that give them a unique and valuable perspective on the community. For example, I contacted several leaders of the faith community, which often feels like an invisible facet of life in Aspen. Additionally, I contacted journalists for their broad insight into the community, young entrepreneurs for their insight into establishing a foothold in the business community, and activists for insight into the political organization and leverage of locals. Finally, I recruited additional respondents by using referral sampling and personal networks. For example, my dad put me in contact with about five of his friends, many of whom had several decades of experience in the Roaring Fork Valley. While this sample is diverse in many respects, because it was intentionally drawn to gather insight into the experiences of longer-term, year-round locals, it does not represent the experiences of those who work in Aspen seasonally, like the young adults who work in the resort and hospitality industry during the summers and winters.

A third and final set of interviews was conducted with Latinos living in the Roaring Fork Valley (N = 16). The goal of these interviews was to examine the experiences of working-class residents of the Roaring Fork Valley and gauge the racial and ethnic dynamics of the community. Initially, I attempted to recruit through community organizations—including a church and social service agency—as a way of establishing trust with Latino residents. Unfortunately, none of the leaders that I contacted via email responded. Although it is possible that they did not receive the email or no longer held the positions listed on their organizations' webpage, it is also likely that they did not wish to cooperate due to fears of privacy and confidentiality. Although a portion of Aspen's Latino community was born in the United States or is otherwise documented, a significant number are undocumented. The Immigration and Customs Enforcement agency (ICE) was not very visible or active in Aspen, but they maintained a threatening presence in nearby Garfield County. After the 2016 election of President Trump, several local municipalities passed policies pledging to protect undocumented residents. Without the assistance of local agencies or contacts, Latino respondents were recruited using convenience and snowball sampling. My research assistants, two female undergraduates, cautiously approached Spanish-speaking individuals in public locations (plazas, bus stops, near their place of employment), explained the purpose of the study, and asked if they would be willing to participate. More than half agreed to be interviewed.

These respondents' characteristics are presented in table A3. Respondents ranged in age from twenty to fifty-five and lived in communities up and down the Roaring Fork Valley, but worked in Aspen and Snowmass. They worked in hotels, as housekeepers and landscapers; in coffee shops and restaurants, including front-of-the-house positions; and in childcare or early childhood education. El Salvador was the most common country of origin, followed by Mexico. These interviews, which typically took place in an outdoor location or a semiprivate location at work, were conducted in Spanish by interviewers whose first language was Spanish. The average length was fifty-one minutes, with a range of sixteen minutes to an hour and a half. At no point were interviewees asked about documentation status. Respondents did, however, make reference to family members who were without documentation and their fears that these family members might have trouble with the law or employers.

Each interview was recorded and transcribed verbatim. Data analysis proceeded in an iterative fashion. At each step in the project, I engaged in analytic memo writing. I sometimes discussed my emerging ideas with contacts in the community, people who did not consent to an interview, but who provided insight and guidance throughout. These individuals included a journalist, an employee in city government, and a program director with the Aspen Ski Company. Once complete, I read each interview transcript several times to familiarize myself with the data. I then proceeded with open coding to identify emerging themes and patterns, followed by focused coding. During focused coding, I applied both descriptive and analytic codes to the data. The descriptive codes helped organize the data into topics of conversation. For example, I established codes that labeled instances where the respondent talked about why they moved to Aspen, how they had navigated the housing market, and how they characterized relationships and interactions between social classes. Next, analytic codes were used to identify the patterns in respondents' answers, as well as deeper conceptual meanings.

Table A3 Respondents: Latino Residents (Pseudonyms)

Name	Residence	Country of Origin	Occupation	Age	Interview Length
Alejandro Torres	El Jebel	El Salvador	Hotel (housekeeping); Construction	20	54
Blanca Guzman	Snowmass	Mexican American	Hospitality (supervisor)	26	34
Lorena Romero	Basalt	El Salvador	Hospitality (supervisor)	46	48
Maria Sandoval	Glenwood	El Salvador	Hospitality	47	32
Carlos Molina	Basalt	El Salvador	Hospitality	20	57
Carolina Menjivar	Basalt	El Salvador	Hotel (housekeeping)	43	51
Ernesto Ayala	Aspen	El Salvador	Hospitality (supervisor)	29	16
Enrique Lopez	—	Mexico	Hospitality	55	87
Guadalupe Martinez	Basalt	Mexico	Teacher	35	60
Javier Contreras	El Jebel	El Salvador	Hotel (housekeeping and landscaping)	23	83
Sofia Barres	Glenwood	Brazil	Aesthetician	45	61
Pancho Sellas	Aspen	Peru	Hotel (housekeeping)	54	99
Perla Gomez	New Castle	Mexican American	Child care	27	37
Paola Salinas	Basalt	Mexico	Hospitality	32	29
José Diaz	Basalt	Puerto Rico	Hospitality	39	48
Monica Duran	Carbondale	El Salvador	Hotel (housekeeping)	28	27
N = 16				35	51

The code "lifestyle migration," for example, might be used to label a respondent's answer for why they moved to Aspen, and "egalitarian," "symbiotic," or "exploitative" might be used to code respondents' descriptions of class relations in Aspen. This process remained flexible throughout, as codes were occasionally combined, separated, or reconceptualized to better reflect emerging understandings of the data. After data were coded, I sought out patterns whereby I looked for common themes and responses, as well as evidence of variation and disconfirming cases. During each phases of analysis, I wrote analytic memos and continued to dialogue with colleagues and my informal contacts in the local community.

Documentary Materials

Documentary materials constitute a final form of data used in this project. Ordinances and reports produced by the city comprised a large portion of these data. These included both initial and final versions of the ordinances that emerged through this process; several versions of the Aspen Area Community Plan; technical reports produced by consultants during the moratorium; and reports on topics such as housing, employment, and tourism. Some of these reports were provided by former mayor Mick Ireland, who independently conducted several studies. I also used newspaper accounts to gain insight into land use issues. Coverage of such topics is often front-page news for Aspen's two free daily papers, *The Aspen Times* and *The Aspen Daily News*, thereby contributing both ongoing and historical accounts of battles over penthouses, the Art Museum, expansion of Mark Hunt's land holdings, affordable housing crises, and so forth. I used these sources to provide background context to Aspen's land use struggles; I also used them to capture the voices of community members, developers, and others who may not routinely provide discourses or testimony in official government meetings. These data are interspersed throughout, giving structure and texture to the field notes and interview data.

IDENTITY IN THE FIELD: NAVIGATING RESEARCH AS BOTH INSIDER AND OUTSIDER

Conducting research in a community where you are at once an insider and an outsider poses both opportunities and challenges. With respect to gaining entrée, having longtime ties to the area facilitated exceptional access to both informal and formal informants. My informal ties—my dad and his wife, old friends like Glenn Smith, and new friends like Skippy Mesirow—provided a constant sounding board for evolving ideas and impressions of the area. These friends also played important roles in connecting me with potential official informants, that is, individuals who were interviewed on the record, with informed consent. Because my dad, Glenn, and Skippy represent different generations, they were able to provide access to people occupying different niches within the community. It was a great relief when hanging out at a bar or outdoor summer concert, Glenn would say, "Let me introduce you to so-and-so." Soon, he would be promoting my project to one of his friends, which might lead to them sharing their contact information, and me following up to request an interview. Whether connected by my dad, Glenn, Skippy, or another informal contact, I never revealed to these friends whether I completed an interview with one of their sources. As a natural introvert, I found it terrifying to have to sell my project when out and about during leisure time. As an ethnographer, I am forever grateful for my friends' enthusiasm and generosity and aware of the reality that you are almost always on the clock and that every interaction could materialize into an opportunity to collect data.

Having insider connections and access to lots of locals also posed occasional challenges. In a community full of overachievers with literary interests and aspirations, at any given moment, many people might claim to be writing a book on Aspen. It is a town with many stories to be told, and many people aspiring to tell the next great Aspen story. Almost invariably, those stories converge on the life and times of gonzo journalist and political aspirant Hunter S. Thompson, some drug-fueled escapade or scandal, or interest in the many innovators, entrepreneurs, and celebrities that have made Aspen their home. One ongoing challenge, then, was having to establish credibility and context for my work. On many occasions I had to assure people that I was explicitly *not* interested in the lives of the rich and famous or stories from Aspen's heady hippie days of the 1970s, but that I was interested in the seemingly mundane stories of the "ordinary" people who live and work in Aspen every day. Similarly, I sought to foreground my academic credentials and record of publication, both to dispel assumptions about the subject matter of the book and to let potential informants know that this work and their contribution to it would likely be headed to press.

My position as both insider and outsider to Aspen and the Roaring Fork Valley also provided me with both a sense of empathy and a sense of distance and perspective—tools that came in handy when collecting data and later analyzing it. Experiences with and interpretations of Aspen's affordable housing program are a prime illustration of this duality. Having observed my father struggle to find affordable housing in the area for nearly thirty years, I understood the frustrations that many locals have with the program. There are simply not enough units to satisfy demand, and especially for working locals looking to purchase a home, there are virtually no options within Aspen's free market, and increasingly fewer options down valley, where median home prices were nearly $600,000 in Carbondale and $700,000 in Basalt as of 2019. Seeing my dad and his family cobble together housing solutions and continually face disappointment in the housing lottery gave me a sense of empathy when collecting the housing stories of locals, who similarly experienced uncertainty in their futures—with rental units increasingly being converted into vacation rentals—and suboptimal conditions, which could involve spending two hours a day commuting to work or renting a room well into your thirties and not being able to use the common space.

As an outsider, however, I was able to put these experiences in context and gain some analytic perspective. Long commute times are not unique to Aspen; in fact, the reliable and subsidized public transit system and the modest levels of traffic make travel to work relatively easy. Additionally, only about 25 percent of renters are "cost burdened" in Aspen, which is considerably lower than in most communities in the United States—and not just cities with well-documented housing woes. The affordable housing program, moreover, maintains nearly three thousand units for a city with 7,400 residents (admittedly, the latter number is misleading due to the fact that people who work in Pitkin County, but reside in other communities are eligible for the program). While residents may face limited housing choices, the options that do exist largely fit the category of affordable and, due to the strong job market, do not cost-burden local workers. Surely, there are problems with the Aspen Pitkin County Housing Authority program: units often fall into disrepair due to limited budgets for capital improvements, and those who purchase through the program are limited in how much equity they can obtain, since units are allowed to appreciate in value only in line with inflation. Despite this extensive program, many locals feel that whatever council officials, the housing authority, or developers are doing to improve their lives is never enough. There is never enough affordable housing, never enough open space and access to nature, or protection of the environment. Meanwhile, there are too many subpar teachers and counselors at the high school and too many cars coming into town. The sense of entitlement among some locals is palpable. Mitch Nelson, an architect from New York, dubbed Aspen's middle-class a "subsidy class," emphasizing the degree to which they benefit from redistributive policies. And developers both on and off the record commented that the degree to which city government caters to the needs of locals results in a sense of entitlement and distorts their sense of reality. As an analyst, I was able to take a step back and examine empirical facts and the discourses of locals, and make connections and draw conclusions about Aspen's place-based class culture when they didn't necessarily line up. Similar thought-processes accompanied my analysis of how seriously Aspenites take their buildings and how intensely they debate the proper height and ornamentation of buildings. While, on the one hand, I fully understand the importance of the built environment and how it structures both interaction and sense of place, on the other hand, their discourses and pride of place occasionally struck me as a bit precious. The notion that buildings should be limited to twenty-eight feet, in particular, struck me as contrary to innovation, spontaneity, and basic premises of urban design. While visiting, a number of my friends and research assistants were amused and troubled by what constitutes a community debate or social problem in Aspen, seeing these as "first-world problems" that are far removed from seemingly intractable challenges facing many large urban areas, including violent crime and homelessness. In these conversations, I found myself torn—in a way that is productive among analysts—in being able to understand and contextualize the experiences of people living in the Roaring Fork Valley, but also being able to put their experiences into perspective. Being faithful to these dual perspectives is challenging, however, and I hope that what I have rendered here is a depiction of a place that is at once resonant among locals and sufficiently critical among scholars of class and community.

Notes

INTRODUCTION

1. Perin 1977, 4.
2. Travis 2007, 132.
3. Gieryn 2000.
4. Gieryn 2000, 465.
5. Giddens 1994; Molotch, Freudenberg, and Paulsen 2000.
6. Molotch et al., 793.
7. McCann 2002.
8. Block 2017.
9. Knight 2018.
10. Blakely and Snyder 1997; Low 2004; Pow 2009; Pow and Kong 2007.
11. Blakely and Snyder 1997, 1.
12. Blakely and Snyder 1997, 40–41.
13. Wilkins 2013.
14. Duncan and Duncan 2004, 7.
15. Dolgon 2005; Duncan and Duncan 2004; Rudel et al. 2011.
16. Farrell 2020.
17. Duncan and Duncan 2004.
18. Duncan and Duncan 2004, 7.
19. Dolgon 2005, 81
20. Harvey 1973.

21. Molotch 1976, 309.

22. Greenberg 2009; Gotham 2007; Busà 2017; also see Logan and Molotch 1987.

23. Busà 2017.

24. The notion of the Aspen Idea—the blend of mind-body, and spirit—emerged in Aspen during its renaissance, under the guidance of Chicago industrialist Walter Paepcke and his wife, Elizabeth. As founders of the Aspen Institute and the Ski Company, they brought internationally known intellectual leaders to town, and encouraged their mixing with global leaders in business, all the while encouraging balanced engagement in mental and physical pursuits.

25. Harvey 2001.

26. Stone 1988.

27. Clavel 1986, 2010.

28. Clavel 1986, 189.

29. Warner and Molotch 2000, 2.

30. Gendron and Domhoff 2009.

31. Molotch 1976, 327.

32. Warner and Molotch 2000, 132

33. Glass, 1964.

34. Lees 2003, 87.

35. Zukin 2009, 543–44.

36. Lees, Slater, and Wyly 2008.

37. Hackworth 2007.

38. Harvey 1989.

39. This refers to Neil Smith's "rent gap theory" of gentrification (1979)

40. Atkinson et al. 2016.

41. Atkinson, Parker, and Burrows 2017, 179.

42. Lees 2019; Lees, Shin, and Lopez-Morales 2016.

43. Lees, Slater, and Wyly 2008.

44. Hackworth 2002.

45. Lee, Shin, and Lopez-Morales 2016.

46. Brown-Saracino 2009.

47. Brown-Saracino 2009.

48. Skeggs 2004, 2011.

49. Benson and Jackson 2018.

50. Dean, 2012, 74; Tyler 2015, 498.

51. Benson and Jackson 2018, 70.

52. Benjamin 2009

53. Because the Aspen Pitkin County Housing Authority does not accept federal funds, it is not mandated to gather data in compliance with the Fair Housing Act. This results in an important number of unanswered questions about why so few Latino residents live within subsidized housing. We do not know, for

example, what proportion of applicants are Latino, making it difficult to know the degree to which they seek to live in these housing units. Some of the Latino respondents to this study qualified for subsidized housing and had lived in the housing at various times. Others suggested, in both direct and indirect ways, that they did not have the necessary documentation or that other family members might lack documentation.

CHAPTER 1. PLACE-BASED CLASS CULTURES

1. Weber 1978.
2. Bourdieu 1986.
3. Bourdieu 1980.
4. Skeggs 2004, 2011; Tyler 2015.
5. Sewell 2004.
6. Sewell 2004, 47.
7. Swidler 1986.
8. Molotch, Freudenberg, and Paulsen 2000.
9. Molotch et al. 2000, 796.
10. Molotch et al. 2000, 793.
11. Sewell 2004, 48.
12. Brown-Saracino 2017.
13. Butler and Robson 2003.
14. Harvey 2016, 272.
15. New York Times, 2017, State of Colorado, n.d.
16. As noted in the introduction, one must be a resident of the United States to apply for housing with the Aspen Pitkin County Housing Authority. This is most often demonstrated by a Social Security card. According to US Census data, 14 percent of Pitkin and 23 percent of adjacent Eagle county are made up of foreign-born residents; the number is likely higher, due to the fact that unauthorized immigrants often elude population counts. Rental and purchase options in the free-market are beyond the reach of nearly everyone who works in Aspen. These economic and political realities render a large number of people ineligible to live in Pitkin County.
17. Seamster 2015.
18. Gilens 1996, 2009.
19. Brown-Saracino 2017, 15.
20. Brown-Saracino 2017, 15.
21. Molotch et al. 2000, 793–94.
22. Everyone I interviewed had lived in Aspen for at least a year at the time that I interviewed them; all but two were planning on living in Aspen for the foreseeable future. I excluded seasonal workers for a number of reasons. For one,

their orientation to place is likely more temporary and what drew them to town is more likely to be engagement with the leisure. For this reason, they may have a narrower orientation to the community. Second, and relatedly, as residents with a shorter tenure and different time line, they are less likely to be politically engaged and focused on local politics as they relate to housing, education, and other social services.

23. Philpott 2013, 172.

24. Philpott 2013, 175.

25. Rothman 1998, 235.

26. Aspen Area Community Plan 2000, 4.

27. Philpott 2013, 33.

28. Rothman 1998, 270.

29. Rothman 1998, 246.

30. Rothman 1998, 246.

31. Benson and Jackson 2018; Butler and Robson 2003; Tyler 2015.

32. Farrell 2020.

33. Aspen Area Community Plan 2000, 7.

34. Travis 2007, 153.

35. The Aspen Pitkin County Housing Program does not receive federal funds and there are no federally subsidized housing projects in Aspen or Pitkin County. The units available through APCHA are generally higher quality than federally subsidized housing. There is, moreover, little if any stigma associated with living in APCHA housing.

36. The remaining third of this tax goes to the Wheeler Opera House, which is then used to fund educational and entertainment programs for the community.

37. City of Aspen and Pitkin County 2012, 38.

38. City of Aspen and Pitkin County 2012, 39.

39. City of Aspen and Pitkin County 2012, 20–21.

40. Warner and Molotch 2000.

41. Aspen provides favorable property taxes, unfavorable sales taxes, and a state income tax of 4.63 percent. Kiplinger 2019.

CHAPTER 2. LIVING THE "ASPEN DREAM"?

1. There are two housing markets in Aspen. The free market consists of homes that are bought and can appreciate in value, as well as rental units—which tend to be either beat-up, odd-ball spaces or ultra-high-end condos. The deed-restricted market consists of units for rent or purchase, that have income or employment restrictions attached. Most of these are managed by the Aspen Pitkin County Housing Authority; some are managed by individual employers, such as the St. Regis Hotel or the school district. The homes that are purchased through this

program do not appreciate in line with the free market, so that when owners sell them, they earn the original purchase price plus the rate of inflation measured by the consumer price index (or CPI).

2. When a unit becomes available in the affordable housing program, local employees are able to enter a lottery to "win" that unit. They qualify to bid on properties or enter a lottery for units based on their income and household size, along with how many years they have been working in the county.

3. Benson and O'Reilly 2009.

4. Gosnell and Abrams 2011.

5. Hoey 2014.

6. O'Reilly and Benson 2009.

7. Nevarez 2011, 164.

8. Cohen, Duncan, and Thulemark 2015, 156.

9. Benson and O'Reilly 2009, 610.

10. Benson 2013, 2015; O'Reilly and Benson 2009.

11. Simon 1959.

12. Bourdieu 1986.

13. Rothman 1998, 215.

14. Accominatti, Khan, and Storer 2018.

15. Seamster 2015.

CHAPTER 3. STEADYING THE PENDULUM

1. A twenty-eight-foot limitation had been passed by city council in 2013 on the south side of the street only, which would reduce the mass and scale of buildings and provide more accessible views of the mountain. The previous height limit was three stories; twenty-eight feet is equivalent to two stories.

2. Lefebvre 1996; Harvey 2016.

3. A comprehensive plan is a vision document that guides development in a municipality. It serves as the basis by which laws and policies are developed; it expresses the goals and aspirations that get encoded in land use regulations. It guides laws and official policies, but it is not a legal document. Municipalities vary in how frequently they revise their "comp plans" (or master plans). Aspen and Pitkin County jointly published theirs in 1992, 2000, and 2012. Comprehensive plans are usually written by a committee composed of elected officials, urban planners, professionals with relevant expertise (architects, environmental scientists), and citizens.

4. Atkinson, Parker, and Burrows 2017.

5. City of Aspen and Pitkin County 2012, 7.

6. City of Aspen and Pitkin County 2012, 6.

7. City of Aspen and Pitkin County 2012, 7.

8. City of Aspen and Pitkin County 2012, 20.
9. City of Aspen and Pitkin County 2012, 26.
10. City of Aspen and Pitkin County 2012, 38.
11. City of Aspen and Pitkin County 2012, 38.
12. City of Aspen and Pitkin County 2012, 38.
13. While growth and sprawl were frequent sources of dread for the Aspen City Council and residents, there was little threat of sprawl occurring in Aspen due to the existence of an urban growth boundary that prevents the building of many types of structures outside of the city boundary. The urban growth boundary was established to protect the rural parts of the county from development. In Aspen, infill was used to encourage growth within the boundary and urban core by giving developers more "space" on their lots to build (by expanding floor-area ratios, or FARs).
14. Associated Press 2013.
15. Carroll 2015.
16. Savail 2013.
17. Centner 2008.
18. The no-complaining clause was attached to this building in 2013; it sold to a new buyer in 2017 with this clause attached. The clause lacks legal teeth, given that noise ordinances supersede this individual land use application, allowing the occupants to make complaints when decibel levels exceed legal limits.
19. Meinhold 2014.
20. Sackariason 2009.
21. Wackerle 2015a.
22. Sackariason 2019a.
23. Carroll 2015.
24. Carroll n.d.
25. Wackerle 2015b.
26. City of Aspen and Pitkin County 2012, 8
27. City of Aspen and Pitkin County 2012, 8.

CHAPTER 4. CONSTRUCTIONS OF "SMALL-TOWN CHARACTER"

1. Duncan and Duncan 2004, 29.
2. City of Aspen and Pitkin County 2012, 24.
3. City of Aspen and Pitkin County 2012, 26.
4. City of Aspen and Pitkin County 2012, 38.
5. City of Aspen and Pitkin County 2012, 21.
6. Gieryn 2000.
7. City of Aspen and Pitkin County 2012, 7.
8. City of Aspen and Pitkin County 2012, 2.

9. City of Aspen 2017a.

10. Harvey 2001, 409.

11. Duncan and Duncan 2004.

12. The twenty-eight-foot limitation would be imposed in all zone districts except the Service-Commercial-Industrial Zone, or SCI, which sits about six blocks off Main Street, and houses more functional, industrial uses in a somewhat out-of-the-way setting.

13. Jacobs 1961.

14. Whyte 1980.

15. Shephard and Smithsimon 2011.

16. City of Aspen and Pitkin County 2012, 21.

17. City of Aspen and Pitkin County 2012, 21.

18. Carr et al. 1992; Loukaitou-Sideris 1993; Madanipour 2010; Stevens 2009.

19. City of Aspen 2017a, 27.

20. City of Aspen 2017c, 33.

21. City of Aspen and Pitkin County 2012, 20.

22. City of Aspen and Pitkin County 2012, 38.

23. City of Aspen and Pitkin County 2012, 38.

CHAPTER 5. "BUT DOES IT DELIVER VALUE?"

1. The Aspen Pitkin County Housing Authority manages affordable housing for those employed in the county through both rental and purchase markets. Units within the purchase market are not allowed to appreciate at a market rate; instead, they can appreciate only in line with cost-of-living adjustments. This limits the profits that can be made when existing owners sell their units.

2. City of Aspen 2018.

3. City of Aspen and Pitkin County 2012, 41, 38.

4. One percent of this tax went to an affordable housing fund; the remaining .5 percent went to the Wheeler Opera House to fund art and cultural events.

5. New Jersey Builders Association v. Mayor and Township Committee of Bernard's Township, Somerset County, 108 N.J. 223, 1987. *Rational nexus* is a term used in land use law. A "rational nexus" exists if mitigation fees are imposed in such a way that they do not violate due process (e.g., that fees are applied equally to all developments within a class) and if it can be determined that a development created the need for infrastructure and the fees required to offset these needs are accurately and appropriately calculated.

6. If a building owner decides to redevelop, their project usually falls into one of three categories: (1) complete redevelopment, or "scrape and replace;" (2) significant remodel, where 30–40 percent of the structure is altered; (3) minor remodel, involving less than 30–40 percent of the structure. The final case does

not "trigger" new mitigations and is the only remodel option not subject to the new code amendments.

7. Warner and Molotch 2000, 10.

8. City of Aspen 2017c.

9. Dal Bó 2006.

10. Sackariason 2019b.

CHAPTER 6. A MALL AT THE BASE OF A MOUNTAIN

1. Zukin et al. 2009.

2. Zukin and Kosta 2004.

3. Oldenberg 1989.

4. Deener 2011, 311.

5. Fainstein and Gladstone, 1999, 23.

6. Zukin, 2009, 545.

7. Burns 2003.

8. City of Aspen and Pitkin Count 2012, 26.

9. City of Aspen and Pitkin Count 2012, 7

10. Hyra 2015.

11. Milias 2017.

12. The city's budget was closer to $120 million at the time he made this statement.

13. City of Aspen 2017b.

14. City of Aspen and Pitkin Count 2012, 20.

15. Molotch 1976.

CHAPTER 7. BUSCANDO EL SUEÑO AMERICANO

1. U.S. Census Bureau 2020b; Public School Review 2020. It is likely that the percentage of Latinos is higher in both locations due to the presence of undocumented residents, who may be less likely to be counted in official government estimates.

2. U.S. Census Bureau 2020b; Public School Review 2020. The U.S. Census estimates that 23 percent of Garfield County is foreign born.

3. Horan 2002.

4. Davis and Moctezuma 1999.

5. Farrell 2020; Travis 2007. The New West typically refers to the geographic regions west of Colorado that have experienced rapid population growth since the 1990s. This population growth has been accompanied by changes in the economy of the American West, from resource extraction and ranching to

tourism and technology. These changes have also brought cultural changes, including a more progressive political approach, especially as pertains to environmental policies. Latino migration has been a part of these transformations, with their labor playing an important role in sustaining the tourist economies and building boom.

6. Park and Pellow 2011.

7. Farrell 2020.

8. City of Aspen 1999; Travers 2011.

9. Duncan and Duncan 2004, 186.

10. Dolgon 2005, 155.

11. Duncan and Duncan 2004, 7.

12. Pulido 2002; Reed 1999.

13. Cravey 2003.

14. Nelson and Hiemstra 2008.

15. Nelson and Hiemstra 2008, 327.

16. Farrell 2020, 182, 185–89.

17. Farrell 2020, 271, 281, 287.

18. American Immigration Council 2017.

19. El Salvador Info, n.d.; Equal Times 2017.

20. The exact phrase used by Maria was Aspen "ha sido nuestra fuente de empleo." One research assistant, a native speaker from Argentina, translated it as "fountain of jobs"—which is a literal translation. Another assistant, a nonnative Spanish speaker, provided a more colloquial translation, "a source of jobs."

21. There is no doubt that there are trailer parks that are overcrowded and provide substandard conditions. None of these respondents currently lived in such a location. One described living in a trailer home when she first moved to the United States, which functioned like a rooming house for newcomers. She moved out within two months, first sharing a room with her supervisor, then moving into the hotel where she worked, and later forming a household of her own. This typifies one common trajectory among recent arrivals.

22. The saga of the Pan and Fork trailer park is one such case. When my family and I lived there in the early 1990s, it was a mixture of White and Hispanic residents. Over time, Hispanic representation grew. In 2010, the city purchased the property because it sat in a flood plain. The plot of land—which once housed thirty-seven trailer homes in a beautiful riverside setting—sat empty for seven years, as local residents fought over how to best use the land. In February 2020, a plan for the site was finally approved by the Basalt City Council. When it opens in 2023, the development will house a community arts center, a restaurant with a rooftop bar, and just four affordable housing units. Gentrification has clearly come to Basalt, erasing and replacing the spot where my own father became a first-time homeowner, alongside numerous Latino neighbors.

23. Bourdieu 1977.

24. Many respondents spoke of being afraid of ICE, especially within adjacent Garfield and Eagle counties, where ICE has been more active. Just one respondent described a specific negative encounter with law enforcement. Alejandro said that his brother had been pulled over—possibly profiled—by a police officer in Eagle County for driving an Audi and having tinted windows.

25. Schmalzbauer 2014.

CONCLUSION

1. Busà 2017; Greenberg 2009; Hackworth 2007.
2. Hyde 2018.
3. Dolgon 2005; Duncan and Duncan 2004.
4. Brown-Saracino 2009.
5. Brown-Saracino 2017.
6. Benson and Jackson 2018; Butler and Robson, 2003; Tyler 2015.
7. Nevarez 2011, 176.
8. Condon 2019; Navigate LLC, Rees Consulting Inc., and WSW Consulting. 2016.
9. Auslander 2017.
10. Herchenroeder. 2014
11. Benjamin 2009, 8.
12. Waxmann 2016.
13. Mengle and Muhlbaum 2019.

APPENDIX

1. Brown-Saracino and Stiman 2017, 88.

References

Accominotti, Fabien, Shamus R. Khan, and Adam Storer. 2018. "How Cultural
  Capital Emerged in Gilded Age America: Musical Purification and Cross-
  Class Inclusion at the New York Philharmonic." *American Journal of
  Sociology* 123(6):1743–83.
American Immigration Council. 2017. "Fact Sheet: Immigrants in Colorado."
  Retrieved June 9, 2020. https://www.americanimmigrationcouncil.org
  /research/immigrants-colorado.
Apartment List. 2020. "National Rent Report." Retrieved on February 8, 2020
  https://www.apartmentlist.com/rentonomics/national-rent-data/.
Associated Press. 2013, October 8. "Aspen Couple on Mission to Quiet Restau-
  rants." *Denver Post*. Retrieved February 5, 2020. https://www.denverpost.com
  /2013/10/08/aspen-couple-on-mission-to-quiet-restaurants/.
Atkinson, Rowland, Roger Burrows, Luna Glucksberg, Hang Kei Ho, Caroline
  Knowles, and David Rhodes. 2016. "Minimum City? The Deeper Impacts of
  the 'Super-Rich' on Urban Life." In *Cities and the Super-Rich: Real Estate,
  Elite Practices and Urban Political Economies*, edited by R. Forrest,
  B. Wissink, and S. Y. Koh, 253–72. London: Palgrave.
Atkinson, Rowland, Simon Parker, and Roger Burrows. 2017. "Elite Formation,
  Power and Space in Contemporary London." *Theory, Society, and Culture*
  34(5–6): 179–200.
Auslander, Jason. 2017. "Aspen Council Votes for Shorter, Smaller Affordable
  Housing at Castle Creek." *Aspen Times*. Retrieved February 8, 2020. https://

www.aspentimes.com/news/aspen-council-votes-for-shorter-smaller
-affordable-housing-at-castle-creek/.

Benjamin, Rich. 2009. *Searching for Whitopia: An Improbable Journey to the Heart of White America*. New York: Hachette Books.

Benson, Michaela. 2013. "Postcoloniality and Privilege in New Lifestyle Flows: The Case of North Americans in Panama." *Mobilities* 8(3): 313–30.

———. 2015. "Class, Race, Privilege: Structuring the Lifestyle Migrant Experience in Boquete, Panama." *Journal of Latin American Geography* 14(1): 19–37.

Benson, Michaela, and Emma Jackson. 2018. "From Class to Gentrification and Back Again." In *The Handbook of Gentrification Studies*, edited by Loretta Lees with Martin Phillips, 63–80. London: Edward Elgar.

Benson, Michaela, and Karen O'Reilly. 2009. "Migration and the Search for a Better Way of Life: A Critical Exploration of Lifestyle Migration." *Sociological Review* 57(4): 608–25.

Blakely, Edward J., and Mary Gail Snyder. 1997. *Fortress America: Gated Communities in the United States*. Washington, DC: Brookings Institution Press.

Block, Fang. 2017. "Aspen, Colorado, Has the Highest Entry Price in the U.S. for Luxury Homes." Mansion Global. Retrieved May 7, 2020. https://www.mansionglobal.com/articles/aspen-colorado-has-the-highest-entry-price-in-the-u-s-for-luxury-homes-69765?mod=article_inline.

Bourdieu, Pierre. 1977. *Outline of a Theory of Practice*. Cambridge: Cambridge University Press.

———. 1980. *The Logic of Practice*. Palo Alto, CA: Stanford University Press.

———. 1986. "Forms of Capital." In *Handbook of Theory and Research for the Sociology of Education*, edited by John Richardson, 241–58. New York: Greenwood.

Brown-Saracino, Japonica. 2009. *A Neighborhood That Never Changes: Gentrification, Social Preservation, and the Search for Authenticity*. Chicago: University of Chicago Press.

———. 2017. *How Places Make Us: Novel LBQ Identities in Four Small Cities*. Chicago: University of Chicago Press.

Brown-Saracino, Japonica, and Meaghan Stiman. 2017. "How to Avoid Getting Stuck in Meetings: On the Value of Recognizing the Limits of Meeting Ethnography for Community Studies." In *Meeting Ethnography: Meetings as Key Technologies of Contemporary Governance, Development, and Resistance*, edited by Jen Sandler and Ranita Thedvall. New York: Routledge.

Burns, Stephen. 2003. "Memo: Regulating Franchises." York, ME: Municipal Planning Board.

Busà, Alessandro. 2017. *The Creative Destruction of New York City: Engineering the City for the Elite*. New York: Oxford University Press.

Butler, Tim, with Garry Robson. 2003. *London Calling: The Middle Classes and the Re-making of Inner London*. London: Berg Publishers.

Carr, Stephen, Mark Francis, Leanne G. Rivlin, and Andrew M. Stone. 1992. *Public Space*. Cambridge: Cambridge University Press.

Carroll, Meredith. 2015, September 3. "Break Out a Tiny Violin for the East Hopkins Avenue Family." *Aspen Times*. Retrieved February 5, 2020. https://www.aspentimes.com/opinion/meredith-carroll-break-out-a-tiny-violin-for-east-hopkins-avenue-family/.

Carroll, Rick. 2015, June 29. "Base2 Lodge Petition Enters Final Stretch" *Aspen Times*. Retrieved February 5, 2020. https://www.aspentimes.com/news/base2-lodge-petition-enters-final-stretch/.

———. Nd. *Aspen Times*. Retrieved February 5, 2020. https://www.aspentimes.com/search/17170841-113/base2-petition-submitted-developer-mark-hunt-plays.

Centner, Ryan. 2008. "Places of Privileged Consumption Practices: Spatial Capital, the Dot-com Habitus, and San Francisco's Internet Boom." *City & Community* 7(3): 193–223.

City of Aspen. 1999. "Resolution #114." Retrieved June 8, 2020. https://www.cairco.org/projects/aspen-resolution/resolution-114-text.

———. 2017a. "Commercial, Lodging, and Historic District Design Standards and Guidelines." Retrieved on February 9, 2020. https://www.cityofaspen.com/DocumentCenter/View/412/Commercial-Design-Standards-Book-PDF.

———. 2017b. Ordinance 6 (Series of 2017). Retrieved on February 9, 2020. http://aspen.siretechnologies.com/SIREPub/cache/2/uva1ecwfcdi2lu3u23ekcgaw/6127802092020093005367.PDF.

———. 2017c. Ordinances 29–34 (Series of 2016) Exhibit B: Scenarios Analysis Summary. January 9 Retrieved February 9, 2020. http://aspen.siretechnologies.com/SIREPub/cache/2/uva1ecwfcdi2lu3u23ekcgaw/5620402092020093304599.PDF.

———. 2018. "Workforce Supply and Match." Retrieved on February 8, 2020 https://www.cityofaspen.com/DocumentCenter/View/712/Workforce-Supply--Match?bidId=.

City of Aspen and Pitkin County. 2000. *Aspen Area Community Plan*. Retrieved October 6, 2020 https://www.pitkincounty.com/DocumentCenter/View/852/2000-Aspen-Area-Community-Master-Plan---Action-Plan-PDF

City of Aspen and Pitkin County. 2012. *Aspen Area Community Plan*. Retrieved December 29, 2017. http://aspenairport.com/sites/default/files/downloads/Aspen%20Area%20Community%20Plan%202012.pdf.

Clavel, Pierre. 1986. *The Progressive City: Planning and Participation, 1969–1984*. New Brunswick, NJ: Rutgers University Press.

———. 2010. *Activists in City Hall: The Progressive Response to the Reagan Era in Boston and Chicago*. Ithaca, NY: Cornell University Press.

Cohen, Scott A., Tara Duncan, and Maria Thulemark. 2015. "Lifestyle Mobilities: The Crossroads of Travel, Leisure and Migration." *Mobilities* 10(1): 155–72.

Condon, Scott. 2019, February 12 "Study Forecasts How Bad Roaring Fork Valley's Affordable Housing Shortage Will Be by 2027." *Aspen Times*. Retrieved February 8, 2020. https://www.aspentimes.com/trending/study-forecasts-how-bad-roaring-fork-valleys-affordable-housing-shortage-will-be-by-2027/

Cravey, Altha J. 2003. "Toque una Ranchera, por Favor." *Antipode* 35(3): 603–21.

Dal Bó, Ernesto. 2006. "Regulatory Capture: A Review." *Oxford Review of Economic Policy* 22(2): 203–25.

Davis, Mike, and Alessandra Moctezuma. 1999. "Policing the Third Border." *Architectural Design* 69: 34–37.

Dean, Jodi. 2012. *The Communist Horizon*. London: Verso.

Deener, Andrew. 2007. "Commerce as the Structure and Symbol of Neighborhood Life: Reshaping the Meaning of Community in Venice, California." *City & Community* 6(4): 291–314.

Dolgon, Corey. 2005. *The End of the Hamptons: Scenes from the Class Struggle in America's Paradise*. New York: New York University Press.

Duncan, James S., and Nancy G. Duncan. 2004. *Landscapes of Privilege: The Politics of the Aesthetic in an American Suburb*. London: Routledge.

El Salvador Info. N.d. "The Minimum Wage in El Salvador in 2020: How Does It Compare?" Retrieved June 14, 2020. https://elsalvadorinfo.net/minimum-wage-in-el-salvador/.

Equal Times. 2017. "As El Salvador Increases Its Minimum Wage, Big Business Increases the Pressure to Reduce Worker Gains." Retrieved June 14, 2020. https://www.equaltimes.org/as-el-salvador-increases-its#.XuaV4kVKiM8.

Fainstein, Susan S., and David Gladstone. 1999. "Evaluating Urban Tourism." In *The Tourist City*, edited by Dennis R. Judd and Susan Fainstein, 21–34. New Haven, CT: Yale University Press.

Farrell, Justin. 2020. *Billionaire Wilderness: The Ultra-Wealthy and the Remaking of the American West*. Princeton, NJ: Princeton University Press.

Gendron, Richard, and G. William Domhoff. 2009. *The Leftmost City: Power and Progressive Politics in Santa Cruz*. Boulder, CO: Westview Press.

Giddens, Anthony. 1984. *The Constitution of Society: Outline of the Theory of Structuration*. Cambridge, UK: Polity Press.

Gieryn, Thomas F. 2000. "A Space for Place in Sociology." *Annual Review of Sociology* 26(1): 463–96.

Gilens, Martin. 1996. "'Race Coding' and White Opposition to Welfare." *American Political Science Review* 90(3): 593–604.

———. 2009 *Why Americans Hate Welfare: Race, Media, and the Politics of Antipoverty Policy*. Chicago: University of Chicago Press.

Glass, Ruth. 1964. *London: Aspects of Change*. London: MacGibbon and Kee.

Gosnell, Hannah, and Jesse Abrams. 2011. "Amenity Migration: Diverse Conceptualizations of Drivers, Socioeconomic Dimensions, and Emerging Challenges." *GeoJournal* 76(4): 303–22.

Gotham, Kevin Fox. 2007. *Authentic New Orleans: Tourism, Culture, and Race in the Big Easy*. New York: New York University Press.

Greenberg, Miriam. 2009. *Branding New York: How a City in Crisis Was Sold to the World*. New York: Routledge.

Hackworth, Jason. 2007. *The Neoliberal City: Governance, Ideology, and Development in American Urbanism*. Ithaca, NY: Cornell University Press.

Harvey, David. 1973. *Social Justice and the City*. Baltimore, MD: Johns Hopkins University Press.

———. 1989. "From Managerialism to Entrepreneurialism: The Transformation of Urban Governance in Late Capitalism." *Geografi ska Annaler* 71(B): 3–17.

———. 2001. *Spaces of Capital: Towards a Critical Geography*. Edinburgh: Edinburgh University Press.

———. 2016 "The Right to the City." In *The City Reader*, 6th ed., edited by Richard T. LeGates and Frederic Stout, 272–78. London: Routledge.

Herchenroeder, Karl. 2014. "Council Adopts New 'Double Basement' Language." Retrieved February 8, 2020 https://www.aspentimes.com/news/council -adopts-new-double-basement-language/.

Hoey, Brian A. 2014. *Opting for Elsewhere: Lifestyle Migration and the American Middle Class*. Nashville, TN: Vanderbilt University Press.

Horan, Cynthia. 2002. "Racializing Regime Politics. *Journal of Urban Affairs* 24(1): 19–33.

Hyde, Zachary. 2018. "Giving Back to Get Ahead: Altruism as a Developer Strategy of Accumulation through Affordable Housing Policy in Toronto and Vancouver." *Geoforum* (published online).

Hyra, Derek. 2015. "The Back-to-the-City Movement: Neighbourhood Redevelopment and Processes of Political and Cultural Displacement." *Urban Studies* 52(10): 1753–73.

Jacobs, Jane. 1961. *The Death and Life of Great American Cities*. New York: Vintage Books.

Kiplinger. 2019. "State-by-State Guide to Taxes." Retrieved May 12, 2020. https://www.kiplinger.com/tool/taxes/T055-S001-kiplinger-tax-map/index .php?map=&state_id=6&state=Colorado.

Knight-Frank. 2018. "The Wealth Report: A Global Perspective on Prime Property and Investment, 12th edition." Retrieved on October 6, 2020 https://content.knightfrank.com/resources/knightfrank.com/wealthreport 2018/the-wealth-report-2018.pdf.

Lees, Loretta. 2003. "Super-gentrification: The Case of Brooklyn Heights, New York City." *Urban Studies* 40(12): 2487–509.

———. 2019. "Planetary Gentrification and Urban (Re) Development." *Urban Development Issues* 61(1): 5–13.

Lees, Loretta, Hyun Bang Shin, and Ernesto López-Morales. 2016. *Planetary Gentrification*. New York: John Wiley & Sons.

Lees, Loretta, Tom Slater, and Elvin Wyly. 2008. *Gentrification*. New York: Routledge.

Lefebvre, Henri. 1996. *Writings on Cities*. Hoboken, NJ: Wiley Blackwell.

Logan, John, and Harvey Molotch. 1987. *Urban Fortunes: The Political Economy of Place*. Berkeley: University of California Press.

Loukaitou-Sideris, Anastasia. 1993 "Privatisation of Public Open Space: The Los Angeles Experience." *Town Planning Review* 64(2): 139–67.

Low, Setha. 2004. *Behind the Gates: Life, Security, and the Pursuit of Happiness in Fortress America*. New York: Routledge.

Madanipour, Ali. 2010. *Whose Public Space? International Case Studies in Urban Design and Development*. New York: Routledge.

McCann, Eugene J. 2002. "The Cultural Politics of Local Economic Development: Meaning-Making, Place-Making, and the Urban Policy Process." *Geoforum* 33(3): 385–98.

Meinhold, Bridgette. 2014, August 13. "Take a Look Inside Shigeru Ban's Spectacular New Aspen Art Museum." Retrieved February 5, 2020. https://inhabitat.com/shigeru-bans-woven-screen-clad-new-aspen-art-museum-is-now-open/.

Mengle, Rocky, and David Muhlbaum. 2019. "The Ten Most Tax-Friendly States in the U.S." Kiplinger. Retrieved May 27, 2020. https://www.kiplinger.com/slideshow/taxes/T054-S001-10-most-tax-friendly-states-in-the-u-s-2019/index.html.

Milias, Elizabeth. 2017, January 1. "Issue #130: How IgnorANT." Retrieved on February 8, 2020. http://www.theredant.com/red-ant-blog/2017/1/23/issue-130-how-arrogant-1192017.html.

Molotch, Harvey. 1976. "The City as a Growth Machine: Toward a Political Economy of Place." *American Journal of Sociology* 82(2): 309–32.

Molotch, Harvey, William Freudenburg, and Krista E. Paulsen. 2000. "History Repeats Itself, but How? City Character, Urban Tradition, and the Accomplishment of Place." *American Sociological Review* 65(6):791–823.

Navigate LLC, Rees Consulting Inc., and WSW Consulting. 2016. "Policy Study: Aspen Pitkin County Housing Authority Affordable Housing Study." Retrieved February 8, 2020. https://www.apcha.org/DocumentCenter/View/119/APCHA-Guidelines-Consultant-Policy-Study-PDF.

Nelson, Lise, and Nancy Hiemstra. 2008. "Latino Immigrants and the Renegotiation of Place and Belonging in Small Town America." *Social & Cultural Geography* 9(3): 319–42.

Nevarez, Leonard. 2011. *Pursuing Quality of Life: From the Affluent Society to the Consumer Society.* New York: Routledge.

New York Times. 2017. Colorado Election Results. Retrieved October 6, 2020 https://www.nytimes.com/elections/2016/results/colorado

Oldenburg, Ray. 1989. *The Great Good Place: Cafes, Coffee Shops, Bookstores, Bars, Hair Salons, and Other Hangouts at the Heart of a Community.* New York: Marlowe and Company.

O'Reilly, Karen, and Michaela Benson. 2009. *Lifestyle Migration.* London: Routledge.

Park, Lisa Sun-Hee, and David N. Pellow. 2011. *The Slums of Aspen: Immigrants vs. the Environment in America's Eden.* New York: New York University Press.

Perin, Constance. 1977. *Everything in Its Place: Social Order and Land Use in America.* Princeton, NJ: Princeton University Press.

Philpott, William. 2013. *Vacationland: Tourism and Environment in the Colorado High Country.* Seattle: University of Washington Press.

Pow, Choon-Piew. 2009. *Gated Communities in China: Class, Privilege and the Moral Politics of the Good Life.* London: Routledge.

Pow, Choon-Piew, and Lily Kong. 2007. "Marketing the Chinese Dream Home: Gated Communities and Representations of the Good Life in (Post-) Socialist Shanghai." *Urban Geography* 28(2): 129–59.

Public School Review. 2020. "Roaring Fork Valley High School." Retrieved on June 8, 2020. https://www.publicschoolreview.com/roaring-fork-high-school -profile.

Pulido, Laura. 2002. "Reflections on a White Discipline." *The Professional Geographer* 54(1): 42–49.

Reed, Adoph. 1999. *Stirrings in the Jug: Black Politics in the Post-Segregation Era.* Minneapolis: University of Minnesota Press.

Rothman, Hal K. 1998. *Devil's Bargains: Tourism in the Twentieth Century West.* Lawrence: University of Kansas Press.

Rudel, Thomas K., Karen O'Neill, Paul Gottlieb, Melanie McDermott, and Colleen Hatfield. 2011. "From Middle to Upper Class Sprawl? Land Use Controls and Changing Patterns of Real Estate Development in Northern New Jersey." *Annals of the Association of American Geographers* 101(3): 609–24.

Sackariason, Carolyn. 2009, July 9. "Weinerstube Owners Hoping to Win Appeal in Development Lawsuit *Post Independent.* Retrieved February 5, 2020. https://www.postindependent.com/news/wienerstube-owners-hoping -to-win-appeal-in-development-lawsuit/.

———. 2019a, July 23. "Mark Hunt Has Big Plans for Downtown Aspen." *Aspen Sojourner.* Retrieved February 5, 2020. https://www.aspensojo.com/home -and-real-estate/2019/07/mark-hunt-has-big-plans-for-downtown-aspen.

———. 2019b, August 25. "Aspen Developer Looks Back on Successes, Challenges as W Aspen Hotel Opens." *Aspen Times*. Retrieved February 8, 2020. https://www.aspentimes.com/news/local/aspen-developer-looks-back-at-successes-challenges-as-w-aspen-hotel-opens/.

Savail, Andre. 2013, August 27. "The Battle for Aspen's Soul?" *Aspen Times*. Retrieved February 5, 2020. https://www.aspentimes.com/news/battle-for-aspens-soul/.

Schmalzbauer, Leah. 2014. *The Last Best Place: Gender, Family and Migration in the New West*. Stanford, CA: Stanford University Press.

Seamster, Louise. 2015. "The White City: Race and Urban Politics." *Sociology Compass* 9(12): 1049–1065.

Sewell, William H. Jr. 2004. "The Concept of Culture(s)." In *Practicing History*, edited by Gabrielle M. Spiegel, 90–110. London: Routledge.

Shepard, Benjamin, and Gregory Smithsimon. 2011. *The Beach Beneath the Streets: Contesting New York City's Public Spaces*. Albany: State University of New York Press.

Simon, Herbert A. 1959. "Theories of Decision-Making in Economics and Behavioral Science." *American Economic Review* 49(3): 253–83.

Skeggs, Beverley. 2004. *Class, Self, Culture*. London: Routledge.

———. 2011. "Imagining Personhood Differently: Person Value and Autonomist Working Class Value Practices." *Sociological Review* 59(3): 579–94.

Smith, Neil. 1979. "Toward a Theory of Gentrification: A Back to the City Movement by Capital, not People." *Journal of the American Planning Association* 45(4): 538–48.

Sommeiller, Estelle, and Mark Price. 2019. "The New Gilded Age." The Economic Policy Institute. Retrieved February 3, 2020. https://www.epi.org/publication/the-new-gilded-age-income-inequality-in-the-u-s-by-state-metropolitan-area-and-county/.

State of Colorado. N.d. "2016 Colorado General Election Turn out by County and Party Affiliation." Retrieved on October 6, 2020 https://www.sos.state.co.us/pubs/elections/ACE/2016GeneralVoterTurnout/atlas.html?indicator=i1&indicator2=i4.

Stevens, Quentin. 2009. "'Broken' Public Spaces in Theory and in Practice." *Town Planning Review* 80(4–5): 371–92.

Stone, Clarence Nathan. 1989. *Regime Politics: Governing Atlanta, 1946–1988*. Lawrence: University Press of Kansas.

Swidler, Ann. 1986. "Culture in Action: Symbols and Strategies." *American Sociological Review* 51(2): 273–86.

Travers, Andrew. 2011. "Elected Officials Counter Book's Criticism of Local Immigration Issues." *Aspen Daily News*, December 9. Retrieved June 8, 2020. https://www.aspendailynews.com/elected-officials-counter-book-s

-criticism-of-local-immigration-issues/article_0078a88e-170d-5265-88eb
-688b43b7249f.html.

Travis, William R. 2007. *New Geographies of the American West: Land Use and the Changing Patterns of Place*. Washington, DC: Island Press.

Tyler, Imogen. 2015. "Classificatory Struggles: Class, Culture and Inequality in Neoliberal Times." *Sociological Review* 63(2): 493–511.

U.S. Census Bureau. 2020a. "Quick Facts." Retrieved February 1, 2020. https://www.census.gov/quickfacts/fact/table/US,pitkincountycolorado,aspencity colorado/HEA775218

———. 2020b. "Quick Facts." Retrieved June 8, 2020. https://www.census.gov /quickfacts/fact/table/carbondaletowncolorado,pitkincountycolorado ,aspencitycolorado,US/PST045219.

Wackerle, Curtis. 2015a, May 6. "Referendum 1 Passes." *Aspen Daily News* Retrieved on February 5, 2020. https://www.aspendailynews.com /referendum-passes/article_8e81a4ed-a390-5b34-af63-ef2e47bf3e46.html.

———. 2015b, November 4. "Voters Reject Base2 by a Large Margin." *Aspen Daily News*. Retrieved on February 5, 2020. https://www.aspendailynews .com/voters-reject-base-by-large-margin/article_d36e26d2-fc86-5f71-87dc -c0dfcff84acd.html.

Warner, Kee, and Harvey Molotch. 2000. *Building Rules: How Local Controls Shape Community Environments and Economies*. Boulder, CO: Westview Press.

Waxmann, Laura. 2016, July 7. "SF Mission Tech Workers Skeptical over Proposed Tech Tax." *Mission Local*. Retrieved February 8, 2020. https://missionlocal.org /2016/07/sf-mission-techies-skeptical-over-proposed-tech-tax/.

Weber, Max. 1978. *Economy and Society: An Outline of Interpretive Sociology* [translation of 1964 edition, of Weber 1922], edited by Guenther Roth and Claus Wittich. Berkeley: University of California Press.

Whyte, William Foote. 1980. *The Social Life of Small Urban Spaces*. New York: Project for Public Places.

Zukin, Sharon. 2009. "Changing Landscapes of Power: Opulence and the Urge for Authenticity." *International Journal of Urban and Regional Research* 33(2): 543–53.

Zukin, Sharon, and Ervin Kosta. 2004. "Bourdieu Off-Broadway: Managing Distinction on a Shopping Block in the East Village." *City & Community* 3(2): 101–14.

Zukin, Sharon, Valerie Trujillo, Peter Frase, Danielle Jackson, Tim Recuber, and Abraham Walker. 2009. "New Retail Capital and Neighborhood Change: Boutiques and Gentrification in New York City." *City & Community* 8(1): 47–64.

Index

breaks, 10, 13; code, 113; coffers, 114; cuts, 3, 23, 160; employment, 189; federal, 216; friendly state, 59, 241; incentives, 2, 12, 238; income, 58–59; levies, 58–59, 241; local, 58, 165, 183,189, 240; progressive, 14; property, 38, 140, 143, 241; real estate, 188, 190–91, 241; retail, 190–91; retroactive, 151; revenues, 11, 19, 23, 34*fig.*, 38, 55, 59, 140–43, 148, 176, 233; revolt, 241; sales, 23, 38, 57, 140, 143, 165, 176, 188, 191; subsidies, 18, 183; supplementary, 23, 234, 241; tech, 241; transfer, 142–43, 168, 241. *See also* Colorado: taxes; mitigation; Real Estate Transfer Tax (RETT); 1992 TABOR Laws (Tax Payer Bill of Rights)
Telpiz, Nadia, 76
Teton County, Wyoming, 4, 9, 24, 48–49, 202, 205, 217–19, 222–23, 231, 241; Grand Teton mountains, 10; Jackson Hole, 4, 123–24, 202
third places, 174–75
Thompson, Hunter S., 13, 44–45, 47, 53–54, 67, 181
tiered-rate, 151–54, 157–59
Torre, 124–26
Torres, Alejandro, 206, 208, 210, 222, 258*table*, 272n24
tourism, 12, 18, 63, 114, 214
Travis, William R., 54
trickle-down economics, 51, 195
Trump, Donald 212, 226
Tyler, Imogen, 21, 32

Ukranians, the, 100–1, 105
undocumented: population, 205, 212; residents, 200, 225; workers, 203, 220, 222
unintended consequences, 27, 92, 129, 135, 145, 147, 159, 168, 238–39
unpretentious luxury, 11, 13, 48–49, 52, 84, 94, 135, 221, 223, 231
upscaling, 19–20, 87, 160, 175, 197; in retail, 86, 173–76. *See also* gentrification; supergentrification
urban growth boundary, 54, 141, 268n13
urban planning, 8, 15, 30, 53–54, 58, 92, 94, 140, 145; department, 57, 126; staff, 2, 115, 153; tools of, 5, 22, 63, 108, 229, 233–35
use mix, 93–94, 135–37, 140; ordinance, 136–37; regulations, 115, 140, 144

use value, 12, 14, 116, 157, 232–34
Ute Indians, 40

Valley, the, 54, 75, 200, 208, 211, 213–14, 218–19, 222; *See also* Pitkin County; Roaring Fork Valley
variance, 92, 107–9, 111, 127, 195
Viceroy Hotel, 132
view plane, 93, 122, 134, 144
visitors, 2, 11, 37, 39–40, 59, 76, 88, 116, 121; affluent, 50, 52, 59, 61, 64, 82, 86, 97, 114, 152, 175, 183, 197, 226, 231, 233; businesses for, 16, 18, 74, 83, 96, 111, 165, 169, 174, 176–77, 186, 189–90, 197, 238; class interests of, 27–28, 37, 50–51, 57, 95, 111–15, 177, 186, 190, 192–93, 197, 231; experience, 97, 149, 152, 154; mingling, 42, 82, 84, 88, 97, 99, 117, 132, 169, 172, 174, 181, 183, 226, 228, 238; revenues from, 16, 50–51, 59, 61, 157, 166, 190, 192–93, 197, 229; space for 23, 27, 102, 118–19, 134, 228

Wackerle, Curtis, 111
Ward, Mason, 49–50, 77–78, 89
Warner, Kee, 16, 57, 155
Weber, Max, 30–31
Weinberg, Boogie, 182
Weinerstube, 103, 175, 182
western arcades (covered walkways), 123, 123*fig.*, 128, 131
Wheeler Opera House, 127, 266, 269
Whipple, John, 105
Whiteness, 25, 38, 90, 200, 204–5, 227, 240, 243
whitopia, 25, 240, 243
W Hotels, 132–33, 133*fig.*, 164
Whyte, William H., 130
Wilkins, Kathryn, 9
Williams, Raymond, 39
Wilson, Toni, 102–3
Wright, Ben, 171
Wyly, Elvin, 18

Yaw, Fletcher, 185
Yeager, Jimmy, 101
York, Maine, 176

Zermatt, Switzerland, 232
zone districts, 93, 139–40, 142, 269n12; commercial, 140, 142–43, 171

Founded in 1893,
UNIVERSITY OF CALIFORNIA PRESS
publishes bold, progressive books and journals
on topics in the arts, humanities, social sciences,
and natural sciences—with a focus on social
justice issues—that inspire thought and action
among readers worldwide.

The UC PRESS FOUNDATION
raises funds to uphold the press's vital role
as an independent, nonprofit publisher, and
receives philanthropic support from a wide
range of individuals and institutions—and from
committed readers like you. To learn more, visit
ucpress.edu/supportus.